D0627160

Technique of Executive Control

TECHNIQUE OF EXECUTIVE CONTROL

by Erwin Haskell Schell
MASSACHUSETTS INSTITUTE OF TECHNOLOGY

EIGHTH EDITION

McGRAW-HILL BOOK COMPANY, INC.
1957 NEW YORK TORONTO LONDON

TECHNIQUE OF EXECUTIVE CONTROL

 Library of Congress Catalog Card Number 24-10224

To My Father and Mother

Preface

To those who are searching for a constructive analysis of executive conduct, I offer this book. It is intended as a manual or guide to executive straight thinking. It does not aim to draw arbitrary conclusions or to determine inflexible standards. Rather it suggests and stimulates new avenues of reflection, and aids in building the executive method best suited to the unique capacities of each personality.

In this, the eighth edition, a new chapter entitled "Executive Self-development" has been introduced for those executives who are especially ambitious to further themselves through meritorious personal effort and conduct. And recent widespread interest in decentralization and expansion problems has prompted the inclusion of chapters on "Executive Delegation" and "Executive Creativeness."

The chapter on executive reading has been revised to include current bibliographical references.

ERWIN HASKELL SCHELL

Contents

Technique of Executive Control

Introduction

This book aims to be of direct, practical usefulness to the line executive, the superintendent, the supervisor, the foreman, and the working boss in their relationships with subordinates, associates, and superiors. Never before in our industrial history have the responsibilities of this group of men [1] been of such great significance to the success and security of the enterprise.

It has become clear that there are certain fundamental principles and basic rules of action which are generally applicable in these relationships. More than this, the methods and techniques of competent executives show definite differences from the procedures used by mediocre or inefficient executives. It is the purpose of this book to describe those executive procedures which the test of time has proved to be sound and effective.

Chapter 1, The Executive. Initially we point out how this book can be used to greatest advantage; we have something to say about the executive as his activities and responsibilities differ from those of administrators and functional officials, and we consider the nature of the

[1] This term is used here and throughout in the generic sense; women have taken their place in many, if not all, the fields dealt with in this book.

executive tasks—the job of the manager. In order that the reader may judge for himself whether he has the capacities for executive ability which the job calls for, we also deal briefly with the traits or characteristics of the executive which are unusually important to his success.

Chapter 2, Executive Attitude and Morale. We realize today more clearly than ever that executive ability and accomplishment rest in large degree upon executive attitude. Once established on a basis of sound principles of human conduct, executive action may respond to an infinite variety of circumstances and situations with consistently constructive results.

More than this, the right attitude toward executive performance provides the basis for executive morale and for the personal satisfaction resulting from responsibility in management. This chapter attempts to define that state of mind and point of view which lead toward positive and constructive attitudes and build a true sense of satisfaction and accomplishment.

Chapter 3, Executive Tools. One of the most helpful concepts concerning the work of the executive is that he, no less than any other artisan, requires tools as well as skill in their use. These tools are somewhat unusual in form and substance, but once they are viewed properly as implements that enable the executive to multiply the effectiveness of his effort, they become quickly susceptible of development and improvement through use. Curiously enough, these tools cannot be purchased; nor can they be fashioned by another. Each executive must make his own equipment for himself.

Chapter 4, Executive Control. Control is inherent in management. It does not mean coercion. Control is largely made up of the flow of orders and instructions in one direction and the flow of reports and comments in the other. In this chapter we consider how authority should relate to control, how orders are to be designed and given, and how the issuing of orders always carries ensuing responsibilities that constitute an important aspect of executive work. In this connection, ways are suggested of dealing with disciplinary problems in a constructive manner.

Chapter 5, Executive Delegation. Here we learn of ways in which the executive multiplies himself through others—assigns responsibility and corresponding authority, yet retains accountability. We further deal with some of the concerns, hesitancies, and uncertainties commonly met with when delegation is undertaken, as well as the significance of delegation as a constructive social act and as a builder of men.

Chapter 6, Executive Stimulation. In this chapter we are concerned with ways and means by which people may be encouraged to work with a will. All people have been found to respond to certain stimuli which provide incentives for their effort and their interest. To a marked degree, executive proficiency rests upon the faculty of the executive to create a stimulating environment for the individual workman.

Chapter 7, Executive Duties. Fortunately, a growing number of specialized industrial activities relating to labor must be dealt with in a unified fashion inasmuch as they affect the plant as a whole; they are, therefore, placed in the province of the personnel manager or director of industrial relations. But there are a number of activities which cannot be divorced from the work of the line executive, and these are considered in this chapter. They include such responsibilities as the introduction of new employees, training, transfer, promotion, and resignation. Finally we give attention to the principles of good conduct which underlie praise and commendation as well as reproof and criticism.

Chapter 8, Executive Collaboration. As our manufacturing processes become more highly integrated, our executives are finding it necessary to collaborate more closely with one another. This chapter discusses ways by which they can think together more effectively as well as some of the problems of collaboration between the executive and his subordinate executives, functional specialists, associate executives, and superiors.

Chapter 9, Executive Public Relations. A fact of great significance to effective executive technique is that every executive has a large audience, or "public," which is deeply interested in his relationships with subordinates and others. Executives are news to many individuals and groups both within and outside the plant. How to capitalize upon this interest and how to avoid the hazards of misinterpretation and misunderstanding are questions of major importance to the executive in his relationships with these third parties.

Chapters 10 and 11, Difficulties with Subordinates. One of the surprising aspects of executive control is the similarity of difficulties experienced by executives in different establishments. Difficulty is an inseparable part of human effort; in this chapter we discuss many of the common problems of the line manager and suggest a number of ways in which their solution may be approached.

Chapter 12, Difficulties with Associates. With the increasing size of our industrial establishments, the problem of horizontal relationships between executives of the same rank becomes more complicated. The thoughtful consideration of possible difficulties and ways of avoiding them has proved to be of marked value to the line executive, who characteristically gives a large part of his attention to his relationships with subordinates. This chapter is directed toward such issues as arise frequently in normal business.

Chapter 13, Difficulties with Superiors. Very little has been written concerning the characteristic problems of the line executive as he relates himself and his work to his superiors. Yet this relationship is of crucial importance to the executive's development and advancement. It is not uncommon to find line executives whose methods of dealing with subordinates and associates are of the best but who are markedly weak in dealings with their superiors. In this chapter we consider a variety of problems likely to arise in ordinary industrial operations, the correct solution of which goes far to maintain a happy and constructive relation between the line executive and his boss.

Chapter 14, Executive Improvement. Executives

may approach the problem of improvement in a surprising number of ways. Improvement may offer itself in extensive or intensive form. For example, it may be disclosed by the use of "new eyes," a study of changes, the use of control checks, and the making of suggestive comparisons. This chapter aims to outline to the executive particular methods whereby he may find personal security through constant developmental improvement.

Chapter 15, Executive Creativeness. The increasing rate of change, as well as the new competitive advantages found in constant evolutionary improvement, make personalized creative ability of constantly greater value to the executive. Accelerative advance in the application of ingenuity has become an important safeguard against obsolescence in executive techniques no less than in areas of new products, materials, and processes.

Chapter 16, Executive Self-development. It is a widely accepted truism that the ability to lead others presupposes the presence of self-leadership. The doorway to executive accomplishment is through self-mastery. In this chapter we give thought to those approaches to self-development that will ensure and assure the most favorable ratio between executive accomplishments and executive talents or capacities.

Chapter 17, Executive Proficiency. Competence in any given field calls for an unusual and unique group of qualities. This is particularly true in the work of the executive. There is a definite *style* to the high quality of accomplishment that marks the exceptional manager, and in this chapter we have aimed to describe some of its aspects.

Executive Reading. During the past several years there has been an increasing flow of literature having to do with the technique of executive control. In this bibliography an attempt has been made to present a selected list of current publications which may profitably be read in conjunction with this book in the interests of acquiring a broader viewpoint and a deeper grasp of the problem of executive control.

Conclusion. The steady demand for this book reflects a deep and continuing desire on the part of executives to improve their performance and to grow in the art of management. The current edition tries on the one hand to introduce concepts, principles, and rules of action which have been newly brought to light, and on the other hand to retain those underlying fundamentals which base all cooperative human relationships, irrespective of time or place.

As Calvin Coolidge said, "We must be as progressive as science, and as conservative as the multiplication table."

CHAPTER 1

The Executive

There seems to be a widespread belief that executive skill is a God-given attribute. It is something that you have or you haven't. Your success as a leader of men is a matter of unchangeable destiny. In some measure, this is true. There are a limited number of essential executive qualities which are doubtless in the nature of a birthright. Without them, one can never hope to aspire to executive success. With them, accomplishment follows naturally.

But between the individuals who have these few qualities in great measure and those who do not have them at all there lies the much larger number of individuals who are gifted in moderate degree. These are the persons whose progress may suffer because of the notion that executive technique is a matter of a sixth sense, an intuitive faculty which defies explanation, a hunch which always tells the right thing to do at the right time. These people tend to close their minds to their problem. If they employ a wrong executive method and arouse antagonism and opposition, they are inclined to place the blame on the unseemly disposition of the employee. If repeated errors cause them to make a poorer showing than other executives in similar positions, they say, in discouragement, "I was never intended for executive work."

Now the truth is that such a viewpoint not only does no good but does great harm. The executive who follows an impulse usually relies upon some emotional stimulus, and in the majority of cases this reaction points to exactly the wrong thing to do. The leader who lets his impulses guide him is a good leader only for a mob, and we have no place for mobs in industry. Good leadership requires careful, penetrative thinking and, in addition, absolute self-control. It is through the mind, with its power to guide emotional pressures into constructive behavior, that man has progressed. If he had depended solely upon his habits and feelings, he would still be living in caves. An organization should be marshaled forward by reason. The executive should think his way along, and his desires and actions should conform to the decisions of his mind rather than to the unguided surges of his emotional nature.

It would be helpful if we were to set down definite rules of conduct to ensure executive success in every case. The difficulty here is that there would be a different rule for each executive-employee relationship, because every person differs from every other. In the chemical laboratory we can mix two reagents and forecast the result precisely. In the human laboratory, when one personality impresses itself upon another, the result is not a simple reaction; it is a complex response springing from the individual consciousness or subconsciousness with a form and intensity that vary with the personality of the person impressed.

This would make our task appear rather hopeless, were it not for two qualifying elements. First, there are certain tendencies and modes of behavior which are common to all of us. These characteristics may be overlaid with differing patterns of personality, but their universal presence gives the executive a basis for a thoughtful study of human behavior. Second, the executive can know himself. He can determine the methods and tools which his personality will allow him to use most effectively, and he can, therefore, lay down rules of self-conduct which will suit his particular capacities.

It is clear, then, that we cannot be arbitrary in our discussion of executive conduct. Although when we say, "Do this, do that," it may appear that we are presenting explicit instructions, they should not be so interpreted. The reader must weigh the text carefully and take from it what will serve him best. Our purpose is not merely to provide information; it is to offer food for thought. The executive cannot advance through gaining knowledge of executive methods unless he considers these methods in the light of his own personality.

We urge that the text be read with constant reference to its personal application. Ask yourself, "Do I entirely agree with this statement?" "Have I a better method than the one suggested?" "How would I conduct myself in a similar situation?" To this end, we have obstructed the text with questions, and we believe that the greatest value to be gained from the book will come through their study. Certain questions serve to amplify the text, others to qualify it, and others are in the form of cases picturing problems that face the executive. The majority of these cases represent actual incidents. We have included no answers to these questions, for the correct answer will vary widely in terms of the personalities involved. We believe that it will be beneficial to the reader to work out for himself the best personal approach to solution. It may be that he will never meet a similar case, but if his mind has been trained to think carefully and precisely on such problems, he will attack an actual situation with greater vigor and certainty of success.

It is clear, therefore, that to get the greatest return from the book, the reader should proceed slowly and thoughtfully. The questions should be considered an integral part of the text and should not be passed over until answered to the reader's "personality satisfaction." We suggest that interleaving paper be placed between pages and the answers to questions jotted down, as the act of writing often leads one to arrange his thoughts in a more orderly form.

The Executive. Let us first define our terms, for industrial nomenclature is far from standardized. An executive, as we define him, is one who is responsible for the execution of work performed by others. We look to him for accomplishment. We find him near the cutting edge of the industrial organization, where the main object is being approached. He is always close to the zone of action. Whether he be office manager in charge of clerks, district sales manager in charge of salesmen, or foreman in charge of workmen, his place is at the firing line.

We may define the executive in another way. He is the medium for the flow of orders and policies from the administrators to the employees. And who are the administrators? They are often termed the chief executives or higher executives. Their major function is to represent equally the rights of the owners, the employees, and the public, a responsibility which has come more and more into their hands with the constantly rising status of management as a profession and with the waning influence of the board of directors as an administrative force in business operation. The administrators determine policy. They guide and control the progress of the enterprise in its fight for existence and advancement. They decide what shall be done, and in large measure their success lies in the quality of business judgment shown in these decisions. They coordinate and keep in proper balance all the factors of the enterprise that are necessary to success. Having provided the agencies and the paths of action, they delegate the action to others. They hold the executives responsible for the work itself. They hold the functional officials responsible for the maintenance of working conditions.

And who are the functional officials? They are the technicians, the experts, who are skilled in some single service which is of value to other members of the organization. The functional official maintains some particular factor necessary to operation. In the factory, the purchasing agent, the traffic manager, the storekeeper, and the move-boss are examples of functional officials who specialize in the maintenance of suitable quantities and qualities of material, while the employment manager, service manager, factory physician, educationalist, and restaurateur specialize in the maintenance of labor. Please note that these specialists are not "executing" in the direct sense but are providing the executives with the wherewithal for the execution of the work which is the justification for the enterprise.

Now it should be said that these divisions do not occur in so pure a form as we have indicated. The administrators are also executives to the degree that they are in turn responsible for the performance and accomplishment of those who report to them. Likewise the executives have limited areas in which they may use their own discretion in the determination of policy, and to this degree they are administrators. The functional officials may also have subordinates and, in the supervision of these assistants, they are doing executive work. Nevertheless, if we examine the organization of any enterprise in terms of basic purpose, we will find administrators at the top, planning and organizing, while delegating the maintenance of conditions suitable for performance to functional officials and delegating performance to executives who are responsible for employee accomplishment.

There are also staff aids and counselors who serve administrative, executive, and functional officials, but their activities do not concern us here. We are interested only in offering a clear picture of the executive's position in any enterprise. We see him receiving orders from the administrators and apportioning them to the employees in such a way that work progresses coordinately and smoothly. We see the executive being assisted by technical specialists who maintain a working environment containing all the factors necessary for performance. We see the employee looking to the executive as his source of authority and direction and receiving from functional experts assistance which enables him to maintain a higher level of productivity.

The Executive Task. In the past, the executive's job included a great miscellany of responsibilities. The dangers of this situation were pointed out by Frederick W. Taylor, who emphasized the impossibility of a high quality of service from one individual who was busying himself in so many activities. Under such organization the executive was doomed to be "Jack of all trades and master of none." Thus American administrators soon began to apply the principle of the division of labor to the managing personnel.

Gradually the activities involving the maintenance of working conditions have been removed from the executive and turned over to the functional specialist. At one time a shop executive purchased and stored his own supplies. Now such work is done by a purchasing agent and a storekeeper. At one time the executive maintained control over the quality of the work done by his employees. Now this responsibility is in the hands of the inspecting division. And so on through the list, until today in many of our highly functionalized organizations the executive finds his materials specified, purchased, expedited, received, stored, issued to him, and moved from his department; his machinery, service equipment, and working quarters maintained; his labor employed, instructed, and cared for in case of injury or illness. Even the orders which he receives are so planned, scheduled, and dispatched that he has merely to place them in the proper rack for the specified employee. All this is done by specialists, and we find the executive asking, "What is there left for me to do?"

Stripped of all the miscellaneous activities of upkeep, the executive is free to face his major task—the organization of the will of his employees, which is defined by Dr. Edward D. Jones as "the means by which you provide in a group of men for harmony of mood, harmony of attitude, or the desire of all to accomplish the same thing. This is what we call cooperation, or the right mental attitude toward the project in hand."

This is the job of the executive. It is plain to see that executives are, in truth, the real managers of labor, that labor management is their great responsibility, and that their success or failure in accomplishing the work which they are to do will be measured primarily, not in terms of their technical knowledge or in terms of their technical skill, but in terms of their effectiveness in organizing the will of the employees—in handling men and women.

Executive Traits. It is useless for us to attempt to list all the traits essential to executive success in its fullest sense, for we should be required to mention all of man's mental, moral, and physical virtues. The omission of any one would surely be damaging in some degree. There are certain traits, however, in which variations in quality more seriously affect executive success than they do in others. To put this thought another way, let us assume that it were possible to assign relative weights to the virtues that an individual possessed but that no person could have full weight of all. The person wishing to become an executive would find a heavy weighting of certain characteristics necessary, while others need not be present in so great a degree. For example, an executive might readily dispense with physical beauty, an attribute which, however, might be of great value to an actor.

Among the traits of which the executive requires an unusually large allotment, we may mention first an *innate interest in, and affection for, people.* Executives, in the last analysis, are molders of human stuff. In the usual organization they are in intimate contact with a larger number of personalities than any other official, unless it be certain functional experts such as the employment manager, company physician, and personnel director. Their problem is that of human relationships, which are ever complex, ever changing, ever defying standardization.

Success in handling people requires, therefore, an abiding interest and continuous thought. To one whose natural tendencies lie in this field, the subject offers constant fascination. To one without this inborn interest, the subject ceases to be appealing after the first flush; the mind closes to progressive thinking, and the ability to guide and direct is enormously weakened. We shall see in the next chapter that many of the executive's most effective tools are forged out of his capacities for human interest and affection.

Again, the element of cooperation within an organization springs from something more than wage-payment systems, delegations of authority and responsibility, and the fear of unemployment. As one administrator remarked, "You cannot throw a crowd of men together and expect to have a successful organization any more than you can place a man, a woman and children within a house and expect a happy family." The executive who has a sincere affection for his workers will find his greatest happiness in hastening their self-improvement and progress. His pleasure lies in the making of men. Such a leader obtains an unusual degree of loyalty and cooperation. The man maker believes in people by and large, searches out the strong points in each individual, and provides the incentive for their translation into economic value.

A second characteristic which executives require is *strength*, or *power of personality*. It is not easy to describe this quality, but we may speak of it as a vigor which seems to spring from the nervous system, a vitality that is not confined to any particular type of physical or intellectual make-up. In many cases this quality does not manifest itself actively but creates the impression of reserve force which may be drawn upon if need be. In other cases it may flower in a characteristic forcefulness of speech or gesture or may find outlet in a sturdy determination that never lessens until the goal is reached.

People are extremely sensitive to the presence of this

characteristic in others. When accompanied by other necessary factors, it becomes of great value in executive work. The administrative and executive group, in reality, represent the nervous system of an organization. Through them the impulses of action are transmitted and finally impressed upon the wills of the employees. The more powerful the impulses, the more pronounced will be the reaction of the employee mind. An effective organization requires executives who have more than average power of personality. It is undoubtedly true that this characteristic is one of the basic elements that seem to justify a natural right to authority.

A third quality which appears essential is a *scientific trend of mind*. The executive is constantly facing problems of the kind that yield most readily to the analytical approach of the scientifically minded thinker. The technical problems involved in coordinating the work of a group of men, materials, and equipment in such a way that maximum quality and quantity are obtained and waste is kept to a minimum are often exceedingly complex. They require solution well in advance. The successful executive wins his victories through preventive rather than curative action. To plan and schedule for the future calls for a process of thought which is distinctly scientific in nature.

This quality brings with it a humility before truth, a subordination of personal feeling, and an ability to discriminate between fact and opinion—an objective approach. The executive so endowed can make an accurate appraisal of existing conditions and, by contrasting these with the ideal, find a proper approach to constructive improvement. There is a practicality in this method of advance which allows progress to be built upon a firm and lasting foundation.

It is further true that the scientific attitude of mind is of value for the greater ease of approach that it affords to the technical problems of machinery, materials, and processes which are becoming more and more prominent in our industrial life. Many executive decisions which affect the employee must rest on a knowledge of the technical activities to be undertaken.

These three traits—interest in and affection for people, power of personality, and a scientific trend of mind—may be said to be the outstanding requirements for executive success.

To be sure, executives should possess moral stamina, but there is no less need for this quality in any other walk of life. It is true that executives should be endowed with energy, but this quality again is needed wherever accomplishment is the goal. We cannot say that the human cost of executive work is any higher than that of technical activities of equal importance. The work of an executive may require a higher level of intelligence than that of his employees, but this characteristic is not what distinguishes him from many other officials who do not occupy executive positions.

In other words, were we looking for executive timber, or promising applicants for any position of similar responsibility, we would look for men of moral uprightness, physical vigor, and a given level of intelligence. If, from this group, we were to select men for executive work, we would increase our requirements to include an interest in and affection for people, power of personality, and a scientific trend of mind. In like manner, there are specific qualities required for salesmen, functional officials, staff assistants, and so on.

Experience and educational training for the particular job are of course requisite to many executive responsibilities, and, indeed, there are very few positions of any rank in which these are not requisites. Such education and training, however, can be only developmental. All they can do is to make effective the innate resources of the man.

Q. *One executive says, "Make better men and women of your employees and better work automatically follows." Another says, "Show employees how to become more efficient in their work and you automatically make them stronger and better men and women." Where should emphasis be directed?*

> Compare the responsibilities of the executive with those of the minister or priest as they affect the employee's relationship with his work, his fellow workmen, and his home and family. Do individual improvements in word (attitude of mind) and in deed (proficiency) occur independently or are they best developed concurrently?

Q. *You are asked to select a man to be given a course of training in your department, after which he will become your assistant. Later, if a branch plant now under consideration is established, he will be placed in an executive position parallel to your own. Assuming that applicants will have had no industrial experience, what questions would you ask them in forming estimates of their potential executive capacity?*

> What are the characteristics essential to executive competence? What is the sort of previous experience or behavior that would indicate capacity in each of these characteristics? What questions would you ask in determining the extent of this capacity?

Q. *You are one of a group of workmen. Your boss has been promoted and your group has been told that one of its members will be selected to fill his place. Contrary to your expectations, you are not chosen; but a fellow workman gets the position. Though you are disappointed, you admit the wisdom of the choice and say, "Well, he deserves it, and I'll be glad to work for and with him." Irrespective of what has been said in the text, what would you list as the qualities of such a person?*

CHAPTER 2

Executive Attitude and Morale

Lasting success in executive accomplishment begins with executive attitude. Far more important than what he does, how he acts, or how much he knows, the way the executive feels toward his responsibilities determines the initial competence of the leader.

Some years ago a young graduate visited his university in order to leave a record of his progress. He said that after a period of apprentice training he had been put in charge of a group of foreign-born laborers. I asked him how he got along. He replied that after the first day one of the workmen came to him and said, "You never do this work before. You don't know much about it but you are all right. We talk it all over and we think you going to be a fine boss. So we going to teach you how."

He was not sure just how he should have felt about this rather frank but friendly overture. I told him it was the highest possible compliment that could have been paid him—that it marked him as a sure-fire executive.

Executive work is a relationship. The executive is always relating himself to someone else. When this is not true, he is doing something that a clerk could do better. How should he feel about his relationships?

The Basis of Executive Attitude. We all have a basis for our attitudes. Sometimes it is just ignorance. There are instances on record of small children found playing with rattlesnakes because they had not been conditioned to fear or to beware of them. To develop a proper attitude toward our executive responsibilities we first must clear away some underbrush in the form of loose thinking about people and keep certain facts clearly before us.

The first of these is that *the common man is not common* at all. He is definitely uncommon—unlike the man who works beside him. The word "common" suggests something that is of little account, like the common pin. Just because there are many millions of us in the world we quickly and falsely assume that we are not distinctive. We are. Do you feel that you are the same as everyone else? I don't. Nor does anyone. True, we have many basic similarities in such matters as bodily construction and functioning—temperature, heartbeat, and the like. But our backgrounds are different. Our experiences have been different. Our hopes and ambitions are different. We are individuals and expect and want to be treated as such.

The second fact is that *each of us is much older than his birthdays indicate*. Our years mark but an infinitesimal part of our real age. No one knows how old we are, but estimates run as high as 300 million years. We are not the product of the war, or the depression, or the gay nineties. We are the fruit of thousands of centuries.

Why is it that when we get on a train we avoid the coach with no one in it, hunt for an empty double seat in a partly filled car, and hope against hope that no one will sit down beside us? It is said that this comes down from our days as monkeys, when two on a limb was not so good for the outermost.

Why is it that in normal times we will not stop at a roadside ice-cream dispensary unless it boasts of at least twenty flavors, and then after looking them over carefully, we choose chocolate, strawberry, or vanilla?

Why is it that when Easter Sunday comes around we feel abashed if we must go to church in last year's headgear, but if we have a new hat hanging on the hatrack at home, we have no qualms about wearing the old one?

These tendencies may reach far back into our inherited way of doing things. When we realize how our millions of years may have conditioned us, we can begin to see why it is worthwhile to think about our relationships with others and not to assume that executive effectiveness is simply acting naturally without thinking.

The third fact is that, in terms of money value, *we are much more valuable individuals than we appear to be.* Let us take a workman with a potential earning rate of $80 a week, or, in rough figures, $4,000 a year, and with perhaps twenty-five useful years before him. In the event of his sudden death, what amount of government bonds at, say, 3 per cent interest would it be necessary to provide for his wife and family in order that this income be continued over such a period? On this basis, the man represents the equivalent of roughly $80,000 as he stands. When we see employees in the factory, we do not realize just what is represented in going value.

When we take any production department in an industry and compare the value of machines, materials, and men, we realize that the capitalized economic value in dollars of our manpower often outruns many times the value of the inanimate elements of production.

The fourth fact is that *each of us is born with extraordinary capacities* and some have special talents which are most unusual. For example, as small children we toss and catch a ball, thereby solving a problem of four variables; we can detect a flavor when it is but one part in several million; the range of our normal hearing is enormous; our internal temperature control holds us to a variance of less than a few degrees in all climates throughout the years of our lifetime. These are but a few of the abilities with which we were born. And many of us can recall the paymaster who could remember all the hundreds of numbers and names on the payroll; the clerk who could multiply four-digit numbers in his head; the repairman who made the engine run when all others threw up their hands.

Employees are like this. We never know what unusual abilities may be concealed behind the routines of our workmen; and, as we live in a country where people have traditionally had a chance to make use of their special abilities, no one looks down upon us if we cultivate the habit of giving men a chance.

The fifth fact that underlies our executive attitude is that *every single person hopes for an ever-better future for himself*. The human creature always has looked upward. Call it ambition, enterprise, initiative or call it dissatisfaction, unrest, discontent, the plain fact is that everyone wants to better his lot and will, under normal circumstances, take constructive steps to do so if given a reasonable chance.

These five characteristics—our employees' individual differences, their long ancestry, their high economic value, their extraordinary talents, and their inborn ambition—if fully appreciated and accepted, provide us with a sound basis for a truly progressive attitude toward our executive responsibilities. We should be aware of one further characteristic of ourselves and our employees before we attempt to define our attitude as executives.

Human Capacity for Growth. We can improve. There seems to be almost no part of our activities in which we cannot do better if we put our minds to it.

We can develop skills past all belief. I recall reading of a prisoner in a French penal colony who, wishing to escape and knowing the necessity of money for the attempt, learned to throw a large knife high in the air and catch it by the point in his teeth. By entertaining visitors with this trick, he collected a few pennies from them which finally accumulated to make his flight possible. An evening spent watching variety shows on TV is usually sufficient for us to prove to ourselves man's gift for growth in skills.

Today we can develop our constructive imagination and practical ingenuity in ways which a few years ago would have been believed impossible. Our departments of research and development have revealed a capacity for increased creativeness that has been far greater than anyone could have dreamed. Properly designed suggestion programs have tapped deep sources of usefulness in our employee group that hitherto have gone to waste. Now we are sure that there is no end to growth in improvement, because new suggestions create new situations and these in turn invite new suggestions.

We learn through experience to evaluate the happenings about us and the motives underlying them. We all seem to have a kind of native wisdom which as years pass enables us to form common-sense judgments in the absence of all formalized rules of logic. In short, every person contains the promise of growing better with time. More than this, such improvement is normally essential to happiness.

Executive Concern. Any person of responsibility is concerned that his responsibilities be competently fulfilled. The attitude of the executive, in the light of the foregoing facts, should be one of *concern for the fullest release of each individual employee toward constant personal growth and self-development.*

Here lies the basic principle upon which rest all subsequent policy, technique, and accomplishment. The certainty that this *is* the prime purpose of the executive rests in turn upon the knowledge that every human being is a person of unique characteristics, the product of ages of evolutional development, having a high economic value, with unknown potential qualities, blessed with a normal unrest and a capacity for growth which make him, in a democracy, a "free and equal" individual.

Executive Attitude and Action. What can the executive do in a practical way to enable employees to improve? How do activities directed to that end relate to other company responsibilities in matters of cost, quality, service, and general departmental effectiveness?

The answer is not difficult. Employee aspirations are like layers in a layer cake, and to provide an outlet for each of these ascending desires requires simultaneous emphasis upon company objectives. The interests of both employee and company must be served at the same time.

The beginning of all efforts to permit the employee to do his best is *the assurance of personal security*. It is one of the earliest rules of leadership that security should be provided in return for willing response. But to make the job secure for the workman calls for more than proper employee selection, training, and equipment to assure satisfactory accomplishment. In addition, the executive has the responsibility that the job itself shall remain secure as a result of constantly lowering departmental costs and improving quality and service. Increasing departmental effectiveness means steadier jobs for all employees.

Next to security, the employee hopes for a job that provides *a good place to work*. Shop facilities and surroundings, particularly the human contacts, make the work pleasant or burdensome. Such satisfactions build loyalty even as security builds willing response.

The company has good reason constantly to improve working conditions, even apart from their effect on the present working force. The living standards of industrial workers as consumers (purchasers of consumer goods) have risen rapidly and are continuing to do so. The living standards of the workers as producers, that is, the factory standards, must also advance if the average concern is to maintain its position in competition with newer establishments in the maintenance of a high-grade employee personnel.

More than this, it has become clear that the more the doing of a piece of work is simplified and made physically convenient, the lower are unit costs and the higher is quality. Frank Gilbreth, the pioneer of motion study, used to pay especial attention to the way in which the overweight operators performed their tasks, as they usually had studied for themselves the elimination of waste motions and in the process had learned to perform their tasks quicker and better.

With job security and working satisfactions taken care of, the workman's interest moves on to *opportunity for advancement* in such matters as over-all experience, personal standing, responsibility, income, and the like. In return, he will give his zeal. To operate a department in which such opportunities are present, the executive must so competently conduct its affairs in the company interest that departmental progress is recognized and rewarded by ever-enlarging activities, output, and responsibilities.

Finally, if the employee is to be stimulated to do his best, he requires, in addition to security, satisfaction, and opportunity, a *truly worthy objective* which he and his associates are convinced is entitled to their highest efforts. To such a cause he will give devotion. To awaken the devotion of a group of employees is the highest accomplishment to which any executive can aspire.

Once more, company objectives should be considered along with employee desires. The commonest of products may offer a high purpose to workmen if its standards of excellence are such as to build a reputation for the best in quality. There are many plants in the United States whose standing in the trade makes their employees proud to work for such organizations.

High-grade executives earn the willing response, the loyalty, the zeal, the devotion of their employees by so strengthening and advancing the effectiveness of departmental operation that each employee is given opportunity to develop his abilities and to enlarge his opportunities. And to provide a reasonable degree of security, of job satisfaction, of personal opportunity and an ideal to work toward is a man-sized job for anyone.

Executive Morale. What keeps the executive's spirits up? In our efforts to provide fullest opportunity for the progress of our men, where shall we look for stimulation and encouragement for ourselves?

Kettering has said, "When you get into business you get into trouble and the nice part of it is that you can pick the kind of trouble that you like to get into."

Executives are constantly getting into trouble *for* people—for their superiors, for their associates, for their subordinates, for the customers who will use the products. It is the kind of trouble that executives like to get into, for it brings the kind of fundamental satisfaction that builds true morale.

Good gardeners have the knack of making plants grow; people say that they have a "green thumb." Good herdsmen have a way with cattle. Good executives are man makers first and foremost and, as such, they are truly happy men, for there are few thrills greater than those of seeing people grow and prosper under one's supervision.

Executive morale does not spring out of wage incentives, working conditions, vacation allowances, or pension plans, although these help. Executive morale springs from the personal certainty that employees have become better and more useful men and women as a result of sound guidance; that the company has become a more effective operating unit because of intelligent efforts; that the executive himself has grown in the art of management.

During a depression year one of my associates revisited a Southern town where he had spent some time as an executive in a large car-building enterprise. As he walked along the main street of the village, he was stopped by a workman who greeted him and said, "You probably don't remember me, Mr. Fernstrom, but I used to work for you down at the car shop. I just wanted to tell you that the seven years I worked for you were the seven happiest years of my life."

Executives do not have to go far in search of evidence to bolster their morale. Wherever they are, whomever they work for, and whatever the difficulties they encounter, they know that they are performing as significant a service as a man can offer—they are helping people to live a more satisfying and self-respecting life.

Discussion. What is your response to the following comments?

1. *I agree that there is work that a clerk can do better than I. If I did not have so many clerical requirements I could be a better executive.*

Is there anything to be gained from clerical activities? How important are facts in the building of plant and employee effectiveness? What assurance about such facts provides greater self-confidence to the user? Are there clerical activities that may ensure and strengthen the executive's position in the eyes of his superior?

2. *It may be true that we are all different, but we cannot expect to have each job exactly tailored to each man. Many operating jobs must be practically identical.*

If we as workmen were required to perform work identical with that of other operators, would it help us to know that our boss was aware of the ways in which we differed from them? If so, why would it help?

3. *The idea that we may have come down from monkeys does not seem to have much relation to the problem of getting out production.*

Did you ever have employees complain that they were away from other employees and lonesome in their work? Why did they feel that way? Have you ever had employees complain that they were forced to work in too crowded surroundings? Why did they think them too crowded? Did you ever have employees object to working where windows could not be seen through? Why do people want to see out of windows?

4. *Maybe employees are worth a lot in terms of money and if this is the case, why aren't they a bit more careful of their own standing and value to the organization?*

> Are employees usually given to calculating their value in terms of money? Is this the way to stimulate workmen to increase their standing and value to the organization? If not, how should we go about doing so?

5. *I have plenty of employees who are aware that they are extraordinary but they don't want to apply their abilities in improving their work or the work of the department.*

> Are employees ordinarily aware of their unusual abilities or capacities? May a workman have a good reason for not wanting to improve his future with his company?

6. *My experience has been that most employees have little ambition. They want a soft job, a big pay check, and nothing to think about.*

> Is it normal for people to be without ambition? If not, why may they find themselves in this state of mind?

7. *Nobody can make a job secure. There is no absolute security that any man or institution can offer.*

> When we speak of job security, just what do we mean? Absolute security? Relative security? Partial security? What would we as executives hope for in the way of security?

8. *It is all very well to talk about outlays for improving working conditions but when such expenditures do not reduce unit costs the proposal is impractical.*

Just how may labor turnover affect unit costs? To what extent are quality of output and general science important as factors to be considered?

9. *Workmen today expect opportunities to be laid before them on a silver platter. They don't want to pay the price of opportunity.*

Should opportunity in work be a reward or an integral part of every job? Should opportunity have a price? Does the presence of opportunity compensate for the absence of complete security?

10. *Devoted employees may be all right in theory but most workers save their devotion, if they have any, for their families. Work is work and not a place for sentiment.*

What makes us want to do our absolute best? Money? Prestige? Security? Personal satisfaction in accomplishment? When we did the best job we ever turned out, what was it that drove us on? Was it feeling or cold calculation?

11. *Some executives may build morale out of making men, but if they don't make money for the company at the same time they won't have a job. No one can live on morale.*

Is it impractical to attempt to make men and to build company security at the same time? Do executives ever do exactly one thing at a time? What do we mean by living? Existing? What do men live by? As executives, why are we in need of morale?

CHAPTER 3

Executive Tools

Tools offer the same advantages to the executive as to the workman, for through them the user may increase the quality and value of his service and eliminate waste of time and effort. The executive's tools, however, are not as tangible as those of the employee, who is dealing with substances instead of personalities. They are in a sense psychological, and their purpose is to assist in the development of employee cooperation to the most effective degree, with a minimizing of the emotional frictions and misunderstandings which are inevitable if the tools are not used. The executive's tools are found in certain qualities of disposition which, if reflected in his conduct, will produce certain definite responses from the employee. These qualities of disposition do not appear in the form of words, and rarely are they the primary cause of an executive act. Rather, they form the atmosphere or background for executive words and acts.

Stimulating Tools. A later chapter is devoted to the avenues through which the executive stimulates performance and accomplishment. Here we are concerned with the tools which he can use. Undoubtedly the quality of *enthusiasm* lies in this category. Enthusiasm is contagious. Enthusiasm in an executive breathes life into a project. It stimulates a desire for action. It concentrates attention upon the work at hand.

EXECUTIVE CONDUCT. Remember that enthusiasm is emotional in nature. Do not stir up too much of it. Too great enthusiasm in work requiring painstaking attention may increase mental tension to such an extent that inaccuracies will result. Remember that enthusiasm, like most emotional tendencies, is not continuous in nature. It waxes and wanes. It is easiest to arouse when a new project is started. It is most difficult to evoke at the time when it is most needed, namely, just before accomplishment is reached. Save your enthusiasm for the home stretch. Do not simulate enthusiasm. Be sincere. The way to arouse it in yourself is to concentrate your attention upon your project; visualize its completion and the accompanying satisfactions of accomplishment, and enthusiasm will follow.

Q. *Does fatigue affect one's sensitiveness to enthusiasm?*

> What is enthusiasm? Is it a real eagerness to accomplish something, or an ebullition of spirits that requires further translation into action? Is enthusiasm desirable if the possibility of such translation is not immediately available? What results from enthusiasms which are allowed to evaporate?

Q. *You have been very successful in developing an enthusiastic spirit in your organization. The employees are doing their best, but because of technical difficulties beyond their control, their efforts are badly hampered and their accomplishment will inevitably be disappointing. Is it advisable to develop enthusiasm under these circumstances?*

If not, where will you draw the line? Is it necessary to be absolutely certain of success before awakening enthusiasm? Can you be? If not, what sort of chances can you legitimately take?

Q. A branch sales manager has found that ten-minute pep talks to salesmen at the beginning of work every morning have a beneficial effect upon sales. He suggests that the practice be instituted in all production departments. Do you agree or disagree, and why?

How does the work of the employee who is engaged in production differ from that of the employee in sales or in clerical work? In which group is outward attitude of greatest importance? What may be other purposes of the sales pep talk? To assure that work is started promptly? To accelerate the warming-up process? To supply a reason for daily personal contact between salesman and executive? Contrast this situation with that of production or clerical work.

Cheerfulness is a never-failing source of stimulation. Many executives have learned the great value of this tool and have consciously developed its use. Cheerfulness begets cheerfulness. Like enthusiasm, it implies faith in the project. It produces an environment favorable to thought and helps to carry the organization through difficulties and over obstacles.

EXECUTIVE CONDUCT. Do not neglect this tool. Do not be afraid of using it. Some beginners in executive work feel that a spirit of cheerfulness may detract from their dignity. This is not true. If you feel that you must wear a grim mouth, wear smiling eyes. But don't wear both grim. To be sincerely cheerful you must take a cheerful view of things. This does not mean that you cannot be serious or grave when need arises. Your normal outward attitude, however, will yield you far greater returns in cooperation and a pleasant working environment for yourself and your organization if it is optimistic.

Q. *Is cheerfulness something that you can assume while you are on duty and discard when your workday is over, or is it a quality that must become habitual in order to be effective?*

> Is cheerfulness subject to control? Or is it our response to the conditions which surround us (when they are pleasant, we are cheerful, and vice versa)? If a person is invariably cheerful, is he not failing to take life as seriously as it deserves? Are there not legitimate times for gravity as well as cheerfulness?

Q. *You are busy in your office; an employee enters and asks to speak to you. You cannot give him any time at the moment and ask him to come back in half an hour. Would it be your natural tendency to speak pleasantly or gruffly when such an interruption occurred? If the latter, could you demand pleasantness of yourself? Is not cheerfulness subject to self-control?*

> Does pleasantness spring from a sense of courtesy or from a feeling of cheerfulness? Should an executive allow employees to interrupt him when busy? What is the most important kind of executive busy-ness?

A spirit of *unselfishness* has a profoundly stimulating effect in certain directions. Employees distrust a selfish boss, particularly if his selfishness leads him to take credit for constructive suggestions which have been made by them. As soon as the workman feels assured that the executive has the interests of his subordinates sincerely at heart, the fundamentals of loyalty are established.

EXECUTIVE CONDUCT. Do not hesitate to demonstrate an attitude of unselfishness. Make it a rule to tell your chief of any constructive suggestion which an employee may offer, and contrive to do this, if you can, in the hearing of the employee, so that there can be no doubt that the credit is rightly assigned. If an employee finds a better opportunity elsewhere, don't stand in his way. Help him to embrace it, even though this may cause temporary embarrassment to your plans.

Q. *If you believe that one of your employees would fill your position better than you do, should you stand in the way of his getting the job? Should you make your attitude known to your chief? Should you urge your chief to make the change?*

> Can you compare yourself with another as accurately as can your chief? Have you as complete a view of the whole situation as has your chief? Is it a human tendency to deprecate one's assets and overemphasize personal weaknesses? Should one ever *urge* his chief to do anything?

Stabilizing Tools. A quality that clearly belongs in this grouping is *calmness*. It is an executive attribute which is very popular with employees. All of us enjoy dealing with a calm person, for we know that he is a person of habitual self-control. Calmness, like other pleasant qualities, is contagious. Where executives are dealing with female employees, it is particularly desirable that this tool be used, for emotionalism spreads very rapidly among women. In times of stress or emergency, employees watch the executive closely and are quick to imitate him. If he is calm, they tend to become so.

EXECUTIVE CONDUCT. Don't affect the quality of calmness. It will give you an appearance of false dignity which is only amusing. Calmness is a product of true thoughtfulness. You will find it hard not to take on the emotional state of those around you, for it is natural that you should do so. Only conscious self-control will enable you to restrain your feelings and allow your mind to work unhampered. Calmness comes with thought. To think requires self-discipline.

Q. *An employee rushes into your office and tells you that a portion of the power shafting is working loose from its fastening and is in danger of falling. You run to shut off the power and then to the point of trouble with a view to keeping employees away from danger. Does this haste necessitate a loss of poise?*

> Are there any grounds for believing that a person in haste cannot be calm? What do you mean by haste?

Q. *Do executives who are quick in speech and action necessarily lack calmness?*

> Should an executive ordinarily be quick or slow in speech? In action?

A tool which arouses a strong responsive feeling of satisfaction and stability is that of *consistency*. The executive who is the same today, tomorrow, and the next day is always welcomed among workmen. Once the will of a group has been organized, and its direction determined and undertaken, the element of momentum appears. The greater the organization the greater the momentum. To change its course or purpose is to meet opposition. The consistent executive is one who does not deviate from his plan. His policies are not changed by every whim of circumstance. He can be depended upon to carry through. His plans are coordinate. There is a rightness in the fitting together of his ideas and a stability to his personality.

EXECUTIVE CONDUCT. Don't vacillate. A poor plan persevered in is better than a good one shifted while being executed. Don't be changeable in temperament—optimistic today, pessimistic tomorrow. Set your standard of conduct and stick to it. Develop a stable personality.

Q. *Under what circumstances should you change a plan in the midst of carrying it out?*

> Should a plan be changed because of increasing employee opposition to its continuation? Because a better method has appeared? Because it is not arriving at the desired objective? How far may a plan be left elastic and still be called a plan?

Q. *You are newly employed as a clerk in an organization. One of your acquaintances comes to you and says, "Let me give you a little advice. If you ever want to get anything from the boss, don't go near him just before lunch or the first thing in the morning, for he's ugly as a bear then. And leave him alone on Mondays. They are always 'Blue Mondays' for him." Would your favorable impression of your boss be increased through this information?*

> Suppose that you have good explanation for periods of depression; can it be offered as an excuse for grumpiness? Does evidence of consistency inspire confidence in a leader? Why? We expect executives to act naturally; we admire them for their self-control. How can these attitudes be reconciled?

Time-saving Tools. Executives who are *receptive* make it possible for their employees to come to them without nervousness or hesitancy and quickly present the matter at hand. Matthew C. Brush, in commenting upon this quality, says:

> I have in mind very clearly an instance of my own experience, where my predecessor had so impressed his subordinates with the importance of their subserviency that in my first interview with one of them he spent all his time, all his thought, and all his energy thinking of how he should conduct himself to show proper respect to a superior officer, and how he could say things which would most please me, with the result that he had left no thought, time, or energy for consideration of the question we were discussing. It took me months to untrain this man so that he would come into the office as a co-worker and not as a slave. A member of a team can have intimate, close, cordial, and even friendly relations with the leader and still not break down any attitude of respect and courtesy.

EXECUTIVE CONDUCT. Remember that when an employee enters your office he is in a strange land. He feels the atmosphere of authority; he is constrained and hesitant. Make him feel at ease. Your method of greeting will help. Some executives make it a rule not to talk across their desks to an employee who is unaccustomed to addressing them. The desk seems to form a barrier to free discussion; it symbolizes authority and creates an atmosphere of homage which is restraining.

Q. *Does the cultivation of approachability mean that you should make yourself available for all manner of minor questions and discussions so that you have a continual stream of employees running to you, making serious inroads upon your time?*

> Where are you going to draw the line? Is it practicable to see employees by appointment? Should they be asked to submit their requests in writing? Should you make it a practice to walk about the department at certain times and be available for advice or discussion? Is the employee's need of conference with his chief symptomatic of any defect in organization or method?

Q. *You have an employee who is well-meaning and loyal but has little sense of proportion. He is constantly importuning you with unimportant matters. He seems to feel that he can do nothing without specifically asking your permission or opinion. How can you help him to overcome his tendency without making him feel that you have taken a dislike to him?*

> Should you: Tell him that he is wasting your time? Ask him questions which demand that he do more thinking?

Obstruct his access in such a way that he will realize that he is unwelcome? Discourage him through a continued rejection of his ideas? Ask him to present in writing the advantages and disadvantages of any future proposals?

Q. *You are filling the position of plant superintendent. You have adopted the "open-door" policy and find that workmen who report to your foremen are coming to see you on many matters. They seem to appreciate the opportunity to talk with you on subjects which they prefer not to discuss with their immediate superior. Is your receptiveness being used properly? Does your policy conflict with the principles of good organization?*

What would be your diagnosis of a situation in which employees wished to talk with you on subjects which they preferred not to discuss with their immediate superior?

Another time-saving tool is the quality of *simplicity*. There is no value in attempting to gain prestige by impressing the employee with your extensive learning or large vocabulary. Simplicity makes for mutual understanding and intimate contact between minds.

EXECUTIVE CONDUCT. A novelist once said, "We should spend more time upon our books so that the reader may spend less." You should apply this rule in your dealings with employees. Work over the facts you wish to present until you can offer them simply and in the language of the listener. The greatest speeches of history have nearly all been so simply presented that anyone could understand them.

Q. Do you consider it advisable to use a slang expression if it enables you to present your thought more effectively? What is the value of refraining from the use of slang?

Why is there such a thing as slang?

Q. You enter an organization as executive and find in use a large number of shop terms which have developed in this particular plant but which are not common elsewhere; you are familiar with others which are more generally accepted. You face the alternative of accustoming yourself to the terms used in the new organization or introducing the unfamiliar but more widely accepted outside nomenclature. What factors will you consider in making your decision?

Would commonly used terms offer any advantage in dealings with distributors or other customers? In dealings with factory employees? What difficulties would you anticipate in introducing the new terms into the factory? How soon should this be undertaken, if at all? Do you think it possible that the factory employees could be brought to *want* to use the new terms, and if so, how? If this seems impossible, have you any counterplan to suggest?

Frankness brings large returns to the executive in time economies, for frankness in an executive encourages frankness in employees. As a result, there is no beating about the bush; no one has mental reservations. The facts, favorable and unfavorable, are laid upon the table and the problem is attacked without delay.

EXECUTIVE CONDUCT. Be receptive to facts, however discouraging, disappointing, or injurious to your personal welfare they may appear to be. Don't let your feelings be hurt by facts. If you cannot avoid feeling hurt, don't show it. Many well-meaning people are not frank because they dislike saying anything which may cause offense. Never become angered by a fact.

Q. *You have been frank with an employee. You have told him of some faults which he can easily rectify if he will. It is evident, however, that you have disturbed and pained him. When he leaves your office, he seems cooperative and appreciative of your frankness, but you are concerned that he will later remember the sting of the facts rather than the facts themselves and become sullen and obdurate. Is there any way that you can follow up this incident so that the sting will be removed but the facts again recalled to his mind?*

> Would you later contrive to talk with him in a friendly way on another subject? Would you take pains to commend him on evidence of improvement? Would it have helped if you had told him, "If I did not think you were worth saving, I shouldn't have taken the trouble to tell you these things"?

Power of personality in the executive often takes the form of *impressiveness*. This does not mean impressiveness in appearance, but rather the ability to impress the mind of another. Executives often do not put enough of themselves behind their words. They make their statements too lightly, they neglect to drive the idea home. As a result, a part of their message does not catch hold, and a repetition is necessary.

EXECUTIVE CONDUCT. Cultivate a tone of voice and manner of speech which will be listened to. Don't speak too rapidly. Give your words a chance to become absorbed. Don't waste your words. Say exactly what you mean. Never spin out conversation with an employee on business matters. If you have nothing to say, say nothing. Safeguard your reputation of being worth listening to.

Q. *Does one necessarily have to speak loudly or pitch one's voice at an unusual point in order to speak impressively? Are clearness and tempo of speech more important factors? Is the reputation of saying something worth listening to of greater importance than the manner of saying?*

> Some executives favor speaking a bit gruffly. What do you think?

Q. *Is impressiveness in appearance an aid to impressiveness in speech? If so, is it an essential?*

> Irrespective of what has been said in the text, what do you find impressive in conversation directed to you? Is it the appearance of the speaker, the manner of speaking, the content of his thought, or is it your expectancy resulting from a knowledge of the man?

Conforming Tools. From the employee viewpoint, *firmness* is a welcome executive quality. This characteristic brings confidence and conformance to the will of the executive. Firmness does not require an emotional background in order to be effective. Many successful executives have the reputation of being "mild but firm." The presence of firmness implies that the executive has shouldered his responsibilities and is facing his problem of organization squarely and with assurance.

EXECUTIVE CONDUCT. To be firm does not mean that you should be obstinate and close your eyes to the truth of a situation. Firmness lies midway between obstinacy and irresolution. It is a quality that protects your judgment from the buffetings of other personalities, but it need never close the door to reason.

Q. *One of your employees has asked to be allowed to change his method of work. You have gone over his suggestion carefully and are convinced that, while the new method would be easier, it would not afford so close a control over quality, and the output would tend to suffer in this respect. You have told the employee that you will not permit the change. He has returned to you twice to ask that you change your decision. Have you been sufficiently firm in your treatment? Has there been an error in properly evidencing your firmness, rather than in the degree of firmness itself? How will you make your position clear to him?*

> Some executives protect themselves from such situations by establishing reputations for not changing decisions—others protect themselves by a show of irritation upon repeated requests for changes—others develop reputations for being right in their judgment. In this case, would you feel that some explanation for your firmness would be desirable? Is the employee probably sincere in his feeling or is he trying to test your firmness? Can an executive develop a reputation for obstinacy with his employees? How?

We have heard a great deal of the value of *tact* in executive work, and the meaning of the word has come to be somewhat misunderstood. Tact is not the avoidance of unpleasant subjects in executive relations. The tactful leader does not necessarily sidestep a discussion of disagreeable, distasteful, or disappointing topics when talking with employees. Tact is merely the ability to appeal to the positive moods of the individual, such as loyalty, duty, justice, and to remove him from the influence of negative moods, such as those of hatred, resentment, suspicion, or anger. When individuals are influenced by these negative moods, they are rarely cooperative for good purpose. Therefore, the executive finds tact a great aid in developing conformance.

EXECUTIVE CONDUCT. It is de-morale-izing to hurt the pride of an employee or to injure his feelings in any way. It is de-morale-izing to arouse his anger or resentment toward another. The tactless person usually does these things unintentionally. Remember that tact is born of a regard for the personality of others.

Q. *If you find that you have made a tactless remark before a group of employees, should you allude to your error and attempt to correct it?*

> What is the result of a tactless remark? Do the harmful effects of tactlessness spring from reaction to the statement or to the attitude of mind implicit in the statement? Can a wrong inference be corrected without reference to the statement from which it was drawn?

Tolerance and *patience* are qualities that reflect the executive's sensitiveness to the rate of advance of his organization. The intolerant or impatient executive is a disorganizing influence. He demands undue haste, which results in undue waste and confusion. It has been said that the great ignorance of our educated classes is their ignorance of ignorance. The executive is too prone to expect more of the employee in the way of knowledge and mental adaptability than is fair and reasonable.

EXECUTIVE CONDUCT. Your cannot expect your organization to improve as rapidly as you can yourself. If your employees could improve at your rate, they would not be employees, but would have qualified for executive work. Your organization has a certain rate of growth and of assimilation of new ideas. Find out what it is. Don't hurry it. You will get better results in the long run. One good executive has said, "It is much harder to determine what it is best to overlook than to discover what to criticize."

Q. *Cannot patience and tolerance be overdone? May not employees misinterpret your patience as a lack of stamina on your part? How can you avoid this misconception?*

> Should you tell them that you are being patient or tolerant? Should patience or tolerance be shown when there is no improvement? What indicates that these qualities are being overemphasized? Underemphasized?

Q. *You have a messenger boy in your organization. He is full of energy and is somewhat mischievous. You have spoken to him about his deportment, and at such times he accepts your criticism in good spirit and restrains his tendencies for a period. Have you any good reasons for tolerance?*

Some executives consider such boys worth watching as possible executive timber. Do you agree, and, if so, why? Should an executive be tolerant of the practical joker in an organization? Would his type of humor affect your decision, and how?

Restraining Tools. There is a requisite degree of *dignity* in every position of authority which the occupant should respect and maintain. Dignity in office is a symbol of assurance that the responsibilities which accompany authority are not being treated lightly.

EXECUTIVE CONDUCT. Dignity does not imply solemnity, nor does it demand a show of ritual or ceremony. Dignity results from a clear appreciation of the significance of the responsibilities that you have shouldered and a sincere and abiding desire to give the best that is in you in meeting these responsibilities. You will acquire a natural dignity if you maintain this attitude of mind. Don't simulate dignity. The mask is easily detected and will harm more than it will help.

Q. *Some executives hold that they should be "one with, but not one of," their employees. Do you agree? To what extent should an executive avoid familiarity with employees?*

For example, should an executive lunch with his employees when business matters are not to be discussed? Should he accept rides in employees' automobiles? Should he invite employees to his home? Employees are human beings like himself—why should they be treated differently from anyone else? What would you consider indicative of too familiar an attitude on the part of an employee?

Q. *Does an atmosphere of natural dignity lessen approachability?*

> Does it lessen misuse of executive time? Why? Some executives believe that gravity is imitated by employees and that in this mood, employees are more apt to think about their work than otherwise. What is your opinion?

Courtesy is the great defensive tool of the executive. It is also an economizer of time. The courteous executive suggests courtesy to his men. In such an atmosphere we find self-control, and where there is self-control there is very little chance of a negative atmosphere of anger, suspicion, or resentment developing. Business can be conducted more rapidly, as reasoning can take place with the least amount of difficulty.

EXECUTIVE CONDUCT. Adopt a uniform standard of courtesy and maintain it. There is no reason for being less courteous to your subordinates than to your chief. Courtesy does not require a deferential spirit and no employee should interpret it in such a way. Courtesy does not require ceremony. It is the outward evidence of a regard for human sensibilities. Your employees will respect you for practicing it.

Q. *You enter an organization as executive and find a standard of courtesy somewhat lower than you desire. Would it be advisable to post a notice requesting improvement? If not, what agency would you employ? Is this an improvement to be sought through the power of example?*

> Suppose that one of your employees does not respond to your examples but shows a chronic tendency to be dis-

courteous to other employees, what would you say to him? Would you threaten him with discharge? Is discourtesy grounds for discharge? Would you attempt to convince him of the error of his ways through their effect upon his usefulness, or through their effect upon his own ultimate satisfactions?

Q. *Can a severe rebuke be administered in a courteous manner? If so, would its effect be increased or decreased by the element of courtesy?*

Should the executive speak in a personal way, or impersonally, as a representative of the company? What should be the basis for such a rebuke—behavior which is below your personal standards of conduct, or behavior which, if continued, will injure the organization or the work?

Tools for Fashioning Loyalty. We should not be doing justice to our subject if we omitted the qualities of *kindness* and *friendliness* from our list of tools. It is true that we like to think of using these qualities solely to develop our own personalities along right paths, and we feel that it is a cheapening thing to exploit them for any other purpose. It is only fair, however, that their great worth to the executive be emphasized.

EXECUTIVE CONDUCT. It is not enough to feel kindly disposed or friendly toward an employee. You should show yourself kind and show yourself friendly. There are countless opportunities for every executive to add this personal touch of interest and friendship to his relations with his workers. Often the employee remembers these acts above all others and builds his loyalty upon them. You will not, as an executive, be in a position to search for opportunities to evidence these qualities, but you should be watchful to capitalize on them when they appear.

Q. *One of your employees is ill. You learn that his sickness appears to be a serious one but that he is in the care of a good physician. He is a man with a family and there is every likelihood that he is worrying about his work and his loss of earnings. If you visited him or his family, would it be appreciated?*

> Wouldn't a letter or a telephone call do as well as a visit? Or could you not send word to him by an employee? Or isn't this a responsibility of the visiting nurse? If you are not in a position to assure the man that his wages will be continued or that his job will be held for him, would it not be better to remain away? Why?

Q. *One of your workmen is a Cuban. He has received several boxes of Cuban cigars from a relative of his and he offers a box to you. You do not smoke cigars. What should you do and say?*

> Is it desirable that there be a shop rule prohibiting executives from receiving presents from groups of employees? From individual employees? Would the nature of the motive behind the giving affect your decision to accept a present from an employee? Why?

Conclusion. These tools cannot be purchased. They cannot be fashioned by another. The executive must make them for himself, and the making is a process of self-discipline. One of the first principles of executive conduct is that to become master of men one must first become master of himself. Self-control lies at the foundation of any plan for executive advancement. There is no easy road to self-control. Benjamin Franklin in his *Autobiography* describes his method of self-development. He took one virtue at a time and trained himself in it until a habit was formed, then turned to another, until he had completed his requirements for self-improvement. Fortunate is the man into whose hands the executive tools fall naturally, but such instances are rare. Almost every successful executive experiences the stress of self-encounter before he finds himself properly equipped to fulfill the responsibilities of a leader.

Discussion. What is your response to the following comments?

1. *Enthusiasm produces an abnormal and temporary emotional condition. Therefore it does not make for steadiness in output or consistency in quality.*

   How about conditions in which unavoidable monotony or unforeseen difficulties have produced a subnormal emotional condition of apathy or discouragement?

2. *Human effort is usually produced at levels far below capacity. The stimulus of enthusiasm tends to raise these levels and thereby increases human usefulness.*

   Can we count on enthusiasm to raise effort to permanently higher levels? Suppose that during the period of enthusiasm, improved work habits are developed?

3. *To assume an attitude of cheerfulness is to be insincere. Sincerity is a fundamental of effective executive conduct.*

What is your reaction to a person who is cheerful in the presence of vicissitude? Is cheerfulness the result of external circumstance or inner philosophy?

4. *Calmness has its place and so has agitation. Organizations are sometimes benefited by a little dynamite.*

Under what conditions are organizations benefited by a little dynamite? How do organizations get into such situations? Is dynamite curative or preventive?

5. *No executive should be asked to gamble his reputation through adherence to a plan which contains unpredictable elements.*

Does the executive usually make the plan? If he does, do employees think less of him if he habitually sticks to it? Can a plan be so termed if it allows for unpredictable elements? Do employees expect the executive to be certain about the future?

6. *Mollycoddling employees does not make them strong. Straightforward statements may carry a sting, but frankness is more effective than tactfulness in the long run.*

Does tactfulness prevent one from being frank? Must frankness carry a sting? Is tact a mollycoddling influence? Just what is tact, as you see it?

7. *One can afford to be tolerant and patient with about one-half of the average group of employees. The others need constant jogging to keep them properly busy. Tolerance with some people only encourages loafing.*

Under what conditions are tolerance and patience justified? Are tolerance and patience to be considered as opportunities for the leakage of executive power, or are they to be viewed as tools which will produce constructive results?

8. *Courtesy may be all right when executives are dealing with women, but men like a boss who will tell them what to do in decisive terms. Too much politeness implies timidity.*

Cannot one be both decisive and courteous? Does politeness imply timidity? If not, what is it in one's manner that implies timidity?

9. *I don't favor the developing of a personal interest in and friendship with workmen. When employees are personal friends, standards of quality and quantity cannot be strictly enforced.*

Does friendship inevitably cause uncertainty regarding precedence in executive loyalties? How can an executive avoid such uncertainty?

CHAPTER 4

Executive Control

Authority. If we are to have control, we must provide avenues through which it can function easily and directly. These avenues we speak of as the paths of authority. They pass from the administrators, who determine policy, to the executives, who are responsible for carrying out the policy, and then to the employees, who perform the actual operations.

It is clear that if these paths are vaguely outlined there will be confusion. The executive must know the precise limitations of his field of authority if he is to function freely and competently, and the employee likewise should know the exact source of control to which he must respond. Furthermore, these paths of authority should not be short-circuited by impatient executives.

EXECUTIVE CONDUCT. See that your employees are thoroughly familiar with the paths of authority. If you interpose any subordinate executive between yourself and the employees, have the extent of his authority clearly interpreted and stated in writing so that there can be no misunderstanding. If you extend authority temporarily to another person, inform the employees affected. For example, if you install a new adding machine which employees must be taught how to use, introduce the instructor to the employees with the understanding that you give him authority to teach and that the employees are supposed to follow his methods. The instructor's position is then clearly established.

Q. *You have appointed one of your employees to act as chief clerk over a group of other clerks. The chief clerk will continue to do his regular work but will supervise the other work as well. You notice that he is wrongly instructing one of the clerks. You tell him and the clerk that the instructions are faulty and then show the clerk the right way to do the work. You have improved the technical process. What have you done to your subordinate executive? What is the effect upon the clerk? What is the right way to take care of this situation?*

> Suppose that you had appointed your employee to train a new employee rather than to act as chief clerk. During the training period, but in the absence of the instructor, you note an error in the method used by the new man. Would you alter your procedure from that previously decided upon?

Q. *Some of your employees are using a chemical which may impair their health unless they take proper precautions, according to the statement of the company physician. He wishes to warn them of the danger and instruct them in proper precautionary measures. How will you place the doctor's expert advice before the employees?*

> After instructions have been issued, you find that certain employees are not following them. Would you consider it advisable to refer these men to the doctor for further and

more emphatic instruction? Suppose that certain employees are not clear as to the exact method recommended; should you refer them to the doctor, or should you advise them according to your own understanding?

Q. *The clerical work of one of your employees is referred to another department for further entries. Your employee takes his completed work to the other department from time to time. You find that the chief clerk in the other department has been instructing your employee to make alterations in his work in order that it may be more acceptable to that department. Is this good organization procedure? How should this situation have been handled?*

Is it permissible for the chief clerk to suggest alterations in method to your employee and ask him to present the suggestions to you? Is such a desire for alteration in method symptomatic of a flaw in organization, and if so, what is it?

The Order. The order is the directive impulse that makes coordinated action possible. It should proceed down the paths of *authority* in proper fashion.

EXECUTIVE CONDUCT. Test every order that you receive or issue with this question: "Has this order the necessary and proper authority behind it?"

When the order reaches the executive from his chief, it may require interpretation. For example, the order "Take inventory of all stocks on shelves as of May 31" may involve considerable organization and planning before it can be presented to the individual employee affected. The task of interpretation must sometimes be delegated to subordinate technicians if the amount of this sort of work is great.

Q. You are an executive in charge of a machine tool department in a large jobbing shop. You have authority over two hundred employees and average fifty production orders a day of this general description: "Make fifty parts as per attached blueprint." Can you see the advantage of having one or more technicians to assist you in determining how, where, when, and by whom the work should be done in order that it be produced with requisite promptness, that the load of work on your department be properly balanced, and that there be minimum waste of effort and material in the process?

Under what circumstances might it be preferable to have such technicians reporting to a central department which, in turn, would report to a higher production executive, rather than to you?

Q. You are a department superintendent in a large branch plant. As a result of charges of paternalism in earlier years, the company and its major executives in the local plant have for some time refrained from support of, cooperation with, or participation in social, political, and community programs such as the Red Cross, Community Fund, and recreational facilities. The company is now returning to activities in this area. Most of the present work on these activities is being performed by the plant personnel director during regular working hours. The plant manager is suggesting very forcibly that you run for member of the school board in the coming local elections. What is the nature of your responsibility here?

Would it make any difference if the recommendations of the plant manager to perform such external activities could be carried out primarily on company time? What if your equal in rank, for example the personnel director, had made the suggestion instead of your superior? Would the personnel director be speaking for the plant manager?

General Brice P. Disque makes the statement that "an executive, before issuing an order, should always know that *compliance is possible and reasonable.*" To fulfill this requirement is often a searching measure of executive ability.

EXECUTIVE CONDUCT. Test every order with this question: "Has everything been provided so that only the addition of a reasonable amount of employee will, energy, and skill is necessary to do this work?"

Q. *In the Taylor system of factory management, the records of the amount of raw material on hand are maintained in the planning department, where the factory production orders are technically prepared for issuance. Does the above principle throw any light upon the reason for this arrangement?*

Does this principle deprive the employee of all opportunity for creative work? Some managers maintain that a certain amount of preparatory work by employees is desirable, as diversification of effort reduces fatigue. What is your opinion?

An order, to be *complete,* should describe the nature of the accomplishment sought for, in terms of quantity and quality, with specified allowable variations in both. It should specify the method of performance; this involves the equipment and labor needed, as well as the process in detail. It should specify the location of performance. It should specify the limitations upon the time of performance. It should specify the individuals who are to be held responsible for the performance.

This is a rather lengthy list of requisites, but as there is often much repetition of orders, it is possible to avoid repetition of detailed instructions. For example, the description of a required accomplishment is often pictured by a drawing, copies of which can be used repeatedly and referred to when the order is duplicated. The necessary method may be incorporated in standard instructions with which the employees familiarize themselves and which need no reiteration. The location of the performance may be indicated by sending the order to a particular executive who has charge of the work in this location. In many cases location becomes a matter of mutual understanding among administrators, executives, and employees. The time limitations are necessarily expressed in the majority of orders, while the individuals responsible for the work are often indicated by the act of assigning the order.

EXECUTIVE CONDUCT. Test every order that you issue with the following question: "Can a complete understanding of what, how, where, when, and by whom the activity is or is not to be carried out be gained from the order together with the standard instructions in use?"

Q. *How does the sign "No Smoking Allowed" which is posted in your department stand this test? Are rules and regulations in reality standing orders?*

Do you favor regulations formulated in positive terms, for example, "Employees are requested to ——" or in negative terms, *i.e.*, "Do not——" or "Employees are prohibited from——"? What different methods are there for acquainting employees with standing orders? Which would appear to be the best?

An order must be *clearly expressed.* The language used should be the terminology of those addressed. There must be no possibility of misunderstanding through ambiguity.

EXECUTIVE CONDUCT. Test the orders that you issue by referring them to an assistant who is not familiar with the matter in hand. If his understanding is slow, confused, or in error, the order should be adjusted. It should be impossible to misconstrue an order if it is carefully read.

Q. *Would you anticipate trouble in understanding this order, "On Thursday at noon hour a new system of paying employees will be instituted. Employees are to line up in alphabetical order in either end of the department. Women operators will receive their pay envelopes from one paymaster and men employees from another"?*

Can you suggest other ways for testing the clarity of an order? What is your opinion of the practice of putting but one fact in a sentence. For example, instead of stating "Office and factory departments will close for the holiday period on Friday at 12:00 noon and 1:00 P.M. respectively and open on Tuesday at 8:30 A.M. and 8:00 A.M. respectively," the notification would read: "Owing to the holiday period, the Company offices will close on Friday at noon. Offices will be opened on Tuesday at 8:30 A.M. Factory departments will close on Friday at 1:00 P.M. They will be opened on Tuesday at 8:00 A.M."

The *issuance* of orders requires careful consideration. There has been much discussion concerning the relative advantages and disadvantages of verbal and written orders. The order issued verbally carries the force of personality with it. In fact, sometimes the manner of speaking allows the employee to read into the directions more meaning than the words themselves express. Written orders, however, have permanence. If not thoroughly understood at first, they can be read again. The record of the exact statement made does not fade as does the memory of it.

EXECUTIVE CONDUCT. As a safeguard against being misunderstood, use written orders whenever feasible. In any case, make sure that you are not being misinterpreted. If you give a verbal order, repetition by the employee affords a check. If the order is written, you can go over it in detail with the recipient. If the order is of a general nature and is posted, you can discuss it with employees picked at random to test their understanding. Do not cause confusion by repeating orders or by allowing orders to overlap so that the same point is covered twice.

Q. *You issue a production order to a group of employees. The work must be rushed, and the order will be so marked. Would the request be more favorably met if an explanation for the need of haste were included? Would you write the explanation on the order, or would you offer it verbally when assigning the order?*

> Would your technique depend upon the extent to which the rush order inconvenienced the employees? Would it depend upon the proportion of rush orders to regular orders?

What do you think of the use of the term "rush"? Are there better expressions? When work is to be rushed, are employees expected to work more rapidly? If not, just what is expected? Is the work rushed, or is it given preference?

The Ensuing Responsibility. Henry L. Gantt stated a fundamental principle of executive conduct when he said, "The authority to issue an order involves the responsibility of seeing that the order is carried out." This responsibility is, indeed, the prime task of the executive, and we may develop a formula to the effect that executive efficiency can be measured in terms of a comparison of that which was ordered with that which was actually accomplished. As Dr. Edward D. Jones puts it:

> In all phases of human affairs there is a friction loss between the will of the executive and the responding will of the subordinate; and that friction loss means that orders must be followed up, by inspection, report, and otherwise, until the intended condition which the order is to bring about becomes a fact.

Some of the means by which executives may stimulate interest and incentive in the employee's performance are presented in Chapter 6. It is important, however, to note that one of the best incentives is the certainty of reward following accomplishment. At one stage in our executive development, penalties were inflicted for nonaccomplishment. This exploitation of fear as a driving force is obsolete. Punishments may rightfully follow voluntary wrongdoing, but their use in executive conduct ends here.

EXECUTIVE CONDUCT. Make it an inflexible rule to see that every order which you issue and do not countermand is carried out. Never let an order be forgotten, no matter how trivial it may be. The effort necessary to see that an order is carried out may be considerable, but you will have safeguarded the habit of full response, which your employees must develop, and your effort will prove a paying investment. If you are new to executive work, you may find that employees will test the degree of your insistence upon prompt accomplishment. They may find reasons for delay or excuses in minor attendant difficulties. Face this situation firmly and see that your standards of response are maintained.

Q. *Is the element of authority of more importance in the issuance of an order or in seeing that it is carried out? In which activity does the educational element play the greater part?*

> Is it the executive's sense of authority or of responsibility that impels him to see that orders are carried out? If the latter, why is the presence of authority needed? Into what groups may the reasons for not carrying out an order be divided? When educational work is needed to see that orders are carried out, what is the inference?

Q. *Will the request that reports on performance or accomplishment be submitted at a stated time after the receipt of an order focus the employee's attention upon the need of a timely and definite response?*

> Under what circumstances would such requests prove impracticable? Is it ever desirable to assign work without some

form of accompanying time requirement? Do time requirements act as incentives? If so, why?

Q. *You have been appointed to executive work and you find that the employees, while apparently kindly disposed toward you, are slow and careless in responding to orders. Do you interpret this as voluntary disobedience or do you feel that it is merely the result of slackness in the executive control developed by your predecessor? What attitude will you take in insisting upon proper response?*

Is it desirable to assume an unfavorable personal attitude until the employee realizes that something is wrong and rectifies his errors, after which you treat him in a more friendly way? Is "keeping on the good side of the boss" an incentive which executives should properly lay before their employees? Should you demand immediate acceptance of your standards of response to orders or should you apply your remedial measures gradually, and why? If the latter, how would you go about it?

Disciplinary Problems. Executives sometimes hesitate in demanding a high degree of discipline, as they fear that this course will make them unpopular and render the maintenance of a working force difficult. Dr. Jones quotes Major Bell as saying:

It makes little difference how rigid the discipline—how taut the requirements: if the discipline is consistent, it will be a happy institution. Everything will run today as it was yesterday, and will be tomorrow, and all hands know what to expect. At all times everybody knows what can and what cannot be done—what is expected of him and what somebody else will do—and can adapt himself accordingly.

And as Dr. Jones further points out: "Consistency is more important than strictness or severity. It is the unfairness that hurts rather than the severity."

EXECUTIVE CONDUCT. Develop an even and unvarying tenor of control. Lay down your course and stick to it. Always interpret your rules and regulations with the same degree of strictness. Show no favoritism to yourself or to others.

Q. *You find that your predecessor in an executive position was much disliked, yet the discipline which he had maintained seems to have been of a high order. Some of the employees criticized his strictness, saying that it was overdone. One employee characterized him as "an old bear" and another termed him a "chronic grouch." In your opinion, was the unpopularity caused by his discipline, or his disposition and its effect upon the manner in which he maintained discipline?*

> Can discipline be maintained in an atmosphere of cheerfulness? Under what conditions would you be happy under strict discipline? If you were certain that such discipline was necessary to success? If you knew that your chief demanded equal discipline of himself? If you knew that you would thus gain greater self-satisfaction from ultimate accomplishment?

Q. *The department of which you are superintendent has a very high capital outlay for heavy equipment. In order to increase production without purchasing expensive additional equipment, your department has been put on a two-shift basis. This solution has the approval of top management, and your department will be the only one operating on this basis (8:00 A.M. to 4:00 P.M. and 4:00 P.M. to 12:00 P.M.). You employ about two hundred and fifty workers on the day shift and one hundred on the evening shift. It has further been agreed that there will be no rotation of the shifts, that is, an employee will work on one specific shift continuously. No complaints have arisen over this policy; however, you learn that some of your foremen have been permitting employees to change back and forth between the two shifts for short periods of time (one day to a week). Such exchanging has had no detrimental effect upon production. What would you do?*

Punctuality is a common disciplinary problem. It becomes particularly acute in organizations where a system of piece-work wage payment is in use. Here the employees claim that they are not paid for their time but for their output, and so long as the latter is satisfactory the executive has no cause to complain.

EXECUTIVE CONDUCT. The requirement of punctuality in yourself is, of course, of first importance. The maintenance of individual employee records upon which tardiness is indicated also offers an incentive. Competition between departments of the organization for highest standing in attendance is often effective and may be continued until the proper habits of punctuality have been established. Don't pay bonuses or offer prizes for punctuality unless you are absolutely forced to this extreme. Punctuality is one of the requirements of the job which should be understood at the time of employment. To comply with this requirement should not merit a reward.

A good punctuality record among your employees is one measure of your ability as an executive.

Q. *One of your employees has outside responsibilities which make tardiness imperative on certain days of the week. How should you handle this situation?*

> Should an employee be given special tardiness privileges of a permanent nature? Of a temporary nature? If so, should other employees be acquainted with these privileges? With the reasons therefor? Should readjustment of wage or arrangement for overtime work accompany such a privilege? How does the appearance of executive favoritism militate against profits?

Q. *You are in charge of a group of clerical employees, who are frequently called upon by the nature of the work to remain after hours. They are paid by salary and no overtime payments are made except for an allowance which is given for their expenses in case evening work is necessary. The punctuality record is very poor. This is partly traceable to transportation facilities, which are extremely congested just before the starting hour. An employee coming to work a little late can avoid this congestion. How would you approach this problem?*

> What factors should be considered in deciding upon the advisability of paying clerical employees for overtime work? Of changing the starting hour? Of insisting upon prompt attendance?

Absenteeism of the avoidable sort is usually found in organizations where the employee earnings are sufficiently above the cost of living so that a surplus of earnings results. The employee prefers to accept this surplus in the form of time instead of money. He also feels assured that supply-demand conditions in the labor market are such that the organization of which he is a member must suffer his absences in preference to a worse condition if he is dismissed.

EXECUTIVE CONDUCT. Obviously, the financial incentive for regular attendance does not exist in this case, nor does the danger of losing the job have any influence. You must find other incentives toward continuous attendance, as in the case of tardiness. The personal regard which the employee has for you will be your strongest support. If you have invested in his friendship and loyalty, he will assist you in maintaining attendance because of his feeling toward you personally; no other incentive will be great enough to equal his desire for free time to himself.

Q. *One of your employees has been very irregular in attendance. His work is excellent and his absences are necessitated by outside interests which add considerably to his income. Although the absences do not materially injure the quality of his service, they affect the morale of other employees, and you feel that the situation cannot continue. Would you dismiss him? Would you advise him to look for another job? Would you advise him to give up his outside work and income and give you his full time? Would you feel that your duty is limited to telling him that the situation cannot continue, that he must give you full time or be dismissed?*

Suppose that he is a man whom you can ill afford to get along without—should this affect your decision or only the time at which you will put it into effect? Are there any principles involved upon which you can base your policy?

Discussion. What is your response to the following comments?

1. *A small amount of vagueness in authority is desirable. If a workman does not know the full extent of the executive's power, he is more easily controlled than when limitations are clearly established.*

It is said that fear feeds upon mystery. What appears to be the incentive to obedience here? (This point will be clarified by the discussion in Chapter 7.)

2. *In our organization, executives are thinking more about responsibilities and talking less about authority.*

Does this statement dismiss the idea of authority as an essential element in executive power? Does it indicate a stage in organization development and mutual understanding?

3. *Orders, in the form of commands or of instructions, are no longer needed in industry. Proper personnel relations make the command unnecessary, and adequate employee training eliminates the need of executive instruction. The order has been superseded by the notification.*

Does the word "notification" indicate the presence of authority? What kind of authority is suggested by the word "command"? What kind of authority, to your mind, is suggested by the word "order"? Is it possible, in all cases, for the executive to divorce himself from responsibility as a teacher?

4. *I don't believe in telling a workman how to carry out an order. I tell him what I want accomplished, let him use his own methods, and hold him responsible for results. If he hasn't enough knowledge of the job to do the work properly, he is not the man to fill the position.*

Compare the validity of this statement when made by a housebuilder employing carpenters and by an executive in a factory where special machinery and processes are in use. Is the trend of the industrial job toward or away from the carpenter type? Is knowledge of, or capacity to perform, a job coming to be the basis of initial fitness?

5. *I refuse to put pressure upon an employee to carry out an order. I will give a man two or three trials, and if he doesn't produce I discharge him. I have no time to bother with men who won't follow directions.*

Why were orders not carried out? In what proportion of cases is executive facilitation, rather than pressure, required? To what extent should executives "bother with men who won't follow directions"?

6. *If the employment department does its work properly, there will be no need of executive follow-up orders. The right kind of man does his work without coercion.*

What requirements other than the right kind of man are necessary to the carrying out of orders? Are there circumstances in which a normally ambitious individual would not want to do his work?

7. The surest cure for tardiness or absenteeism is the fear of discharge. When workmen know the penalty, they stop breaking rules and regulations.

Does the fear of discharge vary in intensity with individuals and circumstances? Is it always the most effective of available forms of incentive? Can it justly be applied to the first offense? Are rewards better than penalties in dealing with tardiness and absenteeism?

CHAPTER 5

Executive Delegation*

When we entrust a task to the care or management of another, we delegate. Delegation is nothing new to executive behavior. Indeed, in Exodus, one of the oldest books of the Bible, we find Moses' father-in-law, Jethro, expressing concern that his son-in-law might "wear away . . . for this thing [the judging of the people] is too heavy for thee; thou art not able to perform it thyself alone." And Jethro further recommends that Moses "provide out of all the people able men . . . and place such over them to be rulers of thousands, and rulers of hundreds, rulers of fifties, and rulers of tens . . . so shall it be easier for thyself, and they shall bear the burden with thee."

This advice Moses accepted, with good results; and in so doing he established one of our earliest records of the application of the principle of delegation.

It can be argued that the evolution of management has been a steady growth in delegation; that at one period in our industrial evolution the master craftsman was both

* Much of the subject matter and topical sequence in this chapter I owe to discussions with friends in the Cleveland Electric Illuminating Company and the Johns-Manville Corporation.

an executive and an operator, and the delegation of his operating activities to others marked his advancement to exclusively managerial responsibilities.

An extensive inquiry made among executives indicated that the most important change of a permanent nature taking place in industrial organization is the delegation of decisions downward to a point as proximate to the scene of action as possible.

Conversely, one of the most difficult transitions required of the proprietor of the small but growing business comes when magnitude makes it necessary for him increasingly to delegate executive responsibilities to others. This he has found very hard to do.

Precisely what do we do when we delegate? In a word, we transfer to someone else a portion of our authority and responsibility, still retaining the accountability for seeing that the assignment is carried out. By this means we may (1) get something done more effectively, and (2) release our time for other—and often more important—duties.

EXECUTIVE CONDUCT. Think of delegation in terms of positive possibilities. When properly performed, delegation contributes in many ways. It means placing faith and trust in subordinates, which usually brings out the best in them. It is a process of sharing, rather than evading, responsibility and authority. Delegation makes for steady growth in the members of the industrial group. Delegation affords deep executive satisfactions in helping others develop managerial skills and in witnessing their growth and improvement. Delegation fosters morale by offering opportunity to others to measure their new responsibilities against their capacities—one of the most precious privileges that can be laid before a subordinate.

Degrees of Delegation. The extent and area of delegation may well vary, depending upon circumstances. You may, for example, wish to delegate responsibilities for a temporary period, pending the return of one who has this responsibility as a regular assignment.

Q. *In the absence of your assistant, due to illness, you have delegated his activities temporarily to three operators, who have agreed to carry the work forward on a part-time basis. Now it appears that your assistant will be incapacitated for a much longer time than you had originally anticipated. Indeed, it is possible that he may never return to his job. What action, if any, should you take?*

> Should you assign someone to the job full-time? Should you consult with your assistant? With those who are carrying on during his illness? What facts are essential to your decision? Are these facts obtainable? If not, what steps, if any, should you take?

You may find it desirable to restrict delegation solely to staff services, such as the making of recommendations, but with no responsibility for action. Here you may face the problem of selecting a staff deputy in a field in which you are not technically versed. Edward D. Jones [1] has laid down four tests which may be applied in such instances, namely:

[1] *The Administration of Industrial Enterprises,* rev. ed., Longmans, Green & Co., Inc., New York, 1935.

Ability to express gist of technical matters in simple terms
Unwillingness to accept measures which would endanger success
Soundness of judgment as revealed in areas of common knowledge
Quickness and facility in dealing with the specific problem presented

Q. *You find, upon delegating an investigation to a staff appointee, that his study will involve interrogating considerable numbers of line executives and operators. How will you go about arranging for these contacts in such a way as to minimize tensions and antagonisms and to maximize collaboration and morale?*

You may require that your deputy (delegatee) acquaint you with his plans and proposed procedures before any action is taken.

Q. *Under what circumstances would this be a desirable restriction? When the deputy is initially uninformed concerning the nature of the difficulties that may be encountered? When errors may prove particularly costly? Or when?*

Under certain circumstances it may prove wise for the delegator to place full responsibility, with attendant authority, upon his deputy, but to require that he—the delegator—be kept advised of decisions and actions as the work proceeds, or as soon as action is taken.

Q. *Might a situation conceivably arise in which the delegator would not require or wish any report or further communication with the deputy once the delegation was effected and understood?*

Q. *A large public utility holding company engaged a firm of contractors to build a new power station in a distant state, the new station to incorporate the most recent advances in power generation. Shortly after the placing of the contract, a power unit in an equally distant area was partially destroyed by fire, and the contracting firm was also retained to make repairs and return the station to service in the shortest possible time.*

Would the extent and nature of the authority extended to the construction managers assigned to each of these plants properly differ in any degree?

Q. *The president of a multiplant company appointed five vice-presidents to act for him in five functional divisions of the business. Said the president, "They are empowered to take presidential action in their respective fields without consulting me. Of course, I know that they would not do this."*

What are your comments?

Extremes and Optima in Delegation. We now have witnessed a wide spectrum of possibilities in the degree to which we may delegate our responsibilities. Let us first consider the executive who desires to delegate the least possible amount of authority. What will be the effect upon his deputy?

To withhold from a deputy an appropriate amount of authority lessens his feeling of responsibility for the success of the project, and at the same time does nothing to lighten the responsibilities of his superior officer. More than this, the deputy lacks the rewards of recognition of good work and of the interest of his superiors in his progress. He to whom work is unwillingly delegated is probably allowed insufficient scope to come near to the limit of his abilities.

Conversely, the executive who delegates too easily and is inclined to wash his hands of the responsibility once it is delegated is probably evidencing a personal distaste for responsibility. His deputies, lacking the sense of corporate interest and guidance that a competent leader would provide, lack the impelling force of certainty as to direction that is necessary to arouse their best efforts.

Where lies the optimum in delegation? Just what should we expect from the executive in the form of action and relationship to his supporters as well as to his deputies?

To begin with, the executive cannot evade his accountability for the ultimate success and accomplishment of the delegated activity. This means that he must at all times be aware of progress made in relation to progress planned, so that he may introduce corrective measures if need be. An executive with only enough information to apply remedial rather than preventive measures is obviously not in a position to justify his responsibilities to top management. He is manifestly out of control.

Just what should his relationship be toward his deputies? He will tell his deputies what to do, why it should be done—but not how to do it. He will open himself to their ideas, recommendations, and suggestions; he will ask their collaboration in any major decisions directly affecting their activities; he will develop in them a sense of responsibility, being careful not to burden them with responsibilities which they have no authority to execute. He should never forget that he cannot blame his failures upon his deputies, for, in the last analysis, the delegation of a job to a man who is incapable of accomplishing it satisfactorily is as much a reflection on the administrator's judgment as it is on the deputy's competence. The administrator should possess the valuable ability to hand over, with faith and trust, a well-defined area of authority while yet retaining interest in, and ultimate accountability for, the function delegated. Finally, he should see in delegation a powerful tool for executive development.

Q. *Is it conceivable that an executive might delegate all his responsibilities to deputies? If so, what responsibilities would be the most difficult to delegate? Are there activities which are better delegated than retained by the executive?*

Q. *How can an executive be assured that the optimum of delegation has been reached? Is such an optimum static or dynamic in nature?*

The Process of Delegation. First, define the job or the responsibility which is to be delegated. Care at this stage will avoid subsequent difficulty. Establish such details as:

1. The precise activity to be delegated
2. The facilities or services to be assigned to the deputy

3. His place in the organization
4. The extent of his authority and responsibility
5. The proposed method of evaluating accomplishment

Q. *What factors should be considered in determining the best method of organizing the above specifications for later presentation to the new deputy? Under what circumstances would word of mouth be sufficient? Informal memo? Official statement?*

Second, select the deputy. On no other act in this procedure does success more importantly hinge. It is not enough that he should have the ability to undertake this activity. He should also, having been told of it, have the desire to do it under the circumstances laid down.

Q. *It has been said that if you want to get something done:*
Find someone who can do it.
Find someone who wants to do it.
Find someone who will continue to want to do it.
Provide him with that which he needs to do it and do it well.
Reward him fairly for his accomplishment.
Give him nothing else to do.
Let him go!

Are there other requirements for the ideal deputy?

Third, lay the opportunity before the selected deputy and see if he takes to it. Timing is important here. Look with him at the situation, the need, the problem, before turning to personalities or qualifications. Often the best deputy is one who is not too quick to accept additional responsibilities. Let him think it over. Remember that you are entering into a copartnership with your deputy and that it is important that both you and he look forward with anticipation to this new relationship.

Q. *A distinguished public servant once said, "I have seen many men undertake new responsibilities as a matter of duty, and I have also seen men undertake new responsibilities because they liked doing them. Over the years it has been the latter group that has accomplished the most."*

> Just how can an executive determine the degree to which a deputy really enjoys the opportunities laid before him?

Fourth, once the deputy has been selected, give him all the information necessary for a good job. He should have a chance to benefit from the experience of those who have preceded him.

Q. *Frederick W. Taylor, in testifying on scientific management before a Senate committee, said in this respect:* [2]
"I do not think anyone for an instant would dream that a surgeon would say to his young men, for instance, 'Now, young men, when we are amputating a leg, for instance, and we come down to the bone, we older surgeons are in the habit of using a saw, and for that purpose we take this particular saw that I am holding before you. We hold it in just this way and we use it in just that way. But, young

[2] *Bulletin of the Taylor Society*, June–August, 1926, p. 164.

men, what we want, of all things, is your initiative. Don't be hampered by any of the prejudices of the older surgeons. What we want is your initiative, your individuality. If you prefer a hatchet or an ax to cut off the bone, why chop away, chop away!' Would this be what the modern surgeon would tell his apprentices? Not on your life! But he says, 'Now, young men, we want your initiative; yes. But we want your initiative, your inventive faculty, to work upward and not downward, and until you have learned how to use the best implements that have been developed in the surgical art during the past hundred years and which are the evolution of the minds of trained men all over the world; until you have learned how to use every instrument that has been developed through years of evolution and which is now recognized as the best of its kind in the surgical art, we won't allow you to use an iota of ingenuity, an iota of initiative. First learn to use the instruments which have been shown by experience to be the best in the surgical art and to use them in the exact way which we will show you, and then when you have risen up to the highest knowledge in the surgical art, then invent, but, for God's sake, invent upward, not downward. Do not reinvent implements and methods abandoned many years ago.' "

Would you agree?

Once informed, the deputy should be free, within technical limitations, to accomplish the delegated objectives in his own way, subject of course to the preliminary review and comments of his chief, which he will properly be quick to obtain.

Q. Why, at this stage, should it seem so desirable for the deputy to draw to the maximum upon his own self-initiative?

Fifth, encourage frequent and perhaps regular contact between yourself and your deputy, as his work proceeds. This should be so approached and implemented that the deputy comes to look forward to these periods of report, discussion, and collaboration with you.

Q. How may this be brought about? What causes a man to find pleasure in discussing his work-in-process with another? What are some of the things the delegator should do if he is to merit this kind of relationship with his deputies? What are the things he should not do?

Q. A successful executive once said to me: "It took a long time before I could train my deputies to hurry to me with their mistakes." Just how would you go about doing this?

Sixth, arrange milestones whereby accomplishment may be summated and measured, methods examined in the light of experience, and improvements planned. Should the delegated responsibility be of a sort that by its nature draws to a close, be sure to introduce a period in which a complete evaluation can be made, to the end that justifiable praise and commendation be given the deputy for work well done. One of the principles of executive development is that personal accomplishment, when properly recognized, provides increased incentive for further achievement. It is our successes that keep kicking us upstairs.

Seventh, after progress has been attained and your relationship with your deputy stabilized, you may consider changes in the direction of less frequent report or review of the work in hand, greater dependence upon the decisions of the deputy, larger areas of discretion in which his personal judgment may be exercised. At this point you may take reasonable pride and gratification that you have been influential in adding to the stature of your deputy—that he has grown under your tutelage.

Difficulties of Delegation. There is often a reluctance on the part of executives to allow subordinates to take personal risks when delegated to important but difficult tasks where the hazard of failure is present and the cost of error is high.

EXECUTIVE CONDUCT. Such risks, particularly physical hazards, should be minimized so far as possible. More than this, the deputy should be armed with adequate and detailed instructions for dealing with such risks. Finally, he should be advised of such hazards and given the opportunity of declining the task without prejudice to him or his future in the company.

The danger of failure in accomplishment is inherent in greater or less degree in every attempted undertaking. When a deputy is required to stretch himself in the attaining of an objective, his chances of success may be lessened but his opportunity for personal development is enhanced. Deputies must be allowed to try if they are to grow.

Q. *It has been said that the greatest self-control required of the executive is called for when he observes a deputy making an error and does not countermand his action. This is difficult, but there are those who argue that it must be done if the organization is to develop the kind of men necessary for steady growth.*

> What is your opinion? Under what circumstances, if any, would you favor preventive action? Absence of preventive action? Is the making of errors essential to the learning process?

There is also the concern that the deputy will fail in his initial attempts and by so doing injure his prospects with the company and possibly even lose the job which he is now filling satisfactorily.

EXECUTIVE CONDUCT. It is a common defect for us to underestimate the capacities and abilities of our subordinates, particularly if they are in a younger age group. Years of experience, while highly valuable, are not always so necessary as they may at first appear, especially if training has been adequate.

Research has been defined as organized failure; that is to say, experimental structures are set up in order that failures may be made cheaply until the correct solution is found. The gasoline component known as ethyl was discovered in this way. Salvarsan was known as "606" because 605 failures preceded its finding.

This principle may frequently be applied to the initial attempts of the deputy in order that his early errors, though real, may be minimized in effect.

Q. *How may the initial activities of a deputy be organized in order to allay the fears of his superior officer that failure will occur or that such occurrence may militate against the future of the deputy?*

A further concern of the delegator is more personal in nature. He may fear that his success in delegating will leave him in the unenviable position of having nothing to do. At least it will give him the outward appearance of idleness.

This concern is not without validity in some industrial organizations. Yet the whole trend of the times is against it. Growing industrial complexities, expansion, and tempo are calling ever more insistently for calm thought and uninterrupted consideration on the part of the line executive. The day of the department head who runs his organization by dead reckoning is passing. In a rapidly changing world, new responsibilities are facing the modern line official which will absorb any spare time released by delegation.

Q. *Just what can the industrial executive do when he has nothing to do? What will he be called upon to do in increasing degree as time passes? Which of his activities will lend themselves more readily to delegation?*

A worry which still exists is that delegation will lessen indispensability; it is argued that as soon as the executive's know-how is sufficiently disseminated to others, he may lose his job.

No statistics are available to refute this opinion, but in the United States at least there is an increasing body of evidence to prove that such strategic indispensability is no longer a widely practiced policy. Modern control methods, scientific purchasing, and the widespread establishment of objective standards of plant operation leave little room today for the executive who carries the secrets of the business in his hat.

Q. *When such uneasiness is prevalent among executives in a plant, of what is this condition symptomatic? What sort of relationships is delegation built upon? How may the actual attitude of top management in these matters of indispensability be determined?*

Finally, there is the feeling that the position or prestige of the executive may be reduced by delegation of responsibilities to others—that he may find his standing among his associates impaired.

EXECUTIVE CONDUCT. Forget it. A man never lowers his position by shedding activities in order that he may concentrate upon more important matters. A man never lowers his standing by giving his subordinates opportunity to grow and develop into more useful employees. A man never suffers in prestige if he builds faith, trust, and confidence in his deputies by offering them a chance to stretch themselves to the limit of their talents.

Q. *You have assigned new responsibilities to one of your staff. Up to this time he has always undertaken such delegated activities in good spirit. Now, however, you are told that he is going about saying that you are passing your work along to him in order that you can have more time for late afternoon golf. In one instance he has been heard to say, "Why doesn't he do his own work instead of pushing it off on me?"*

How would you handle this situation? Would you do anything? Has a mistake been made? If so, where?

Delegation and Succession. Someone has said that the first task of a newly appointed executive is to find his successor. This point of view may be extreme, but it serves to emphasize one of the growing responsibilities of the line official. Slowly it is being recognized that the great majority of our mills and factories will be kept running long after every present employee is dead and gone. If this is true, it is better to prepare the way of succession by careful planning and organization so that such inevitable changes are not allowed to take place on an emergency basis.

Delegation is one of the most effective tools available to an executive in preparing the way for his successor. Indeed, it is the most important tool for the selection and training of successors. Not only does it provide opportunity for latent ability in the organization to show itself, but it also ensures that this talent will ultimately be given a chance to express itself. The company that is organized to build succession from within its own personnel is the company where high morale and motivation are the rule rather than the exception. Moreover, delegation ensures the continuance of the ideals upon which the business rests. It permits such policies to be applied throughout the business and under such circumstances that a minimum of errors in changes affecting executive organization are made.

Q. *An American railroad is said to have an arrangement whereby every mid-zone executive has an understudy who is appointed simultaneously with him. The understudy is perhaps twenty years younger than his chief. The understudy does the leg work, takes care of minor responsibilities —all with the knowledge that upon the retirement of his boss, at age sixty-five, he will succeed him and at the same time be assigned an understudy who will ultimately succeed him.*

How would such a plan work in a manufacturing organization? What advantages and disadvantages do you see?

Delegation and Opportunity. We are living in a ramifying, expanding, accelerating industrial world, filled with dynamic change and flux and bristling with new and enlarged opportunities. To move with the currents of such a world, to advance, to progress, to grow, we must proceed from where we are. Frequently delegation provides this chance, both to executive and to deputy. It has long been known that promotion is most probable where rapid expansion is taking place. Delegation in such an atmosphere provides a testing ground for all parties involved—an opportunity to measure their potential abilities. It is the link or the steppingstone whereby individuals may justify their breakthrough to higher levels of responsibility. Delegation serves its greatest purpose as a threshold to promotion.

EXECUTIVE CONDUCT. Never turn down a delegation proffered by your superior officer. Take it. If it involves responsibilities that you have never shouldered before, take it. If it involves responsibilities that no one has ever shouldered before, take it. If it involves laying aside a degree of security for a degree of risk, take it.

Why? Because no such offer or opportunity will be placed before you by your boss unless he (1) believes you have the ability to capitalize upon it, (2) stands ready to support you in it, and (3) wants you to progress and advance.

Promotion in responsibility is more valuable to the recipient than promotion in rank or in remuneration. Opportunity to grow is still an advantage to be seized upon. Delegation may be the vehicle which brings it to you. Don't fail to grasp the opportunity, for it may not beckon to you long.

Q. *An executive has decided to delegate an important section of his responsibilities to a younger man whose progress he has been furthering. Up to this time the young man has been ready and eager to accept new duties. Now, however, when the executive tentatively discusses the new opportunity with him, he shows little enthusiasm. He continues to do his present work well, and his attitude is cooperative. He gives no reason for his disinclination to undertake the new work. His general comment is, "It might be a good thing to do." But eagerness for it is not evident.*

How should the executive deal with this situation?

Delegation and Change. It has been said that the delegation of responsibilities to a deputy is a dynamic act which should be constantly changed to reflect changing conditions, changing objectives, and, most important, changes in the growing competence of the deputy. For example, it is logical to assume that the degree of delegation may appropriately be increased as the deputy progresses in skill and competence.

Q. *Is there a limit to delegation? If so, what is it? Should every subordinate be the recipient of some form of delegation? Should a deputy be delegated responsibilities up to the limits of his ability? Should the executive delegate all possible responsibilities? Is it the maximum or the optimum that is important here?*

Q. *A mid-zone executive, when privately asked his reasons for hesitating to delegate certain activities, replied: "I am really afraid to delegate certain of my activities because the change in the state of the art is so rapid that I should be running the risk of losing touch with current developments."*

What would be your comments?

Q. *An industrial manager, when questioned concerning delegation, pointed out that in his business important con-*

tracts were frequently the subject of competitive negotiation. In several instances his company had won the order because the president had conducted negotiations with the prospective purchaser, whereas in other companies these activities had been delegated to men lower in executive rank. The company placing the contract had stated: "In these instances we like to deal with principals."

What are your comments?

In an accelerating world, the organization with the best methods of delegation is best able to transfer responsibility and authority, and thereby is in the best position to adjust itself, by virture of its agility and versatility, to the demands of its rapidly changing environment.

Discussion. What is your response to the following comments?

1. *Delegation may have positive qualities. As for me, it has negative qualities also. If the deputy doesn't make good, out he goes.*

Is this point of view debatable? What is implied? What, if anything, do we find wrong with this statement?

2. *There are degrees of delegation, but the halfway mark bears the weakness of both extremes without their strength. Either give your deputy all authority and responsibility or give him none.*

Are these extremes entirely satisfactory to the deputy? What are his reactions likely to be to this policy of all or none?

3. *The process of delegation can be overdone. It is easy to get so entangled in complexities that nothing is ever accomplished.*

What may happen if we overlook any of the five steps listed? Should the deputy be required to find his own way to perform the task delegated to him? If not, why?

4. *There are plenty of difficulties in delegation. An executive heaps up trouble for himself when he starts delegating and supervising. It takes more time to follow up after delegation than to do it yourself.*

What seem to be the current trends in delegation? How do you explain them? Are there instances when more executive time is spent in supervising than in performing? Does this necessarily make delegation undesirable?

5. *Every dog has his day and every dog has his night. When you are no longer the white-haired boy, it is good to have a few activities that will suffer seriously if you are eliminated.*

What light does this atttiude throw on executive relationships where such a viewpoint might be justified? How does such an attitude harmonize with our current industrial trends?

6. *My experience has been that whenever delegation is suggested to an executive, he is on the way out. Delegation is a nice way to put skids under the man who is slated to go.*

What long-term effect will this use of delegation have upon executive activities in an expanding company? In an organization where flexibility is especially required? In a company where executive morale is unusually desirable?

7. *There is a limit to delegation, and that is the minimum amount that you can get away with. Don't delegate any more than you can help. Do what your job requires of you. Collaborate as little as possible. Keep the tricks of your trade out of circulation and don't talk.*

If every executive in a company followed this policy, what would be the end result? What type of executive organizations are likely to grow and prosper in industry today and tomorrow?

CHAPTER 6

Executive Stimulation

One measure of executive success is the ability to get employees to work with a will. The task is to stimulate *the driving force which is within the individual* so that he faces his work with a self-inspired eagerness. The days of the driving type of executive are past. The present-day leader uses far more effective agencies than coercion or the power of fear in motivating his workmen.

A logical approach to a person's will is through the intellect, and this is the path to which many leaders who have rejected the ineffective methods of fear and force have turned. The approach has not been entirely satisfactory, however. As Herbert Spencer wrote with respect to certain economic conditions: "Under your present condition, men could not be got to listen. Even if they listened, they would not be convinced. And even if they were convinced, their conduct would not be appreciably affected."

This indicates that there are other wellsprings of human behavior than those of the intellect, and the psychologists tell us that man's action is impelled by a considerable number of "inherited or innate dispositions" which are called instincts. These in turn are modified by his tendency to imitate others, as well as his facility in forming habits. The executive should be thoroughly familiar with these natural tendencies, for such knowledge will aid him in explaining much of the unreasonable behavior of employees and will furnish him with powerful means of directing their behavior.

The degree to which the executive will stimulate emotional response in place of intellectual response will vary with the level of intelligence of his employees. Those of high intelligence require only logic and a true picture of the facts in order to give cooperation. With employees of lower intelligence the objective must be reflected to them in terms of their innate satisfactions if interest and incentive are to be fully aroused.

The following pages are concerned with ways in which the executive may effectively appeal to employee will through instinctive responses.

Constructiveness. The popularity of building toys is an indication of the inborn desire, active in children, to build and create. It is probable that the drudgery of the old apprenticeship system was somewhat offset by the constructive satisfactions which were offered. The low wage scale in teaching and publishing, for example, has been explained by the fact that the creative satisfactions of the work add to the desirability of positions in these fields and affect the supply-demand balance upon which the wage is built.

EXECUTIVE CONDUCT. Employees will take satisfaction in the knowledge that you welcome constructive suggestions. They will find new interest in their work if they are encouraged to study their job with a view to improving it. Unless you make your position clear, however, employees will hesitate to offer constructive suggestions for fear that they will not be welcomed. It is said that one of the most profitable results of shop committees has been the surprising savings effected by tapping the constructive resources of the employees who have been given a channel for suggestions.

Let the employees understand the significance of their work. Show them how their work coordinates with that of others in the attainment of the final result. Allow them to visualize the constructiveness of what they are doing. The realization will bring gratification and will provide a definite incentive. The administrator who had charge of a factory making aircraft capitalized his knowledge of human nature when he instructed his executives to stop all work for thirty minutes so that the employees could go to the factory yard and see the first plane circling above them.

Everyone likes to feel that he is doing something worthwhile in life aside from earning a living. If you can show your employees that the result of their effort is of real benefit to society, you will provide a natural basis for greater effort.

You can often arouse interest by pointing out the constructive characteristics of the job itself. The development of a balance sheet, the formation of an inventory report, the assembly of a machine offer problems of construction, and, if properly presented to the employee so that he can see the steps toward the finished product, his constructive tendencies may be strongly aroused.

Q. *You are in charge of a group of operators in a textile mill manufacturing cloth for coat and suit linings. A motion picture of the work done in each department and the final use of the cloth in the making of clothing and its wear by the ultimate buyer has been prepared for consumer advertising purposes. The film is to be exhibited to all employees and the question has arisen, "Should the employees be shown the entire film or only that part which represents the work in the textile mill?" Your opinion is asked. What is your answer and why?*

> How would you arrange to exhibit this film? Would you obtain a theater and charge admission to employees, to relatives and friends of employees, or to the public? Is there any value in allowing others than employees to see the film? If you arranged to show the film in the factory, would you require attendance? Would you show it during or out of working hours? If the former, would you pay wages to employees during the time of exhibition? If so, and if they are on a wage incentive system, how would their wages be determined?

Possession. We all enjoy the feeling of ownership even though it be but a nominal ownership. This instinctive satisfaction probably arises from the sense of control which we have over what is ours rather than the mere fact of possession.

EXECUTIVE CONDUCT. As far as possible, develop the employee's sense of responsibility through the capitalization of this tendency. Give him a workplace which he can consider his own, with equipment for his sole use. Give him a locker of his own and a timecard with his name on it, if these items are called for in the nature of the job. Then hold him responsible for the care of these things. This nominal proprietorship will reflect itself in a higher quality of work and a lower labor turnover.

The plan which offers the individual an opportunity to share in the holdings of the enterprise in which he is employed satisfies this tendency. The consequent feeling of responsibility strengthens the spirit of cooperation.

The incentive which the possibility of promotion affords is partly based upon this instinct, for promotion may be a means toward the acquisition of many things which have been denied the employee at his present wage.

Q. *You are in charge of a group of foreign-born employees who have worked for many years on individual machines and the system has been such that each man has been assigned a machine for his sole use. A new system of operation is advocated which will require the men to change from one machine to another during the day. You have spoken to the workmen of the plan and they have objected strongly, each saying in substance: "This is my machine. I have worked on it for a long time. No one else should use it. I don't want to use any other." They offer no other explanation but their feeling is very strong. How will you explain this situation to your chief?*

What will you say to the employees? Might there be any legitimate technical reasons for their attitude? Under what conditions, if any, would you recommend that the feelings of the employees be acceded to?

Q. *Do you see reason for the lowering of morale of day workers in a machine shop when a night shift is undertaken, even though there is plenty of work for all?*

Where machines are attended by one group of employees and adjusted by another group, would you favor staggering the shifts so that the working periods of the two groups would overlap? Can the loss of the possessive satisfactions through the shift system be compensated for in any way?

Q. *You have charge of the maintenance of a large office building. Would your recognition of the possessive instinct assist you in determining the best way to lay out the organization and work of the cleaning and janitor service?*

It has been argued that the practice of assigning different employees to the same area on sequential days develops a competitive spirit which enhances quality. What is your opinion?

Self-assertion and Self-expression. We all dislike being known as "average" individuals. We wish to be recognized as distinctive personalities, and we have a common desire to have heed taken of our ideas and wishes. The employee who is not given channels for self-expression within his organization will look for them elsewhere.

EXECUTIVE CONDUCT. Provide "complaint drainage" for your employees. Give them opportunity to tell of their difficulties. The value of this outlet is well known to practical-minded leaders. The remark is often heard,

"Let him get it off his chest!" This subject is dealt with in further detail in Chapter 12.

You will find in every employee a desire for approval which is one expression of self-assertion. Approval to the workman does not necessarily mean outward praise, but he wants to feel sure that you are watching his efforts and that you will give credit where and when it is due. Maintain proper employee records. Set aside a portion of your time to familiarize yourself with them. Let the workmen know that you are interested in watching the progress of each one, and an increase in interest and incentive will naturally result.

There is another effective approach to the employee in the appeal to pride. For example, one executive who employs salesmen in a field calling for extreme doggedness and persistence makes it a practice to employ college men who have been football or baseball stars. In moments of discouragement the executive remarks, "When you were on the ——— team, you didn't let obstacles discourage you and you are not going to let this setback disturb you if you are the kind of man I think you are."

Self-assertion also fosters a spirit of rivalry or competition. Be careful that you do not carry this application to a harmful extreme. I can recall a number of cases in which group rivalry as well as individual competition grew so keen that the participants clearly overexerted themselves in the heat of the contest. The basis of effectiveness in employee records is here, for they give the individual opportunity to measure his status against past accomplishment, and any progress brings satisfaction.

The success of the "task" (work with a standard time of accomplishment) is traceable to the employee's natural gratification. He measures his achievement against a standard, and the satisfaction which comes with reaching or passing it is a form of incentive entirely lacking where time standards have not been incorporated.

Q. *You receive a petition signed by the majority of your employees asking that hot water be supplied in the washrooms. Is the use of the petition as a form of communication a compliment or a criticism of your executive method?*

> Why would a group of employees determine upon a petition as a means of communication? What motives might impel an employee to sign a petition which was referred to him? What facts would assist you in determining the extent to which the petition represented the actual desires of the employees? Would you consider the employee who organized the petition worthy of scrutiny as possible executive timber? Why?

Q. *You plan to make a new arrangement of equipment in your organization to increase its convenience for the operators. You face three alternate methods: to make a new layout and order the changes made without referring them to the employees; to make a new layout and refer it to the employees for suggestions before declaring it final; to state the need of a new layout to the employees and receive their suggestions before you develop any plan. Which is the best plan and why?*

The Fighting Spirit. This is found in every red-blooded person. The task of the leader is to divert it into useful channels. Man's progress has been an immemorial fight against nature. Industrial work is also a fight against material forces. The work may often be unpleasant, but there is a joy of achievement which makes the fight worthwhile.

On the other hand, it is a well-known psychological principle that this instinct is easily fired by an attempt to override or overrun the rights or privileges of the individual. The flash of anger that comes over us when we signal the bus and it goes by unheeding is a common experience. In like manner the executive who autocratically attempts to overrule his employee's suggestions or complaints is likely to ignite an emotional tinder which may inflame the entire organization and result in a crisis.

EXECUTIVE CONDUCT. Show your men the main objective toward which your organization is directed. Keep this objective constantly before them in visual form if possible. Show them the obstacles which confront them and the challenge which is laid down before them. Express your confidence in your men. Let them know you are behind them and believe in their ability to win. Then put each individual's part in the enterprise clearly before him and release him to action. Make him feel that his success now rests upon his own efforts and his own fighting spirit.

Never upbraid an employee in an emotional manner; under no circumstances should you make a man obey you against his will, unless the act which you require is to compensate for a wrong which he knowingly committed. Never ride roughshod over the feelings of another. Such acts are not constructive; they arouse harmful resentment. The value of self-control is obvious in protecting the executive against such errors in method.

Q. *One of your employees enters your department during the late morning in an intoxicated condition. You are not aware of his entrance until he slaps you on the back and shouts, "Hello, boss, how are you this morning?" He is amiable but boisterous. How are you going to handle the situation?*

> What, in general, is the effect of alcoholic stimulants upon thinking power and upon the emotions? Although this employee's approach is unreasonable, is it indicative of his basic attitude toward you? Should you discharge him?

Q. *A large number of employees in your organization have gone on strike. You are transferred from your executive duties and asked to take charge of guarding the building and premises and providing safe access for working employees. With the knowledge of this instinct, what instructions will you give your guards in dealing with the crowds of strikers who will be about the entrance?*

> What type of men will you select to act as guards? Will you select loyal employees, or retain outsiders who have not hitherto been employed by the company?

Q. *While you are filling the position of foreman, one of your employees comes to you during the noon hour to report that two of the workmen are engaged in a fist fight in the street in front of the office building. What should your procedure be in such an instance?*

> Are they under your jurisdiction as employees? What may be the consequences of their acts? Is it your responsibility as an executive to prevail upon them to stop fighting? To stop fighting in that particular locality, and at that particular time? Why?

Curiosity. We need only to look at the rapid increase in the use of correspondence schools and at the spread of industrial education to appreciate the universal extent of the desire to learn. The extensive sale of encyclopedias is an evidence of the capitalization of this tendency. The job that gives a man a chance to learn as he works offers a strong appeal.

The shortsighted executive takes the stand that the new employee should know his job, that for the employee to ask questions is evidence of ignorance and reason for dismissal. The workman, aware of this attitude, fears to learn openly and in many cases quits the job before his lack of information can cause dismissal.

EXECUTIVE CONDUCT. Make it clear that no matter how well qualified the new employee may be, you plan to give him careful and complete instruction in his work. Take the attitude that you consider it a point of merit if an employee seeks information on things which are not clear to him, and that you will interpret the act as an evidence of a desire to learn and improve rather than an admission of ignorance and unfitness for the job.

Endeavor to obtain for your organization the reputation of being one in which employees are gaining useful knowledge. Encourage outside educational pursuits among your men. Be prepared to advise them of correspondence- and night-school courses which will improve their chances for success. Show that you are interested in their progress. Give them opportunity to gain experience on different jobs so that they may attain a broader usefulness. Never hold a man back on the basis that otherwise he may outgrow his job and find a better position elsewhere. A few examples of your willingness for your employees to accept other positions which involve promotion will prove an excellent investment, for they will bring high-grade applicants to you for employment.

Q. *An employee asks your advice concerning a correspondence-school course and you recommend one and commend his interest. He then asks you, "If I take this course, will it mean promotion for me here?" How would you answer him, bearing in mind that it would be unwise to commit yourself on this point but that the employee's initiative should not be discouraged?*

> Should employees be promoted on a basis of potential possibilities or of past results? Is increased knowledge a reason for promotion? What makes a man qualified for promotion? (The subject of promotion is dealt with in Chapter 8.)

Q. *You have an employee who has been with you for a number of years. He is faithful and industrious but he cannot seem to get past his present job and grasp the broader aspect of the job ahead. You have given him every encouragement to undertake educational work but he never finds time for it. He seems contented with his present work and you face the necessity of taking someone in from outside your organization to fill the coming vacancy just ahead of him. Is there anything more that you can do?*

> Do you believe that there are variations in individual capacities? Do you favor giving an employee a job which is commensurate with his capacity or somewhat below, and why? How can you tell if a job is commensurate with the capacity of the employee? If his capacity is exceeded? If it is not being utilized? Can you rely upon an employee's judgment of his own capacity?

Association. We all enjoy our environment better if we know that there are people about us. Though we may not care for intimate acquaintance with others, we like to feel that they are in the "near distance." This is probably the same impulse that accounts for the herd, the flock, and the swarm in other forms of life.

The associative atmosphere of the workplace certainly has an appeal to the employee. There are many cases of young women who, after marriage, return to their work largely for this satisfaction. We find also that jobs such as night-watching and tasks requiring solitary work often have a high labor turnover. It has been said that the feeling of group satisfaction varies with the number in the working area, reaching a maximum between twenty and twenty-five employees and decreasing slowly with larger groups.

We must also remember that people in a group are much more sensitive to mass suggestion than people taken individually. Fear, anger, enthusiasm are contagious and will spread rapidly. In fact, there is a group psychology which is quite at variance with individual behavior and which we must study in order to understand certain aspects of industrial behavior.

EXECUTIVE CONDUCT. Avoid locating workbenches in out-of-the-way, lonely places. Keep employees in sight of one another. See that each employee is acquainted with those who are working immediately adjacent. This matter is dealt with at greater length in Chapter 8.

Sex. We cannot and should not evade the fact that sex plays a strong part in human behavior. The desire for finery on the part of young working people is doubtless traceable in part to this instinct. Neatness and cleanliness in appearance are most desirable and should be commended in workmen, for they tend toward care and precision in the work performed.

The organization where the younger employees can meet one another is satisfying a normal human need. The executive who, by assistance in housing or by hastening promotion through factory educational work, makes marriage an economic possibility for the young man will receive dividends in increased loyalty and length of service.

EXECUTIVE CONDUCT. Teach the young employee to look ahead. Show him the value of proper habits of work, of thrift, and of self-advancement if he is ultimately to undertake the responsibilities of a home and family. Guard him from blind-alley jobs. If you are employing young women, keep your standards of selection high. If they feel that by such employment their standing is not injured in the eyes of their friends, you will find the problem of maintaining a sufficient labor force simplified.

Q. You have charge of several departments in a factory, some of which employ men and others girls and women. The forelady in one of the latter departments advises you that the large majority of the girls in her department are living at home and are not required to supplement the family income. Many of them are apparently spending their entire income on clothing. She feels that this condition is wrong and wishes that you would issue regulations specifying a less expensive type of work clothing or require the use of shop uniforms, to be designed and supplied for use inside the factory, by the company. What are the various points to be weighed in considering such a proposal?

What might be the effect of the forelady's proposal upon wage incentive? Upon the desirability of the job? If the use of shop uniforms was decided upon, how would you suggest that this ruling should be enforced with minimum effect upon morale? Should the uniforms be designed by a company official? By a committee of employees? By an outside specialist? Or how?

Q. One of the young men in your employ comes to you and asks for an increase in wages, stating that he is to be married and he understands that married men are entitled to a higher wage than unmarried men. He is a good man and worth developing, although his value recently has been lessened through inattentiveness to his work. Develop a presentation which will set him right regarding the factors which determine the amount of a wage, and will provide him with the necessary incentive to put his best effort behind his work.

Are married men entitled to a higher wage than unmarried men? Is the promise of greater dependability entitled to an additional wage? Should not marriage properly produce a greater incentive to improve work quality and quantity, which normally results in greater income? Should an executive offer anything other than opportunity for increased earning power whenever warranted by the employee's record?

Home and Family. We all feel a powerful urge to further the existence and happiness of our immediate family. This desire may cause opposite actions in different people. One immigrant will not come to America until his family can come under his care; another will not let his family come until he has gone ahead and prepared a home and developed a livelihood.

When an executive who is laying off workmen is approached by an employee and asked if there is a job for his son, the executive, if understanding, will sense the pressure behind the parental desire and treat the employee considerately. The executive who finds the workman stalling on the job when work is slack remembers the impelling force urging him to continue as long as possible in support of his family. A knowledge of motivations thus serves to explain conduct, although such conduct may be inexcusable.

The factory magazine editor who, under the caption "Why Doesn't Father Come Home?" wrote of the little daughter at the gate of the workman's home, waiting for the return of her father who is lying in the hospital, a victim of carelessness, used a powerful influence in arousing the proper attitude toward accident prevention.

EXECUTIVE CONTROL. The worker who has dependents

can often be effectively appealed to through this avenue of responsibility. The consequences of dismissal are most keenly sensed in this relation. You must not be tempted to exploit this natural wish to safeguard one's family through using it to arouse fear or uncertainty. The executive who purposely keeps a man guessing about his job under such circumstances is guilty of a crime of management. If you are willing to employ the children of one of your employees, you may fairly ask the parents' cooperation in making the son or daughter a valuable member of your group, and their response will undoubtedly prove helpful to you. You may place greater reliance, in point of service, upon men or women with dependents than upon those without, as the former have responsibilities which make steady employment much more desirable to them. As a result they try somewhat harder to deserve it. Show your employees how they may become of sufficient value to own a home of their own and rear and educate their children and you have capitalized upon one of the strongest desires in human life.

Q. *While an addition is being erected in your department, a timber falls, striking one of your employees and knocking him senseless. His father, who is also employed in your department, rushes out and attacks the workman responsible for the mishap. Should the father be discharged for this?*

> What should you say to the father? To the workman? To the foreman who has charge of the workman? Would you advocate that the workman be transferred elsewhere?

Q. The mother of one of your employees comes to your office and complains bitterly that her son, who has been dismissed, has been unfairly treated by you. She is clearly in the wrong and has evidently been misinformed. Understanding the reason for her strong feeling, do you think that you are in position to convince her to the contrary, or would your superior officer stand more chance of success?

> Would it be desirable to listen to her tirade before referring her to your superior? Is the inference that her son believed that he was unfairly treated indicative of a possible error in the technique of discharge? Would it be desirable to refuse to talk with her unless her son accompanies her?

Leadership. The desire to be led is sometimes called the submissive instinct. We like to think of it, however, as the desire to work under a good executive. The three hundred workmen who, during wartime, followed their contracting foreman to a town some hundreds of miles distant from their last job and worked for three weeks without an exact knowledge of the wage to be paid must have been impelled largely by satisfactions gained under his direction.

The presence of this desire is of great assistance to the executive. If he succeeds as a leader, he will find a growing spirit of cooperation and group loyalty. His men will shout for him. He will find the word being passed around, "Get a job with Mr. ———. He is a good boss." The work of the executive is made immensely easier as soon as he has shown promise of satisfying this desire in his men.

EXECUTIVE CONDUCT. The privilege of capitalizing this

instinct comes as a reward for good leadership. You will find that employees will carry out your wishes with alacrity. You will no longer find it necessary to lean upon your authority when giving orders, as orders will be needed only to give direction to the work. When you gain this form of cooperation, cherish it. Work harder to deserve the attitude which your employees take toward you. Take care, however, that your employees do not lean too heavily upon your leadership. Stimulate them to think for themselves and in other ways foster their initiative.

Q. *In your opinion, would the submissiveness born of fear bring any quality of satisfaction? How does this form of submissiveness vary from that which is born of admiration?*

> Does good leadership make us feel submissive or cooperative? When employees have such confidence in their superior that they follow his directions unthinkingly, is response dissimilar to that incited through the use of fear? Does the prevalence of an unthinking confidence among employees make for the greatest progress of the group and of its effectiveness? What form of relationship do you recommend?

Q. *One of the employees in your department is outstandingly popular owing to his sense of humor. He is the center of amusement in any recreational gathering of employees and is of definite assistance to you in the maintenance of a cheerful organization. Does his popularity in this respect mark him as desirable executive timber?*

> Would opportunity for his humor be increased or lessened by assigning him executive responsibilities? Do humorous propensities indicate an interest in or understanding of

human nature or the presence of an unusual point of view? How would you define popularity?

Justice. No human desire seems more insistent than the demand for fair treatment. In industrial life the presence of a smoldering sense of injustice is as dangerous a menace to the organization as is a flame within the walls of the surrounding building. When employees feel that the treatment accorded them, though unfair, represents the convictions of fair-minded but misguided executives, their sense of rebellion is slow to take active form. It is when employees believe that the executives are knowingly exacting unfair requirements that their tempers rise rapidly to white heat. Conversely, the executive who has gained a reputation for being a just man has forged for himself a lever of control that will make possible accomplishments which no other agency can offer. Such a leader becomes a marked man among workmen, and phrases are coined for his description. He is spoken of as being "on the level," "on the square," "a regular guy," and he gains through reputation a measure of confidence which he may count among his greatest assets.

EXECUTIVE CONDUCT. Remember that justice does not spring from the emotions; it is born of the intellect. Its base lies in conformance to divine or human law. It is impartial. Therefore, in matters of justice you should completely control your feelings so that you may deal with the facts in a thoroughly impersonal manner. It is important that you become thoroughly conversant with all details on both sides of the issue. Human judgment most frequently errs because certain factors are left out in the reasoning. Above all other attributes, employees will respect you for your willingness to do the just thing, even though the doing will place your personal interests at a disadvantage.

Q. *During a national emergency you are placed in charge of an essential industrial development. You have in your employ men of great ability who are receiving a nominal wage but who wish thus to serve their country. The emergency ceases and leaves you with the responsibility of liquidating the enterprise. The members of your organization wish to return at once to their own personal affairs, but for them to do so will place you in great difficulty. What might be their sole reason for remaining with you at further personal loss to themselves?*

Is loyalty possible without justice? Is justice the only requirement?

Q. *You are in charge of a group of clerical employees on salary. No payment for overtime work is allowed. A temporary and unexpected increase in work occurs. In order to meet requirements, all employees will have to work every evening for a week. What official pressure can you bring to bear upon your employees to carry out this program? What personal resource may be of assistance to you?*

Should executive resources in the form of employee loyalties be drawn upon for the consummation of unjust administrative requirements? Under what circumstances might this request for overtime work be a just one?

Q. *Due to certain competitive reasons which must be kept confidential for several weeks, your chief finds it necessary* *to adopt a change in policy. You are acquainted with the reasons for the change and agree to the necessity. Without this information, the new policy would appear to be unwise and likely to arouse employee opposition. Under what circumstances could you say to your employees, "I know that this step appears to be an unwise one but I am certain that it is the right one and I will ask you to trust in my judgment," and feel confident of their support?*

Does their attitude infer something more than their confidence in your sense of justice? Would such expression of confidence be indicative of administrative as well as executive ability?

Imitation. We find within us a tendency to imitate others, particularly those whom we admire. The executive finds this impulse of great value to him in coordination of employee effort. Often through his personal example he can bring about changes in an organization without the necessity of orders or any other form of communication. This is particularly true of personal relationships in the organization. If the executive is courteous, the employees will be courteous, and if the executive is curt and peremptory, the employees will be likewise. A good example appeals not only to our imitativeness but to our reason as well. We are constantly measuring ourselves against others, and where we find traits that we admire, we try to develop them in ourselves. An admirable personality will thus impress itself very rapidly upon an organization and will soon be reflected in the conduct of each member. Some salesmen make it a practice to study the treatment accorded them by clerks and secretaries prior to meeting the executive, as they profess to find a striking similarity between the conduct of the employees and that of their chief and are thus enabled to formulate the proper method of approach.

EXECUTIVE CONDUCT. You are being studied by your employees, for they are interested in you. If their attitude is friendly, they are looking for things to admire. If their attitude is inimical, they are looking for things to criticize. Their interest does not cease with the close of the working period. Sooner or later they will know something of your home life, your recreations, and your outside friends. Intuitively, they are hoping that they may find no flaw—that they may accept you with no reservations—for they want the satisfaction that comes with thoroughly good leadership. They will measure you by the little things you do as well as the big, and will imitate you in them. The power of your example will reach past that part of their lives spent in the workplace. Weigh this responsibility carefully. You inevitably shoulder it when you undertake the leadership of men.

One administrator capitalized this imitative tendency with remarkable effectiveness by telling his subordinate executives:

> I shall not ask you to do anything that I do not require of myself, and furthermore you may commit any of the faults that you see me commit. For example, if you find that I am tardy, you may be tardy. If you hear me cursing employees, then you may curse employees. But not otherwise.

This method is worthy of careful consideration.

Q. *You are in charge of a group of floor salesmen in a men's apparel shop. You feel that your employees are not sufficiently attentive to the matter of personal appearance. You are considering two plans: first, to issue a general notice requesting improvement; second, to exaggerate the well-kept condition of your own attire, being careful not to give the impression of unduly expensive or pretentious clothing, and to place a full-length mirror in the washroom. Which of these plans would you prefer and why?*

It is said that actions speak louder than words. Into what groups might such actions be divided? Those that are capable of imitation? Those that are proof of sincerity? Those that show willingness to practice preachments?

The Force of Habit. We are too inclined to think of habits as something to be avoided, as obstructions through which we must break if we are to progress. In reality they are of enormous value to humanity. As the automatic machine effects great savings over the nonautomatic type, so does habitual conduct effect great savings over that which is not habitual.

EXECUTIVE CONDUCT. Remember that old habits cannot be cast aside and new ones acquired overnight. Such changes require time, and during the transition period, when "automaticity," as Frank Gilbreth used to call it, is absent, production will be abnormally low. Therefore a new method of doing work, though theoretically simpler and shorter than the old, may take longer at the outset, until the new habit is firmly established. Prepare for this period of transition and provide the perseverance and enthusiasm necessary to carry the employees through this stage. The new plan demands conscious attention; it requires greater mental effort. This explains the universal "pain of a new idea." Never be impressed with the excellence of a given method merely because the employee has used it for many years. After his habit was formed, the act probably received little, if any, conscious attention. In instituting a rule or regulation among employees, provide continuous executive pressure until you are certain that obedience has become habitual. The issuance of an order is not enough where habits are to be formed; it must be followed by rigid inspection and report.

Q. *Would it have been as easy to arise an hour earlier during the summer under the daylight-saving plan had the people been instructed to move their activities ahead an hour instead of moving the clock ahead?*

> If working hours are to be increased by fifteen minutes each day, would it seem best, from the standpoint of habits, to add them to the beginning or end of the morning period or the beginning or end of the afternoon period?

Q. *Why is careful preliminary training in the right method likely to prove a very profitable investment in organizations where repetitive work is carried on?*

Q. *In military control, when a soldier is under emotional stress, commanders often find that giving a routine command to the soldier will assist in getting him into a more normal frame of mind. Why is this?*

> One explanation is that habits affect actions and actions affect emotions. The routine command plays upon the

habit of routine response, and the routine response stimulates a normal attitude of mind.

Discussion. What is your response to the following comments?

1. *The use of fear as a stimulant is not wholly wrong. The error is found in its excessive use. A little fear mixed with the hope of reward adds potency to incentive.*

Is not the line between reward and penalty a varying one in terms of personality? Is not the fear of losing the reward present, in some degree, in every application of incentive? Is it desirable for the executive to increase this feeling of fear?

2. *Force is not an obsolete element in executive control. Employees welcome forceful leadership.*

Does forceful leadership necessarily mean coercive leadership? What is the proper use of personal force in leadership?

3. *If the executive concentrates his attention on production and not on the study of instincts and habits, he will find that employees will do likewise.*

Just what is production? Is it affected by the behavior of employees? What, in turn, affects employee behavior?

4. *Explanations of unreasonable acts are interesting, but the executive who insists upon proper conduct and who doesn't know too much about explanations meets with less unreasonable behavior from employees.*

Should the executive's knowledge of forces influencing human behavior make him less eager to organize and develop the employee "will to do"? Do you think that the repression of impulses through the use of fear, is an essentially constructive technique?

5. *I do not favor showing employees how their work coordinates with that of others. The less they see of other jobs the better they will like their own.*

What do you think would be the attitude of employees toward a rule requiring transfer to another job at least once a year? (Such an announcement nearly caused a strike in one large plant.) Can the employee's ambition to obtain a different and better job be used to improve his work on his present job? Of two jobs offering the same wage, if one seems generally more desirable, how should parity be established?

6. *We employ specialists for the improvement of equipment and methods—we employ operators to produce with existing facilities. We expect that these groups will give their entire attention to their own responsibilities.*

The manager of one large organization requires every employee to present at least one constructive suggestion each month. Compare this policy with the one stated above.

7. *Catering to the possessive instinct is a dangerous practice. Employees can easily be led to believe that they own the entire establishment.*

Does not the sense of nominal ownership lead to a greater sense of responsibility rather than to a sense of power? Does not the desire to own (control) the establishment spring from a feeling of rebellion against autocratic policies rather than from management's willingness to share responsibility?

8. *Competitions are undesirable forms of production incentive. They stimulate abnormal effort, their effect is temporary, and discontent frequently follows the disposition of awards.*

Is there a distinction between competitions which naturally result from a sense of rivalry and those which are stimulated by reward through victory?

9. *It is desirable to stimulate curiosity in those employees who are paid to think. For most workmen, however, the less curiosity the better. Too many things to think about bring restlessness and a desire for a better job.*

Cannot curiosity be directed along profitable channels? Would curiosity concerning ways and means of improving the quantity and quality of work being done tend to increase or decrease restlessness? Would the degree of management's sensitiveness to resulting suggestions be a factor in your decision? Cannot the desire for a better job be translated into a desire to make the present job better?

10. *I never put a new employee in a department where he has friends. Production and sociability do not mix well.*

Is a congenial atmosphere conducive to better or poorer work? Need the privilege of congeniality be misused? Does the proposed policy prohibit the possibility of forming friendships with present members of the department?

11. *When an executive shows an interest in the workman's home and family affairs, he is at once burdened with their*

troubles, solicited for loans or wage advances, and asked to excuse tardiness and absence from work.

Is it to be inferred that an executive who is not so burdened is therefore a better executive? Is it not true that every executive, irrespective of policy, meets such problems? With greater knowledge of conditions, would he not be in better position to deal justly?

12. *Leadership—that's what they want. Don't let them forget that you are the boss!*

What seems to you to be the best way of causing them to remember it?

13. *Justice—yes, if they deserve it. Most employees don't appreciate fair treatment and respond by taking advantage of the executive at the first opportunity.*

Is justice to be a reward of conduct? Is it a quality necessary to the proper measurement of conduct? What is the cure for the sort of employee response referred to?

14. *I don't want any employees to imitate me. Their job is to produce—my job is to see that they do it. Let them imitate the work that they did yesterday—and continue to imitate it.*

Are there not different forms of imitation—imitation of activity, imitation of mental attitude, imitation of emotional attitude, imitation of moral and ethical attitude? Judging from this remark, would you consider this executive's attitude to be worth imitating?

CHAPTER 7

Executive Duties

In discussing those activities which are inherently a part of executive responsibilities we shall assume that the problems of employment, health, safety, nutrition, recreation, and formal educational work are handled by functional officials who are specialists in their particular fields. We shall also view the problems of wages (in so far as job evaluation, merit rating, and the system of wage payment are concerned) and of joint relations between management and men as matters of administrative rather than executive responsibility.

Analysis of Labor Requirements. The executive will find it necessary to requisition labor from the employment manager just as he requisitions material or supplies from the purchasing agent or storekeeper. In both cases he should specify the nature of his requirements. The clearer and more precise the specifications, the more satisfactorily will he be served.

EXECUTIVE CONDUCT. The employment manager must sell jobs. If he is to sell any of yours, you should provide him with descriptions and talking points and also inform him of the type of buyers who form a satisfactory market. (Remember that all jobs are "guaranteed"—employees can give them back at will.) One of the best ways to describe a job is by means of a photograph, because people learn more easily through their eyes than through their ears. Give the applicants an opportunity to see how the work looks. If you fear that the work environment is such that photographs would deter rather than attract, then improvement of the workplace is in order.

When you specify the kind of person you wish to employ, there is no need to point out that the applicant should be honest, industrious, prompt, efficient, and have the rest of the virtues. These characteristics are desirable in every employee. Tell the employment manager the unique requirements of the job. For example, it may require exceptional strength, exceptional physical activity, exceptional penmanship, exceptional skill, exceptional experience. The way to detect these unusual requirements is to proceed indirectly by asking yourself, "Why would an average person fail to fill this position satisfactorily?"

Q. *Do you think it a good plan to have every new employee understand that his employment is probational for a stated period (two weeks, for example) and that at the end of that time you will tell him definitely if it seems wise for him to remain?*

> Would the amount of preliminary training necessary affect your decision? When does any employee cease to be on probation? It is said that any employee must fit the job and fit the organization. Might there by any variation in the length of probationary periods in terms of these capacities?

Q. You accept an applicant who fulfills all the requirements for the job which you indicated in your specifications. You soon find, however, that he is a trouble maker and must be dismissed. Should you add to your specification, "Should not be a trouble maker"?

> Can you hold the employment department to account on the basis of a preventable error in selection? Are trouble makers sometimes developed after employment? How?

Introduction of the New Employee. It is a well-known fact that in any new experience the two points of greatest sensitiveness are at the beginning and at the end of the experience, the former being the greater of the two. Therefore, a most important opportunity exists when the new employee is introduced to the organization and the workplace. Some concerns are using this opportunity for well-organized familiarization work under the control of a functional official, such as the personnel manager. By means of an introductory booklet, a trip through the department, well-planned introductions and work assignment, the employee is thoroughly informed about his new environment and is made to feel at home.

EXECUTIVE CONDUCT. There is a simple rule which will help you in forming a suitable method of introduction. It is to introduce the new employee as you would introduce a guest into your own family. This does not call for unctuous geniality, but it involves an atmosphere of hospitality and a thoughtfulness in eliminating the unfamiliarity of the newcomer. Never treat a new employee as a suspicious character who requires watching until he has proved his honesty and worth.

The list of information which the employee requires at the outset is surprisingly long. It includes such broad divisions as organization policy, wages, hours of work, rules and regulations, and also such specific concerns as employee service, restaurant service, employee organizations, etc. A printed booklet will relieve you of reiterating much of this data and will give the employee something for permanent reference. It is worth noting that the employee who finds the new job waiting for him with everything in first-class order at once gains an impression of the organization which more than repays the slight preparatory effort. Remember that you are a salesman. You must constantly sell your organization to your employees. You will have no more favorable moment to gain careful attention than when the employee first starts his work. See that he gets a clear and true picture of his opportunity and his environment.

Q. *You learn that girls entering your department have difficulty in becoming acquainted with others in the lunchroom and find the first few days somewhat disheartening. How will you arrange to overcome this condition?*

Should introductions be made by a representative of the management or by another employee? Why?

Q. *To what length should the introduction of a new employee to others be carried? Is introduction to employees adjacent to the workplace sufficient?*

Is it a good plan to arrange with one of the adjacent employees to introduce the new employee to other members of the group when occasion arises?

Q. *How important do you consider the argument that if the employees are given information booklets the morning they are employed, they will not refer to them while at work, as they dislike appearing ignorant? Would this feeling be lessened if the booklets were organized and published by an employee association?*

> Just how would you divide between the management and the employees the process of inducting a new employee into an organization? Should management take the entire responsibility?

Q. *Where should an executive make his introductory remarks to the new employee—at the employee's workplace or in the executive office?*

> Are there advantages and disadvantages in either alternative? Should such remarks be presented before the employee enters the department? Consider optional methods from the standpoint of attentiveness, executive time and convenience, ease of presentation, etc.

Training. The executive naturally desires that the new employee shall gain facility in correct methods of work. There is a definite technique in administering such training. The executive may undertake this work personally or may delegate it to an employee who has educative ability. In large establishments training may be included in a general educational program which is under the jurisdiction of a functional official who specializes in such work. The executive, however, is rarely free from the responsibility of maintaining standard work methods.

EXECUTIVE CONDUCT. There are certain fundamentals

in successful training with which you should be familiar. The first fundamental is that work should be broken down into its elemental parts and the standard method applied to each element. The second fundamental is that correctness in method should precede speed in operation. The beginner should retard his movements at the outset until he can consciously control them and make them correctly. Only in this way can the establishment of habits involving incorrect method be avoided. This rule applies to mental as well as physical activities.

The third fundamental is that the employee should not be urged to increase his speed to a point which endangers his learning of the proper method. The employee who is put on a job with a daywork rate and then told, "Now I want you to get your production up to a point where you can earn piece-rates as soon as possible," is likely to sacrifice method for speed. The employee is likely to attempt too rapid advancement if he is led to feel that his wage during the learning period is directly related to his production during that time instead of being a subsistence allowance chargeable to training expense. Do not put an employee on a production wage-basis until you are sure that he is in a position to earn a satisfactory return through his newly acquired work habits. It is nearly always true that inferior habits of work can be acquired more quickly than those which ultimately yield the high returns. If the employee has not had enough practice to "make his earnings" by using the right method, he often will shift to a method which will yield a large quantity of work of poorer quality. Allow the employee a normal amount of time to learn his job. If he is earnest, though dull or awkward, this period can be fairly lengthened beyond the normal. Make it clear, however, that you expect a gradual and continual increase in productive rate until a satisfactory pace is attained.

The fourth fundamental is the use of patience. You may require the utmost precision in conforming to the standard method and your insistence may require repeated efforts by the learner, but there will be no opposition so long as you remain cheerful in your demands and patient in the face of his unsuccessful attempts.

Out of the vast development of new training techniques which have occurred during recent years, Glenn Gardiner's brilliant slogan "Tell 'em, show 'em, watch 'em, check 'em" has stripped involved training methods down to their simplest fundamentals. Put this cycle into operation and results may startle you.

Q. *You find that a new employee who has had experience with the work in hand has learned an ineffective and careless method. He considers himself a skilled operator, however. How will you interest him in the proper method in such a way that he will be eager to accept it?*

> What will be the value to the employee of the proper method? Should he be criticized for learning an improper one? Will you object to the period of lowered production which will occur during his mastery of the proper method? Will you be willing to pay him the average previous wage during this period?

Q. *If the learning wage is, in reality, a wage of subsistence, should a married man with a family be entitled to a larger learning wage than an unmarried man with no responsibilities?*

What is the purpose of the learning wage from the company standpoint? Will a married man with a family be of greater value to the company than an unmarried man? Is it desirable that an employee make a financial sacrifice during the learning period?

Q. *Are there cases in which the learning wage should not necessarily be considered a subsistence wage?*

When employees, because of merit, have been transferred to a better position? When circumstances require transfer of an employee to another job demanding an equal grade, though different form of skill?

Transfer. The executive is inclined to look askance at the employee transfer. The act implies a change, and it seems to him that there are changes enough in his personnel without further self-inspired alteration. Furthermore, transfers disturb habit formations and in a measure lower effectiveness. On the other hand, a reasonable movement of employees among jobs tends to relieve monotony and offers an excellent means of insurance against the breakdown of chains of routine, since, in case of absences, there will be other employees present who are familiar with the work and can undertake it during the emergency. A third advantage is that transfers, while not immediately resulting in promotion, usually offer increased opportunity to earn promotion and are therefore a direct form of incentive.

EXECUTIVE CONDUCT. Don't be afraid to transfer an

employee if he deserves an increased opportunity. The transfer may temporarily inconvenience you, but it will bring later returns in developing your reputation for giving a man a chance to advance. In dull times, shift your employees about so that they may learn more than one task. This is a most effective method of giving an employee a chance to grow and improve his value to you and to himself. View the act of transfer as an opportunity in human research. You cannot always tell what an employee is best fitted for until you have tried him. The trial-and-error method is sometimes the only way of finding out the one best place for each man in your organization.

Q. *You have transferred an employee to a new position offering greater opportunities but he does not seem to be able to handle the job. It is a clear case of lack of capacity. Would you advocate dismissing the employee? If not, would you advocate transferring him to a lesser job or back to his old job? If the latter, how would you approach him in order to return him to his previous work with a minimum loss of morale? Would it have been easier had you placed him probationally on the new job?*

> Is it possible entirely to avoid such errors in judgment? Is it probable that errors in the judgment of human capacities usually are in the nature of underestimates?

Q. *You propose to transfer an employee to a more promising occupation. The employee objects. He says, "I'm all right here. I'm perfectly contented." When told of the brighter future ahead in the other work, he responds by saying that he doesn't care for the new work, as it has too much responsibility attached to it. What can you do, if anything?*

Should you coerce him? Urge him? Stimulate his ambition? Express your confidence in him? Insist upon a probationary trial? What is the executive's responsibility toward a man whose ambitions are not commensurate with his capacities? What are the executive's responsibilities to the company in dealing with such a man?

Q. *Do you think that a raise in pay should or should not accompany a transfer to new work? Which situation would be better if the employee should fail to make good on the new job? Should an employee be transferred to another job if you are not reasonably sure that he will succeed?*

Should an employee expect an immediate increase in wage when receiving a transfer as the result of merit? Do you think it desirable to ask an employee to carry on temporarily other work offering greater opportunity for advancement, with the mental reservation that, should he prove fitted, the change will be made a permanent one?

Q. *As superintendent of a research department in one of the many plants of a major company, you have been predominantly hiring college graduates. Apparently your selection has been satisfactory, as the performance of the new men is generally excellent. However, these men come to you frequently to request transfer.*

Should an executive expect to lose some men this way? What if they request transfer to a similar department of a plant located in another area? Transfer to another department in your plant? Can a research department be used as a training ground for operating departments? What if you feel that it would be to company advantage to retain these men, even if not in your department? What if considerable time and effort has been given to the training of these men?

Promotion. The possibility of promotion is a great provider of incentive. Its potency is so obvious that executives have been known to exploit its worth, wrongly stimulating employees by vague allusions to future advancements to positions which the worker has not the capacity to fill. To develop a yearning for that which cannot be reached is as wrong as to retard achievement. Someone has commented upon the fact that although Napoleon's soldiers carried marshal's batons in their knapsacks, there were very few who rose to that position. Even though hope does spring eternal in the human breast, we have no right to lead it along false pathways.

EXECUTIVE CONDUCT. Never stimulate employees by allusion to promotion unless you are convinced that they have the necessary resources of capacity and ability to achieve the goal if they will. Provide paths of promotion in your organization as far as it is possible to do so, and don't hesitate to let the path run out of your organization and into another if further advancement is thus possible. If you have blind-alley jobs, and you doubtless will have some, be frank in telling your employees of them. If possible, arrange promotional possibilities *within* every job. Where this is not possible the presence of a base or minimum rate, to be followed by successive increases as the employee shows greater facility, develops incentive toward improving the given job and diverts attention from the hope of promotion through transfer.

Found your decision regarding promotion upon a basis of incontrovertible fact. The proper employee records should show you when the promotion is earned. Never be swayed by emotional pressure in this matter. Work on a basis of objective results and proved accomplishments. Don't wait for employees to ask for rate increases before considering their cases. Either have it understood that at certain periods each year you will review the rate situation and confer the merited increases, or, better still, develop a plan whereby increases take place automatically when earned. The problem of getting rate increases approved by your chief is considered in Chapter 15.

Q. *Do you believe that an employee should receive a wage increase only when he has demonstrated that he has earned it, or do you believe that a wage increase acts as a definite incentive in some cases?*

> Would your answer turn upon the degree to which you were certain of the presence of capacity?

Q. *One of your newer employees shows unusual ability. You are convinced that he can satisfactorily fill a new position which carries promotion with it. There are older employees, however, who have not the necessary qualifications for the job but who will doubtless feel offended at the appointment. Should you advise them of your proposed change before making it? If so, how will you present the matter to them?*

Do you think that employees, in general, have a rather definite knowledge of the status of their capacities as compared with those of their associates? Is this a problem in which amenities should be observed rather than facts or knowledge imparted?

Praise and Commendation. The giving of praise or commendation gratifies the instinctive desire for approval. Some executives do not favor its use. They adopt the policy of taking exceptional work for granted. They argue that the employee will then infer that what he considered unusually good was no more than what was expected. He will then set higher standards of achievement for himself. The error in this logic is found in the conclusion. Only the rare employee finds incentive in passive acceptance of good work by his chief. The usual result of this policy is to bring discouragement or the feeling that the boss is unappreciative.

EXECUTIVE CONDUCT. Do not be fulsome in your praise. A little is often better than too much. It is not necessary to give praise immediately after the act. Wait until the situation seems right, a time which may be better sensed than reasoned. If you have opportunity, give it in the presence of others. Present it in an official sense, though with your personal support. You will find that it is best given in a sober spirit, for it should seem unmistakably sincere. Make certain that in your commendation you do not indicate that the employee's performance represents the best he can do. If you do this, you will take away his incentive for further effort.

Q. *You find that despite your efforts to the contrary, your commendation of an employee's work has gone to his head. He is apparently the type of person whose ego fattens on praise. When you are in his vicinity, he calls you over to see his work again, in the hope that you will make some further comment. You find that you have unfortunately stimulated a latent tendency toward conceit. How will you handle the situation?*

> By making additional commendation dependent upon specific improvements which you call to his attention, could you not capitalize his desire for further praise?

Q. *After commending the progress record of one of your employees, you learn that your clerk has made a mistake and the record is not so good as you had understood it to be. The employee had made no definite answer to your commendation, which was given in the presence of several other workmen. How can you advise the employee of your error and turn it to good account by giving him an incentive to better his actual standing?*

> Is the purpose of commendation to reward or to stimulate further? Or both? If used solely as a reward, what attitude may result? If used solely as an incentive?

Reproof and Criticism. We may make a distinction between reproof and criticism. Reproof is essential in the case of voluntary or repeated error on the part of an employee. Criticism serves in the case of an unintentional error or omission. Reproof calls attention to a volitional act, while criticism may be directed at an unrecognized mistake.

It is safe to say that more errors are made by executives in administering reproof and criticism than in any other of their recurrent activities. There seems to be a delusive cloud hanging over this technique which makes reproof synonymous with "bawling a man out" and criticism unavailing without a mustered display of temper.

EXECUTIVE CONDUCT. Administer reproof and criticism as soon after the act as possible, but not so soon as to indicate any emotionalism. If the employee feels that you are acting in anger, he will very largely discount your statements. Never give reproof or criticism in public or to any employee who is not under your direct authority. Never present your attitude on a personal basis; make it clear that you are acting as an agent of the organization. Never offer reproof or criticism in an emotional way, or in a way which would tend to rouse emotion. In the case of criticism, you will find that intense seriousness is not always essential. The most important thing to remember in offering reproof or criticism is that *it is the application of a force calculated to act constructively*. The result should be the awakening of a desire on the part of the employee to improve his conduct. Any technique which leaves the workman sullen, discouraged, or emotionally excited is obviously not effective.

Q. *One of your employees tends to take your criticism as indicating a personal animosity. You understand that he believes you are trying to make things unpleasant for him so that he will resign. How can you effectively overcome his misunderstanding?*

Is such an error on the part of the employee indicative of faulty executive technique? How can an executive make sure that such a misunderstanding will not occur? If you do not introduce personal feeling into reproof, how can you feel certain that you appear to be sincere?

Q. *You have reproved an employee and he denies the act. While you are certain that he was responsible, you cannot prove it. Should you have reproved the employee under these circumstances? Should you have reproved him conditionally? For example, "Now, Frank, I don't know whether you did this or not, but if you did do it, you must realize that it cannot be repeated."*

In such a case, can the suspicion of guilt be evidenced without the use of direct reproof? What would you advise?

Q. *One of your fellow employees with whom you have frequent contact is continually being openly and intentionally criticized and rebuffed by his superior. Your superior is an associate of his superior. Although much of the criticism is well founded, you feel that the way in which it has been presented is causing considerable harm to the morale and performance, not only of the individual concerned, but also of the employees in his department. What should be your action?*

Would you take any formal action? Would you act differently if you were a close friend of the employee being criticized? Of his superior? Of your superior? What if the situation did not affect production or performance in your department? If it did affect them?

Dismissal or Discharge. In many organizations executives are permitted to dismiss employees from the department but are not permitted to discharge them from the organization payrolls. In either case the act is never one which should be entered into lightly. It often represents the final experience of the employee in the organization and is strongly impressed upon his memory. As time passes, his feeling toward the organization is largely colored by the treatment which he received upon dismissal.

EXECUTIVE CONDUCT. You should never dismiss an employee without giving his case a thorough and impartial investigation. In cases requiring immediate action, you may find it necessary to remove the employee from your department at once, but your decision should not be made until it is very clear to you and to others that you are acting with no emotion, with evident open-mindedness, and with the feeling that you must prove the guilt rather than that the employee must prove himself innocent.

The acts which are grounds for dismissal or discharge should be known to all employees. In any given instance your task is then one of establishing the occurrence of the act.

If it is possible to avoid it, do not dismiss or discharge an employee in the presence of others. Make it clear that your action is impersonal and, in a sense, automatic. Again, the important result of your action should be to leave the individual with a sincere desire to improve his conduct and the feeling that he can do so.

Q. An employee whom you discharged returns to you two weeks later and asks to be reinstated. What factors would you consider in forming your decision?

Group the factors into those affecting the employee, other employees, the executive, and company policy. Are there certain acts which may cause discharge but which would not prohibit reinstatement? If so, in the case under discussion was discharge the best remedy?

Q. Your plant has six thousand employees working in three major manufacturing divisions. The industrial engineering department is organized along the same major division lines as the operating divisions, with an industrial engineering director and a supervisor in each of the three divisions. As a supervisor of one of the industrial engineering divisions of twelve employees, you have set up your division on a functional basis. You have two men employed in analyzing costs and developing standards for the standard cost program. One of the two men has had considerable experience with your company in standard cost work. He is a very willing and rapid worker. The second man knows very little, and cares less, about costs, and works under the close direction of the first man. You have limited experience in this type of work and so rely heavily upon the first man; however, you find that he makes frequent errors, so that you continually have to check his calculations. Criticism has been ineffective. Your efforts to impress him with the fact that you would prefer more accurate work at a corresponding sacrifice in speed have been of no avail. What is your next move in your cost division?

Would you act differently if other qualified cost personnel were immediately available? What if your man with considerable cost experience has a long company service record? Would you retain him if this seemed to be the best position for him in the company? If you feel that you cannot recommend him for promotion or transfer, should you so inform him?

Resignation. Executives are often too prone to take a disgruntled attitude toward an employee who terminates employment with the organization. This is a mistake, even when the employee is leaving because of dissatisfaction. If the workman has performed his work satisfactorily and has been cooperative, he is entitled to the good will of the organization even though misconceptions on his part do not allow him to respond in kind. Later he may alter his views and wish to return. He will not consider doing so if the parting seemed unfriendly. Far-sighted executives always leave this door open to competent employees, and over a period of years the policy is found to bring good returns.

EXECUTIVE CONDUCT. Take the time to say good-by to your terminating employee. Let him know that he has your friendship and the good will of the organization behind him, if he deserves it. If he has been a desirable worker, tell him that if he wishes to return at some time in the future, you will be glad to consider it. The fact that he is leaving because of dissatisfaction should not deter you from making this remark. *Distinguish between the man's value and his viewpoint.*

Q. *An employee who has not been particularly satisfactory is terminating employment and he asks you if he may refer prospective employers to you when he applies for future positions. How should you answer him?*

Is this a difficulty or an opportunity? If you had maintained comprehensive employee records, would your answer be simplified? What are your responsibilities to the employee, and to the inquirer when receiving such a request for reference?

Q. *A terminating employee enters your office with the remark "I've come to tell you what I think of your entire outfit here." While he has a degree of self-control, his comments are insolent, sarcastic, and rude. How should you handle this situation? Is it a happening which might occur to any executive, irrespective of ability?*

With whom may lie the error of which this experience is the result? What attitude of mind should you desire in such an employee when he leaves your office? How would you proceed to attain it?

Discussion. What is your response to the following comments?

1. *It is not my job to sell the organization to the employee. It is the employee's job to sell himself to me.*

Is it not the employee's relationship to his job that will primarily determine his fitness, rather than his personal relationship with the executive? Does fitness for a job necessarily imply a desire to fit into the organization? Does the proper presentation of an organization to an employee tend to lessen the prestige of the executive?

2. *Whenever I train a man for a job, someone offers him a higher wage and he leaves. Hereafter, I shall let the other fellow do the training.*

What would you infer from this executive's experience? Should an executive expect to lose a certain proportion of newly trained employees in this way? Is his proposal technically sound? Is it industrially sound?

3. *Let the new employee watch other operators and learn for himself. Kindergarten methods are not necessary for grown men.*

Discuss instruction through inspection and imitation versus instruction which includes the addition of competent educational supervision. When employees err in observation in the first method, how can their mistakes be corrected prior to habit formation?

4. *The greater the opportunity for transfer, the less the employee's interest in his present job.*

Is this generally true in your opinion? When true, of what defects in organization is it symptomatic? Inequalities in wage-skill relationships? Inequalities in wage–working-conditions relationships?

5. *It is not my duty to point out the blind-alley jobs. Employees should assume the responsibility for their own futures.*

Is an applicant in position to judge of the opportunity for promotion when considering an opportunity for employment? Is he to be expected to give due weight to these considerations at such a time? If an employee is given responsibilities which are not commensurate with his capacities, is it good policy from the company standpoint to retain him in this position? Is the knowledge of a policy of promotion on merit likely to attract a higher or a lower type of employee to the organization?

6. *When executives are already beset by requests for wage increases, further talk about promotion merely aggravates a difficult situation.*

What do you infer from the situation described? Should executives be beset for wage increases? Whose fault is it if they are? Should an employee be considered for a wage increase only if he has asked for one? Is there a distinction between employee requests for wage increases and opportunities for promotion?

7. *Praise may be helpful to the individual worker, but its value is more than offset by the demoralizing jealousy and envy aroused in nearby employees.*

How can the demoralizing effects of praise be avoided without prohibiting its publicity? Cannot the commendation be so presented that the reason for its giving is clearly evidenced?

8. *I make it a practice to give reprimands rarely but when I do so, I make them so severe that I never have to repeat them.*

What will be the effect of this practice, in your opinion? Will it lead to closer work relationships between executive and employee? What will be the incentive for proper conduct? Is this the best form of incentive? What do you recommend as good practice?

9. *I believe that the constructive value of discharge is lost unless the man is stirred emotionally and awakened to an*

adequate sense of his wrongdoing. Otherwise, he is likely to go to another job and repeat the same offense.

Is not the act of discharge a sufficient emotional disturbance to satisfy the purposes specified? Does executive anger tend to further improvement of the emotional attitude of the employee? Can executive forcefulness in statement be shown without the presence of emotion? Does impressiveness demand emotion?

10. *When I discharge a man I contrive to do it in the presence of other employees. It sets a healthy precedent.*

Does the fear of disgrace through discharge have any effect upon the number of voluntary terminations, in your opinion? Do you favor the development of righteousness through fear? Has the executive a right to use individual misconduct as a means of influencing other employees?

11. *I have no desire to talk in a friendly way with men who are terminating employment. I have no affection for quitters, and no one who leaves my organization is invited to return.*

Does the act of termination necessarily characterize an employee as a quitter? Does this remark represent the attitude of the company or of the executive? In talking with the terminating employee, which attitude should the executive take? What are the advantages and disadvantages of company policy which is (*a*) favorable to later reemployment of terminating employees, (*b*) unfavorable to the same?

CHAPTER 8

Executive Collaboration

To collaborate is to co-labor, to work *with*. Sometimes the work takes the form of concerted action. Sometimes it takes the form of group thinking. Greater progress results when executives of every rank in industry learn to think as well as act together. The newer methods of highly coordinated production call for an equally high coordination of ideas.

The job of thinking together does not require a book of parliamentary rules and a gavel. Nor does it require a well-developed technique and a special list of commandments. The work can best be done in an informal manner. Ordinarily, only a few executives are required. Like any other form of effort, it benefits by a little planning; it is subject to normal hazards of inefficiency and misuse [1]; it requires a reasonable knowledge of human nature.

Executives should be called upon to think together when there are situations to be met and problems to be considered the solution of which directly affects the responsibilities of each participant. A common mistake

[1] Group thinking is misused when it is construed into an opportunity for the placing of blame, the selling of ideas, or the giving of indirect instruction.

has been overemphasis upon schedules and routines. Work of this sort is important only as situations are demanding, as problems are pressing, and not because a given hour of a given day has been set for weekly meetings.

When men are called upon to think together, the presence of an unsolved problem must be accepted in good faith by all. No one should initiate such work without full anticipation that his first ideas may be materially altered as joint effort is given to the solution. The more clearly problems are stated, the better will be the thinking. Problems usually become specific when the precise difficulties that obstruct the group objectives are plainly defined. Of the three questions "What do we want to accomplish?" "What stands in our way?" and "How can we overcome the obstacle?"—the second is the one which points the problem, while the answer to the third is the objective of the discussion.

Collaboration among executives means *acting* as well as *thinking* together. Problems proper for executive collaboration therefore should be those which lead to ultimate action of some sort. Speculative discussions have no place in this area. It should be clear that the job is not finished when the thinking is done. Results should follow promptly, unless there is clear reason for delay.

Collaboration with Subordinate Executives. Every executive knows that the ideas of his assistants next in rank are of direct value to the solution of problems which affect their work and their responsibilities. The objective therefore should be to assemble and discuss these difficulties as expeditiously as possible. The unit cost of sound solutions is of practical significance.

EXECUTIVE CONDUCT. When you are calling your assistants together, tell them why. Give them a chance to do a little mulling beforehand. They will appreciate this opportunity, and your discussion will get under way more rapidly. At the outset, don't hesitate to point out any uncertainties which are in your own mind. State the several sides of the problem. Let your assistants realize your sincerity in desiring their point of view. If you find difference of opinion, give each man a chance to state his case fully, for in these differences lies your greatest basis for progress toward the correct solution. Make it easy for your men to talk. Remember that an active and impersonal discussion stimulates thought. Keep the work on an informal level. Call your men by their first names if by so doing you make them feel more at ease. Be cheerful. When different points of view become too sharply defined, you may have to introduce a little humor in order to relieve the tension. Make sure that everyone present has fair opportunity to contribute his ideas. Frequently some of your best thinkers will be men who need a little encouragement in expressing themselves.

It will be your job finally to summarize the discussion and to draw the conclusion. If you are successful, your decision will usually be based on some obvious principle brought out by the discussion, and you will feel a certain warmth of general approval and willingness to collaborate in subsequent action. No matter how definite your conclusions have become or how unanimously they have been supported, be quick to open the entire problem for reconsideration in the light of new evidence. Never let personal pride stand in the way of getting the right answer. As soon as your men discover your adherence to this principle, your influence as an executive will be multiplied.

If action is to follow, be sure that each participant knows precisely what he is to do. If you have an active part in applying the plan, make doubly sure that you do your bit promptly in such a way as to set an example for the others. The fact that you are the superior member of the group makes this essential.

Don't keep any written minutes of these meetings, unless clearly necessary. If they are essential, keep them in such a way that names are not coupled with remarks, as men rapidly become "gun-shy" when they believe that their statements are to become a matter of formal record.

Q. *For some time it has been a requirement of your company that each production employee should be proficient in the operation of at least two distinctly different types of machines and pass certain tests to prove his facility. During this learning period he is paid the base daywork rate for the job, which ordinarily is considerably below the average piece-rate earnings. He has not been allowed to work on piece-rates during this learning period because of the hazard of spoiled work, accidents, and machine breakdown.*

This plan has never been enthusiastically accepted by the employees, and you have called the working foremen in your department together to discuss ways and means of expediting these activities. During the discussion it becomes evident that your subordinate executives are unanimous in the opinion that the company policy is a poor one and should be changed. You advise them that this question is out of your hands and that you know it has had a good deal of thought by the higher executives, who believe that the advantages of the plan outweigh its weaknesses. From this statement the discussion dwindles and your men finally state that they have very little to offer in the way of constructive suggestion. How should you handle this situation?

Should you have called the meeting in the first place? How should the problem have been put to the group? Is it reasonable to expect constructive suggestions from the men who are opposed to the policy involved?

Q. *A knotty problem involving the question of operations in your department and their relationship to later processes in an adjoining department has been the basis of a discussion between you and your working foremen. A solution has been arrived at, involving the cooperation of the adjacent department head. You have agreed to confer with him as the first step. You now learn that a change in organization is in prospect which will affect the standing of this department head, rendering it undesirable for you to take the matter up with him just at this time. This change, however, is still a confidential matter. It is clear that you must delay any action for some time. How will you justify your hesitancy to your working foremen?*

Should you find a plausible excuse? Should you tell them that you cannot go forward at this time but are unable to give them the real reason? Should you tell them that word has come from your superiors to hold matters up for a while? Should you tell them the true situation and pledge them to secrecy?

Collaboration with Functional Specialists. Executives find it necessary to collaborate closely with the representatives of the many service departments which supply their area. Specialized plant activities involving labor control, material control, equipment control, quality control, intrafactory transportation, and production control are of importance. They must be closely and precisely coordinated with the work of the department.

EXECUTIVE CONDUCT. It is imperative that you keep intimately in touch with these men, for their work is inextricably allied with yours and they must necessarily be consulted if you are to solve many of the technical difficulties of coordination. Inasmuch as these men are not reporting to you, your discussions with them may not at once be translated into authority for action. It will be possible, however, for some unanimity of proposal to be developed, after which the specialists involved may approach their superior officers for authorization. The sincerity of your desire to work out with them proper and practical solutions to difficulties, your open-mindedness to outside suggestion, and your sympathy for their point of view will obtain their cooperation, not only in thought but in action.

In asking for a conference, be sure to make clear that it is a request rather than an order. After such a session a word of appreciation or thanks is always in order. In stating the difficulty you should take care that your remarks do not carry any critical implications as to the manner in which these representatives are servicing your department. Make it plain that you are hunting for a cure rather than a culprit. Take care not to place these men in the awkward position of having to criticize the policies of their superior officers. The purpose of your collaboration is not to bring pressure to bear upon present policies but to work out proper plans of action under them. Never quote the remarks of these specialists to others. The general conclusions arrived at from your discussion are all that need repetition. In stating your difficulty to these men, have at least on tentative solution which you can offer, in order to make it clear that you are not calling them together in order to put them in a defensive position.

Q. *Several of your working bosses have complained that they are not getting satisfactory service from the stores department and the transportation department. They ask that you invite the storekeeper and the division manager having charge of the intrafactory transportation in your area to be present at a meeting in which you put the following question to your subexecutives: "Why doesn't our department get better service from transportation and stores?" How would you handle this situation?*

> Would you call the meeting? Would you prefer to talk with the heads of these two service departments without your subexecutives being present? Would you desire to talk with them together or singly? How would you present the problem to them?

Collaboration with Associate Executives. Industrial organizations find it desirable to maintain horizontal contacts in the form of committee structures. Frequently these committees are given considerable authority in such matters as safety, plant maintenance, and budget development. In some instances special problems such as the rearrangement of facilities, redevelopment of processing, or relocation of plant require the appointment of special groups. Not infrequently these joint efforts are presided over by a major official of the company.

EXECUTIVE CONDUCT. Your greatest hazard will be that of underestimating the importance of this form of activity. When these meetings are properly conducted, they are frequently quite informal in character and altogether pleasant. It is very easy to take the attitude of a spectator—to enjoy the interplay of ideas without taking active part. This procedure also has an appeal because your chances of making mistakes are thereby reduced. Don't fall into this error. Collaboration of this sort means hard work. Before the meeting you should equip yourself with as many facts as possible concerning the problem to be discussed. You should organize your own thinking to the point where you have some ideas on the subject. You should go to the meeting realizing that you will be expected to earn your salt by making constructive and valuable contributions to the job of joint thinking. Frequently your contribution takes the form of presenting ideas for targets, the shooting down of which will expedite the process of "finding out together." Remember that these conferences are not the place to build a reputation for always being right. If your proposals are found to be in error, learn the art of admitting your mistake quickly and easily. It is much more important to detect the proper solution when it appears in discussion, for frequently it is a composite of the ideas of several individuals.

In group thinking of this sort be sure to place the interest of the company ahead of the interest of your own department. Develop the ability to see the broad picture. Do not confuse a part with the whole. Be frank and completely straightforward in your discussion. Lay your cards on the table. Don't scheme—don't bargain—and above all don't endorse others' opinions unless you sincerely support them. You are not invited to these meetings to make someone else's contribution. Don't maneuver. Nothing is more irritating to the presiding officer than to discover that his collaborators have negotiated preagreements as to the stand which they will take when certain subjects are brought up in conference.

If the final decision and plan of action assign specific responsibilities to you, do not rest content until you have put them into effect. Delays in this matter are a frequent and serious mistake of inexperienced executives. Remember that thinking together when well done is never conducive to personal pride. After an active discussion you may lament a number of early suggestions which later required amendment and even rejection. You may recall statements which you wish you had not made. You may think how much better it would have been if you had withheld your ideas until the others had shot their bolt, so that you could have had the benefit of their point of view before expressing yours. This sort of speculation is fruitless and beside the point. The prime question which you should be able to answer in the affirmative is, "Did I *help* with the thinking?"

Q. *The company in which you hold an executive position is conservatively managed and has an enviable record of consistent profits. Located in a small community, it has recently become sensitive to the necessity of maintaining a particularly neat and attractive outward appearance. For the last few years the directors of the company have laid aside a sum of money to be expended on the further development of the grounds surrounding the plant. The precise allocation of these funds is placed in the hands of a special committee composed of executives, of which you are a member. As the plant fronts an arterial highway, it was considered wise to give first attention to the area along this road. For the last several years most of the appropriations have gone to this end. Your department is situated in the building at the rear of the main plant, overlooking a marshy area traversed by a canal. The employees in your department have been urgent in requesting that this area be improved and made more attractive. Upon making the appropriations last year it was the general consensus of the committee that a reasonable sum of money would be appropriated for this purpose at the next annual meeting. With this in mind the employees in your department have given a considerable amount of their time out of hours to grading and otherwise initiating the work with the expectancy that it would be completed by means of funds to be made available.*

However, the past winter has been an exceedingly destructive one and the committee now finds that many of the shrubs and much of the planting previously introduced in front of the building have been killed. In view of the possible publicity value of this area, it is obvious that consideration will have to be given to replacement. Many of your employees, anticipating this issue, have come to you and expressed the hope that you will strenuously represent their interest in the committee meeting in order that the improvement of the area at the rear of the plant will not be further delayed. How will you proceed in this situation?

> Should you make it a point to discuss this situation with your subordinate executives, your associates, or your superior officers prior to the committee meeting? Are there any activities which you should pursue prior to the meeting? What should be your procedure at the meeting in order to assure yourself that the committee will make as nearly a proper decision as possible? Are you in a position at this time to decide in your own mind what is the proper thing to do?

Q. *You are in general agreement with the suggestions made in this chapter, but you find yourself a member of a committee which is intensely partisan. Owing to a long series of past happenings, the executives in the plant are now ranged in two groups. There are the older and more conservative members who are the remnants of the old regime. There are the younger members brought in under new management when the ownership of the company changed hands. You feel that the thinking of the men on this committee is highly colored as the result of this situation. Is there anything that you as a member of the committee can do to alleviate this condition?*

> Is the subject one which could be discussed openly at the committee meeting? Is it one which you could properly discuss with the chairman of the committee? Is it one which you can best approach through your own example to other members of the committee? What are the possible disadvantages to you if you do not ally yourself to one or the other faction?

Collaboration with Superiors. From time to time executives may be called into counsel with their superior officers. This usually comes about when the executive is in position to present specific information or a viewpoint relating to some field with which he is especially familiar. If the problem is of a particularly important nature, he may be temporarily transferred from his other duties in order that he may proceed actively in this joint enterprise. Usually, however, he is called into conference for the purpose of presenting specialized information or of explaining certain circumstances within an area with which he is particularly familiar.

EXECUTIVE CONDUCT. Make adequate preparation. Find out precisely the sort of activity which is expected of you. Organize to perform it as directly, as clearly, as briefly as possible. If you are to make recommendations, be in a position to justify them. Think of possible questions which might be asked you, and organize your answers. It is more than likely that you will experience difference of opinion. This will not call for argument on your part but will require that you explain precisely why you have come to your personal conclusions. If you have a considerable statement to make, feel free to use an outline in order to speak more directly and clearly. State your convictions without hesitation, but be sure you believe them with your head as well as your heart. Remember that you are attending a thinking party. If an ultimate opinion is expected from you, do not hesitate to ask for enlightenment on any points in the ensuing discussion which are not clear to you. Keep in mind your precise relationship to the discussion. Limit your remarks to that particular aspect of the problem in which you are experienced. In this way you will justify your invitation to the conference. At the close of the meeting it may be well to ask the chairman if there is anything more that he would like you to do.

Later you may have a natural desire to recount the happenings to your friends and associates. Overcome it. It is obvious that no group of men can be expected to think freely together if their formative ideas are going to be broadcast. You will doubtless be dissatisfied with your efforts. You will think of a number of points which you might have made: some ideas which could have been stated more clearly. This reaction is common to everyone and should not trouble you further.

Q. *You have recently been placed in charge of a special processing division in a manufacturing concern. Prior to this time you were in charge of a similar department of another organization manufacturing a noncompetitive product. Upon undertaking your new work you find that the process in use is antiquated and obsolete. You learn, however, that the installation and procedure were developed by your present superior, who at one time was in charge of this work. He still believes it to be the proper procedure to use and claims that it has certain points of advantage in the way of quality which offset its high unit cost and slowness. Your present relations with your chief are of the best. Indeed it was largely through his influence that this new and more promising opportunity was opened to you.*

Your chief informs you that the executive committee, of which he is a member, has requested that you present your point of view concerning the methods of processing in your department. The company is planning to move the plant to a new location and to make the most up-to-date installations possible. The executive committee has called in representatives of equipment manufacturers, who have recommended a radical renovation of present operating methods. You learn that they have proposed the precise method of operation which you favor and that their point of view has been strongly opposed by your present chief. You also learn that it was at their suggestion that you were asked to present your experience to the executive committee. How should you handle this situation?

Should you discuss the whole situation and your own point of view with your chief prior to the meeting? At the conference should you offer your point of view with vigor and directness, letting the chips fall where they may, or should you allow the knowledge of your chief's adverse opinion to affect your presentation? Is it conceivable that this situation could be so handled as to win you the admiration and respect not only of the executive committee but of your chief? If so, how?

Discussion. What are your responses to the following comments?

1. *We have proved that thinking together is an unnecessary frill. During hard times we discontinued all committees and conferences and the work went along better than ever.*

Does this mean that all group thinking was discontinued? Might the work have gone along still better if meetings had been continued? Should policies with regard to collaboration vary in terms of good times and hard times? Other things being equal, if work improves when collaboration is discontinued, what has been the difficulty?

2. *I say, let somebody else do the collaborating. You get nothing for your effort but blame if you don't win for your own side.*

What part does "taking sides" play in thinking together? Should an executive give no consideration to the interests of his particular group when he collaborates with other executives? If thinking together is a form of work, on what basis should anyone's participation be criticized?

3. *Informal conferences may be good in theory but my experience has been that if a regular schedule of meetings is not arranged, their use tends to lessen.*

When a sound executive device needs a system to maintain it, what is wrong? Is there anything wrong in arranging a specified schedule of meetings? Do people require practice in thinking together in order fully to appreciate its value?

4. *When subordinate executives are properly busy they have enough to do without helping to think out someone*

else's problems. A little collaboration may be a good idea, but even this offers incentive for a man to take his mind off his own job.

What constitutes the job of a subordinate executive? Should he be thinking about his own job when he is thinking along with others? Why should he be invited to confer?

5. *My method of discussing problems with my subordinate executives is to lay down a proposition, find out who disagrees with it, and then challenge their point of view. If they are men of spirit they accept the challenge, and then we talk it out.*

Are you sure that this is good technique? When would you consider it undesirable to use this method? What are the usual objectives of collaboration? Does this procedure satisfy them?

6. *If I have a problem to discuss with my men, I don't start with a question. I prefer to outline a solution. Sometimes I recommend a wrong one just to see what the men will do.*

What will be the probable result of this method upon discussion? Are there conditions under which it may prove effective? What do you consider to be the form of introduction most stimulating to discussion?

7. *I don't favor too much thinking together among subordinate executives. This policy is one of drift. Important decisions should not appear to rest on the combined judgment of juniors.*

Is it important that decisions be generally acceptable to those who are to put them into effect? What is the nature of problems which are best fitted for collaborative thought? How would problems which you would discuss with your subordinates differ from problems which you would discuss with your associates?

8. *Committees are frequently wasteful substitutes for the work of one qualified individual. They are an excuse to increase executive work without adding to the payroll.*

May this be true? What kinds of committees do not merit this criticism? How can you tell if the use of committees is being overdone?

9. *As an executive I do not favor bringing technical specialists who report to other departments into my office for informal discussions. If I have anything to take up with them, I go out into the department and meet them on their own ground, and the more informal the conversation the better.*

Under what circumstances would you disagree with this point of view?

10. *An executive should be held responsible solely for results and should be allowed to conduct the work as he sees fit. The need of conference between administrators and executives on operating problems indicates that executives are being hampered or that they have not the requisite capacity for their responsibilities.*

Should operating standards be entirely determined by executive experience and judgment? Why? What is the purpose of conferences? To obtain the benefits of group experience? To obtain the benefits of discussion? What are the benefits of discussion?

CHAPTER 9

Executive Public Relations

Every executive has an ever-present audience. Whether his activities have to do with subordinates, associates, or superiors, there will always be the third party—the interested bystander. Particularly is this true of the executive's relationships with his employees. What he does no less than what he says is constantly subject to the observation, interpretation, and judgment of others for whom his comments, directions, or decisions are of absorbing interest. As an executive he is news to a considerably larger group of people than he may realize.

First, there are the witnesses to executive statement or action—the nearby listeners. Many executive activities take place outside the executive office and are inevitably subject to the scrutiny of others. Then there are the families of the workers who hear of the day's happenings across the dinner table, the friends and cronies who discuss such matters over a cigarette or a glass of beer. Some executive pronouncements are significant to the immediate working group or even to the employee group as a whole; and it may well be that sections of the community become close observers, especially when such matters as layoffs are under consideration. Indirectly, the executive's activities are of real interest to distributors and customers as well as to directors and stockholders. And there is usually the "grapevine," which trades upon general gossip concerning all company executives.

Why all this interest? It is the same impulse that causes investors to read the market columns, to subscribe to financial services, and sometimes to listen to tipsters. Executive action may affect these listeners either directly or indirectly. They wish to be constantly informed of managerial steps taken and, more important, of managerial attitude, intent, and motive so that they may better gauge future action and its possible effect upon them. Executive acts are official acts; executive comments are official statements; executive positions taken presumably reflect company policy.

Far from being a source of difficulty, this interest is a resource to any executive. To put it in another way, should an executive discover that his activities were of no consequence to such audiences, he would have real reason for concern, if not for alarm. Such a relationship is in no sense a restriction; rather, it should be viewed as an opportunity which, in the days ahead, will become of constantly increasing significance.

Obviously there are hazards of misuse to be avoided. Misunderstandings, rumors, exaggerations, and misinterpretations of a serious nature may curse executive footsteps if certain simple rules of action are not followed. An important and growing sector of executive time is now being given to this aspect of managerial responsibilities; and, though we are only on the threshold of new knowledge, we can say with certainty that the executive's relationship to his public is fast becoming a responsibility of major significance.

The Family Group. Executives rarely have opportunity to speak to, or to deal directly with, the employee's family. Whatever information reaches this group usually comes through the employee himself, through the comparing of information by members of the family where more than one is employed in the given establishment, or through the plant paper.

EXECUTIVE CONDUCT. In your conversations with employees on any subject, your presentation will always be improved if you are careful to put your statements in such a way that when repeated by the employee across his dinner table they will convey the meaning and motive that you intend. In other words, express your ideas in such a manner that he will wish to repeat them as nearly verbatim as possible.

This is not easy. Particularly in those instances where there may be an honest difference of opinion with respect to executive decisions, an unusually judicial statement is called for in order that the employee may clearly see both sides of the situation. Yet family accord and cooperation with the company in which the chief breadwinner earns his living is a most important resource and worth the effort of gaining.

Q. *You have on the night shift a relatively new employee who is a man of family responsibility and a homeowner in a newly developed section of the city. He is particularly anxious to get on the day shift, as he wishes to continue his participation in community activities and to maintain a more normal family life.*

Your company has a rule that new employees shall spend at least six months on night-shift work before their application for day-shift operation is considered. The employee is aware of this regulation but inquires if there is any way in which he can earn the right to make this change at an earlier date. The company rule is one to which exception cannot be made.

> How will you organize your discussion with him, having the family's reaction in mind?

Outside Friends and Cronies. A workman's friends and acquaintances outside the plant are frequently a stabilizing factor in his thinking and attitude. He will often discuss with them issues on which he feels strongly and on which he welcomes their point of view. In the case of his family, there may be an emotional element involved which is not present in his conversations with his cronies. Usually such listeners have a general knowledge of company standing and policy upon which they can base their comments. Often they have in the past been employees of the same concern.

EXECUTIVE CONDUCT. Make certain that your position is entirely in accordance with general company policy in order that the employee's advisers may not find reason to view your stand as illogical or uncalled for.

Remember that an employee's personal status in the eyes of his friends is as important to him as his prestige within his own family. The less your actions or your statements lower a man's standing in the eyes of his acquaintances, the less will the employee be tempted to color his version of the actual occurrence when talking with his friends.

Even more important is the principle that the executive can build no stronger tie of loyalty than so to deal with each employee that he will have reason to be constantly elevated in the eyes of his outside associates. Commendatory statements, particularly in writing, as well as awards of merit and other similar devices, play a most important role in executive public relations.

Q. *You are informed by your chief that the company plans a reduction in working force to take place on a gradual basis to extend over the coming year; that this policy is not to be announced until it is determined that the normal rate of employee terminations will not be sufficient to care for the contraction in working force.*

One of your employees comes to you and says his neighbor has told him that he heard a gradual layoff was in prospect, and he (the employee) would like to know the answer.

How will you respond to his inquiry?

The Immediate Working Group. An employee, to be entirely happy in his working environment, should properly become an active part of his immediate working group, with a correspondingly close acquaintanceship with other members which may extend to activities outside of the factory. Under such circumstances, the group is naturally interested in the happenings between any workman and his superior officer, inasmuch as what happens to one workman may equally readily happen to others.

With the working group the executive has direct contact, and he is in a better position to protect its members from misunderstanding or misinterpretation as third parties to his actions or statements.

EXECUTIVE CONDUCT. A cardinal rule, previously applied in our discussion of commendation versus criticism, is that all matters of good report may well be discussed with the employee in the presence of others and that adverse criticism should be made in privacy to increase its constructive effect and lessen its sting.

In the interest of good public relations it is highly desirable to deal with employees at their workplace with a minimum of secrecy and mystery. When other employees realize that there is nothing to be concealed and that departmental matters are properly everyone's business in so far as general familiarity and understanding are concerned, much of the basis for misunderstanding and suspicion will be removed. When the executive treats all employees with uniform justice and with open matter-of-factness, a quality of group confidence develops that makes for an effective working atmosphere.

Q. *You have made it a practice each day to walk about in your department in an unhurried fashion in order that employees may find it easy to speak with you concerning any matters that are on their minds.*

On one occasion, an employee leaves his machine and

talks with you briefly on an unimportant subject. You later discover that he had previously been criticizing one of his fellow workmen for his lack of cooperation in the work at hand, that after talking with you he had told his associate that he had passed his complaint on up to you, and that his associate is much concerned and now plans to talk with you.

How will you handle this situation?

The Total Employee Group. Collective bargaining introduced new formalities into what had hitherto been relatively simple relationships between the executive and his employees. His every official act and statement may now come under formal scrutiny. If the employee organization has an agreement or contract with the company, executive behavior is measured against the terms of this agreement. If an action does not fall within the scope of the contract, it may again be examined to see if it contains the basis for establishing a precedent which may be applied to the company as a whole. Finally, there are innumerable instances where the exact significance of an executive act is open to honest difference of opinion; and it is here that time-consuming discussions may occur unless initial care is taken.

EXECUTIVE CONDUCT. Where your every act or statement is subject to examination in relation either to an existing contract or to a future precedent, it is important that before taking a step you verify the correctness of your position in terms of existing company policies and agreements. Again, human memory is fallible, and it is equally important that you make a record of your action or comment in such form that it may be referred to authoritatively should the question ever be raised. Finally, it is especially important that there be a minimum of ambiguity or vagueness in your position—a requirement calling for careful thought and planning.

Q. *You are in charge of a branch plant which performs certain preparatory operations upon a component machine part later to be assembled with other components at the main plant of the company. Because of extremely severe winter weather conditions and resulting transportation delays, the assembly lines at the central plant are at the week end threatened with shutdown due to lack of components.*

The company is in the midst of negotiations with the employee group relative to the piece-rates to be used on the current components which are part of a new model just entering upon assembly. The company has a prior agreement with the employee group that overtime will not be required of any employee against his will.

Word comes to you that overtime output should be resorted to at once to meet the present emergency. After you have presented the situation to the employees, a counterrequest is received that this overtime work be viewed as special and made subject to the piece-rate scale favored by the employee group in their current negotiations.

Upon telephoning the main plant you find that negotiations are still in progress but have been halted over the week end and that executives are not available for counsel.

What steps, if any, should you take, and what effect would you expect them to have upon the employee group?

The Community. Executive public relations differ widely in the extent to which they include community relations. In a small town, where the company dominates industrial activity, almost every executive decision must be weighed in the light of its effect upon the community. In the large city, where a firm is occupying rented space and drawing its labor from a widely varied suburban area, the community factor as an element of public relations is obviously of far less concern.

There seems to be considerable evidence that the best training ground for competent industrial executives is to be found in plants having suburban or rural locations, as such managers have opportunity to form executive judgments that incorporate the complete round of public relations responsibilities, including the external, as well as the internal, group concerned.

EXECUTIVE CONDUCT. Here your public relations activities may take an interesting turn. It may well be that your greatest opportunity to relate yourself constructively to this group lies in community activities or in their support. By thus becoming an active participant in community affairs you may build an acquaintance and personal standing that will strengthen community attitude toward your policies or decisions affecting employees who live in the same locality. It is fast becoming a principle that an executive should be personally known in the community in which the majority of his employees reside, if he is to maintain and further the best type of community relations for his plant.

Q. *You have been given the opportunity to set up a small new manufacturing establishment in an industrial town where labor of the type suitable for your work is normally available. Because of the entirely novel nature of your manufacturing, which is the result of a new technical development, you are free to establish wage scales in terms of your own evaluation of the work to be done, without the limitations of custom or precedent.*

Owing to the profit margins possible in the sale of the new product, you are in a position to establish wages on any reasonable scale.

> What will be your decision in the light of a sound community relations policy?

Distributors and Customers. Here are groups who are closely interested, as third parties, in the executive's relationship with his subordinates. Is he likely to create antagonisms that will bring delays or work stoppages? Is he going to stimulate and maintain consistently dependable levels of quality so that the product of his department will bring steady satisfaction to the user? Is he to be depended upon so to handle his men that production schedules and planned deliveries will be met? In short, is he a competent manager and can his efforts and abilities as a department head be relied upon?

EXECUTIVE CONDUCT. You and your subordinates may never meet any of this portion of your public. You may never, even indirectly, learn of their attitudes or comments. Yet their support and good will are as vital to your success as is the attitude of your superiors. It is an inescapable principle of manufacturing in a free society, which enjoys freedom of choice, that production must obey the law of the market. Your real boss is made up of the many customers for the final product, who, in the last analysis, decide whether they will buy your product or that of a competitor and, therefore, whether you and your company will stay in business.

If you are truly concerned to maintain the long-term security of your departmental jobs, you will be equally concerned that your efforts completely satisfy the desires of the company's market in point of quantity, price, and service. More than this, you are wise to be informed of market conditions and attitudes in order that you may the more closely harmonize your efforts with the current needs and desires of the distributor and the consumer.

Q. *As a department head in a plant manufacturing specialty castings of malleable iron and alloy metals, you are having difficulty in maintaining specifications owing to uncontrollable fluctuations in the metallurgical characteristics of the scrap which composes a large proportion of the daily melt. When specifications are not met, rejections result, together with a loss of good will. Yet the demand for these specialized castings is so great that departmental production requirements continue to rise steadily, customers having no other source for the particular type of castings which your company produces.*

To what extent should you shoulder this responsibility for quality, and what steps, if any, should you take to deal with the current difficulty?

Directors and Stockholders. In many respects the interest of these groups is not unlike that of the distributors and customers. There is one marked difference. These groups represent ownership and are definitely concerned with the health of the business. Although one measure of good health is the presence of profits, this is only one criterion. Company standing in the eyes of prospective customers as well as employees, constant improvement in operating techniques, financial soundness—these are other objectives which directors and stockholders view as important.

EXECUTIVE CONDUCT. This audience usually learns of your accomplishments or difficulties through the medium of the higher executives. And the new measuring sticks now being applied to executive proficiency are showing marked changes. As you deal with your employees, it is well to remember that company directors are showing surprising interest in such matters as the number and disposition of departmental employee complaints, the attitude of employees toward their boss, the willingness of the executive to accept and to act upon new management objectives and methods, his standing with relation to other executives of equal rank in the company.

There is a real hazard that an executive and his accomplishments may be misunderstood or misinterpreted by upper management because he fails to give enough care and attention to his reports to superiors. Where this condition is present, the executive has no one but himself to blame. In other words, it is your opportunity and responsibility to keep your superior so well informed of all phases of your activities that errors in the transmission of information to the higher-ups simply cannot take place.

Q. *You have charge of a major department in a manufacturing plant which occupies a large, multistoried building. The elevator which takes you to your office also serves the executives' office on the top floor of the building. For some time you have been making it a practice to concentrate upon the work of the day while en route to your office, and you have been preoccupied when entering the plant.*

Your chief sends for you and remarks, "A curious thing happened at the Board meeting last week. You may not have noticed, but one of our directors, a banker in town, rode up in the elevator with you and after you had left the car, he overheard the elevator girl remark, 'There goes Old Grouch.' He wanted to know how labor conditions were in your department. I took care of the situation all right, but thought you had better know about it."

Should you explain? Apologetically? Should you have safeguarded yourself from such an occurrence? Should you be expected constantly to guard your tongue and actions in the interest of public relations? Should directors concern themselves with elevator conversations? Do they?

Gossip and the Grapevine. Monkeys chatter to one another in the treetops, and it is entirely likely that many of their remarks are in the nature of gossip. Thus it is for us an inherited trait. In any event, we cannot be realistic about executive public relations without admitting that every human organization of normal size is likely to contain those who delight in gossip even to the point of coordinating their enjoyment with that of others in the organization of the so-called grapevine. But this form of vegetation, which sprouts ears instead of blossoms, does not confine itself to information within the shop. Nothing awakens interest so much as the juicy bit which begins, "I passed the boss coming out of the Community Center last night, and he was saying. . . ." Unfortunately the vine flourishes upon human weaknesses and foibles rather than upon the positive virtues; and, as it lives in the twilight zones of shoptalk, it has little to attract the high-grade executive. Yet it is a factor to be reckoned with.

EXECUTIVE CONDUCT. As an executive you may be certain that there are people in the world who are alert for reason to say ill of you. This is because there is a small proportion of human beings who consider it their province to criticize or to defame anyone who shows greater than ordinary ability or accomplishment. These persons seem to be rather evenly spread throughout the population.

Take care. We all know of instances where promising careers have been blighted by the magnifying and disseminating of minor indiscretions or thoughtless remarks. As long as you hold an official position you will be a subject of interest, of praise, and of attack. Guard yourself from the effects of each.

Q. You have recently been put in charge of an important department in one of several plants operated by a relatively large company with centralized executive offices in New York City. You find that the major divisions of each plant report in some instances to the plant manager and in other instances to New York.

Your assistant has been with the company for a number of years and has been helpful and industrious. You discover that he is active in a so-called "underground" which relays plant gossip to New York, whence it is returned to plant employees in other divisions of your plant. You test the system by commenting on an employee whose future career with the company has been under discussion. You find that your word reaches New York and is returned to an executive in another division of your plant within forty-eight hours.

What should be your policy and procedure in dealing with this situation?

Public Relations. It now becomes clear that every executive has an audience—a public composed of many segments, some of which he never meets or deals with directly. Furthermore, there is hardly an act or an utterance of his that is not of absorbing interest to one or another of these listeners. Is it possible to find a working rule or principle that will apply equally to all situations?

Public relations is a functional activity which is a relative newcomer in industry. Is it really something new or just an old idea in a new garb? Perhaps the answer lies in the matter of relative emphasis. No executive can hope to be successful over a period of time without the element of personal character. This is usually thought of as an inner moral and ethical state of mind which guides his behavior.

We also have an outer character, the person and personality which we turn to the world. It is this outer personal standing which we call our reputation and which we shall in the years ahead consider increasingly. This is because the affairs of industry move more rapidly than before, and the slower processes of acquaintance and evaluation are not sufficiently effective to avoid misunderstandings and misinterpretations.

There *is* an underlying principle in all executive public relations and it is this: It is an executive responsibility effectively to acquaint by open action or by frank utterance all parties at interest with the truth regarding the company's sincere attitude, basic motives, and real objectives, so that early impressions will be confirmed as time passes and familiarity or acquaintance increases.

EXECUTIVE CONDUCT. Your first and most difficult job is to establish a position which you can maintain with the confidence that it is your sincere belief and that you are ready to stand for it. Ask yourself, "Just how do I really feel toward the men in my department—exactly how?" You will run through a lot of generalized answers to begin with, but you can finally force yourself to tell yourself the exact truth in simple words. The same questions may be driven squarely at other executive responsibilities such as costs, quality, output, orderliness, planning and scheduling routines, and the like.

Next, see how your convictions jibe with company policy. They will rarely agree exactly. See if you can support company policy without moral or ethical compromises with your own established principles. This seems unduly involved, but it is most essential that you establish in your own mind a position which you can consistently support so that, when members of your public compare notes, their stories will check.

Finally, view as important resources those many people who follow your official words and acts. The more widely a company policy is understood, the greater its constructive influence can become. If you can build for your organization and yourself a constructive relationship and reputation with the families of your employees, their immediate working group, the employee personnel as a whole, the market, the community, and the ownership group, you will be in a position not only to accomplish larger tasks but to minimize the danger of being misunderstood or misinterpreted.

It is as fundamentally important that the executive "let his light shine" as that he "doeth the thing that is right and speaketh the truth from his heart."

Discussion. What is your response to the following comments?

1. *It is hopeless to expect that executive acts or statements will ever be presented correctly to the employee's family by the employee himself. The workman is normally prejudiced with respect to any executive action that affects him and inevitably will color the story that he tells his family.*

What encourages an employee so to color his statements? Under what circumstances is the employee likely to repeat the statements or the decisions of the executive with greatest accuracy?

2. *The executive who permits his procedures to be affected by the reactions of an employee's friends and cronies is not reflecting the firmness that is essential to competent executive accomplishment.*

Is the executive really being affected by the reactions of these friends of the employee, or is he, rather, attempting to affect their reactions?

3. *It may be good policy to discuss matters with the employee at his workplace, where others may be within hearing distance. I consider it a discourtesy not to permit the employee the privilege of privacy which the executive's office offers. He does not usually wish to have his conversations with his boss open to the hearing and comments of his immediate associates.*

If an employee's conversations with his boss deal largely with troubles and difficulties requiring privacy, is this symptomatic of fundamental weakness in the departmental situation?

Under what conditions is the employee likely to feel more at ease when talking with his boss if the conversation takes place at the workplace? In the executive's office?

4. *It is all very well to consult top management, to make a record, and to talk straight every time you turn around, but what about executive initiative and authority? Cannot an executive call his soul his own when dealing with his departmental workmen?*

Can the executive deal personally with his employees, or as an official does he inevitably represent company policy in the eyes of the workmen? Are there instances where the executive's comments to an employee are of as great, or greater, interest to the employee association as to the workman receiving them?

5. *The closer the executive gets to the industrial community the more trouble he builds for himself. Everyone seizes upon him for a job; complaints and silly suggestions are the rule, and anything he does may involve him in community politics or bring on the charge of favoritism. The farther the executive stays away from community contacts, the freer are his hands in the conduct of his executive responsibilities.*

Can industrial establishments afford to stay clear of their communities? Can management depend upon the absence of misunderstanding, misinformation, and misinterpretation without the presence of closer relationships? What new elements have appeared which may render faulty community relations a severe handicap to the operation of the business?

6. *It may be that the executive's public relations extend to the distributors and consumers, but most companies have competent distribution executives whose job it is to take care of these relationships. The departmental executive who meets specifications and schedules and keeps his costs down does not need to concern himself about satisfying anyone but his own boss.*

Who or what is the real boss over the operating executive? Is it a person? Is it a condition or circumstance? Is it a mass reaction from those who are served? Can an executive afford to limit his efforts to the satisfaction of his superior officer?

7. *Most top managements do not feel the need for any contact or relationship between line-operating executives and the directors and stockholders. Indeed, top management may resent any such group being included under the "public relations" of the departmental chief.*

Good public relations are a process of conveying the truth about matters of mutual interest to the executive's "public." What advantages result from directors and stockholders knowing the truth? What hazards are eliminated? Is this elimination worth the effort? Need such a safeguard disregard the usual avenues of communication between the executive and his superior?

8. *Everybody knows that the executive is a human being and that his activities out of hours are strictly his own business as a private citizen. No one can live happily if he feels that anything that he may say or do at any time may be used against him.*

When an executive influences the future welfare of his employees in terms of their employment, nature of work, and earnings, can the employee think of him as anything other than the company representative, either inside or outside the shop?

9. *An executive cannot hold his job and be sincere. He has to say what the company tells him to say whether he agrees with it or not. It is all very well to let your light shine, but look out for a bucket of very cold water from upstairs.*

Suppose that company policy does not conflict with the executive's personal principles; does his statement of company policy still involve insincerity? Does agreement or lack of agreement with a company policy necessarily label an executive as sincere or insincere?

CHAPTER 10

Difficulties with Subordinates

In the process of organizing the will of a group of employees, the executive will meet with difficulties. He will find that friction points are quite as numerous in organizations of men as in assemblies of machine parts, and he must adopt the same preventive policy as the engineer. Such problems incorporate two elements of difficulty: first, the degree of complexity, and second, the restrictions in the time allowed for solution. The knowledge that an executive is meeting with trouble in dealing with one or more of his employees sometimes spreads with great rapidity throughout the working group, and an error in executive technique may bring about a stress of feeling which results in the destruction of morale.

Often these crises demand immediate action. Usually the circumstance is surrounded by an emotional complex —an atmosphere of strong feeling that is quickly contagious. If the executive is at all susceptible to the influence of the excitement, he finds his reasoning ability hampered by a lack of sufficient time for thought and by a confusing emotional pressure. It is doubly important, then, that he should prepare himself for these difficulties by studying them hypothetically, establishing a plan of procedure in advance. He is then in a position to act in the face of an emergency with promptness and upon a basis of precise and balanced reasoning.

The Basis of Approach. It must be assumed at the start that the executive is qualified for his job from the various standpoints outlined in previous chapters. In approaching his problem he must keep constantly in mind that he is dealing with persons whose actions may be largely influenced by their feelings, that there may be emotional excitement which paralyzes reasoning ability, and that, because of the sensitiveness of the group, the contagion may spread rapidly. He must first guard himself from a like emotional infection. This is a matter of self-control. He must next eliminate the emotional pressure in the employee and make deliberation possible. Last, he must develop a cooperative or positive mood on the part of the employee.

To illustrate, many executive difficulties are based upon the behavior of employees who are in negative moods, influenced by hatred, fear, suspicion, or revenge. The skillful executive

1. Refuses to respond or react in kind.
2. Eliminates the pressure of feeling upon the employee so that reason can freely function.
3. Appeals to the positive moods (such as loyalty, duty, unselfishness, service) in the employee. While this influence may reduce reasoning ability, it will tend to influence behavior in accordance with ethical and moral standards of conduct.

Successful executives are constantly following this procedure. We hear them spoken of as men who keep everyone happy. It is interesting to observe how this method suggests a possible technique for dealing with the complaint.

The Complaint. The act of making complaint is usually a behavior resulting from the pressure of feelings. The employee is urged forward by a strong sense of righteous indignation, or it may be by the stress of fear, hatred, or jealousy, or a longing for revenge.

To attempt to curb or restrict the employee in presenting his grievance can only make matters worse, as such an overruling action will tend to rouse his fighting spirit. This principle applies not only to the technique of the executive in dealing with the complaint but also to the rules of the organization. These should offer to the employee opportunity for the presentation of reasonable grievances in such a way that the action is not a hazard to his further employment. Such an arrangement provides the complaint drainage.

The procedure in dealing with a complaint should then have as a first step:

1. *The knowledge on the part of the employees that the executive will be receptive to the expression of reasonable grievances.*

This attitude, of course, can easily be overdone and result in a flood of petty criticisms. One large office organization limits such expressions by requiring that the grievance be stated in writing and sworn to before a notary public. This procedure probably errs too far in the direction of limiting complaints to be serviceable in the average case. The executive's attitude, however, if it is consistent, will soon define his interpretation of the term "reasonable complaint," and the development of a supercritical employee attitude can be overcome.

The next requirement would seem to be:

2. *The elimination of interruptions or distractions during the presentation of the grievance.*

One of the arguments for the executive's private office is that it provides a place in which his employees can speak to him without interruption and without the danger of being overheard. The strong feeling which usually surrounds a sense of grievance calls for expression, and ordinarily it is best to provide avenues for such expression if we are to satisfy the third requisite in this technique, namely:

3. *The restoration of the employee's normal state of mind as the result of the elimination of emotional pressures.*

To accomplish this result, the executive must fit his method to the case at hand. The majority of persons relieve their feelings through expression, but there are some who grow more excited as they advance in the telling. In the latter case the executive must take the helm of the conversation and guide it into smoother waters. One executive has stated that he never feels that the time is ripe to discuss a grievance with an employee until he has won a smile from him, for he claims that a smile is possible only after a person has attained a reasonably normal state of mind and feeling. Abraham Lincoln was particularly adept in the use of this technique. When persons in argument came clamorously to him for decision, he would often remark that the case in point reminded him of a story, and through its telling he would bring about a calmer and happier frame of mind in his listeners, so that they were ready to listen to his decision.

The value of this state of mind lies in the restored ability of the employee to reason clearly and logically. When this condition has been attained, we come to the fourth requisite:

4. *The evident desire of the executive to get at the facts and motives involved.*

The executive who refuses to make arbitrary decisions, and who requires a thorough knowledge of circumstances and motives, inspires confidence in the employee. The fact that he is viewing the matter calmly further strengthens the employee's belief that the executive is repressing any personal bias or prejudice in a sincere effort to act upon facts.

In the majority of grievances more data are necessary for decision than are offered by the complainant, and executives may find it hard to convince the employee that both sides of the question are entitled to a hearing, particularly when the complaint is against another employee. One executive effectively meets this difficulty by saying to the complainant, "Now, suppose that the other fellow had come to me first and told me his story. You wouldn't have wanted me to decide on his version alone, would you?" The complainant usually sees the point and is willing to have the matter throughly investigated.

Then follows:

5. *The assignment of a definite decision.*

This should be as prompt as possible. Delay means uncertainty, and its continuance is very harmful to the morale of any organization. If time is required to get the facts, a definite future time for decision should be stated.

Finally:

6. *The executive's willingness that the complainant appeal the decision if he desires to do so.*

The employee should know that if he sincerely believes that injustice is being done, he can take the case to the next higher executive with the knowledge that his employer will hold no grudge for his so doing. Machinery for such cases of appeal is fairly common, and its presence in the organization is salutary, for the position of the executive then becomes that of a cooperator in the search for justice rather than that of an arbitrary dictator of conduct.

The reader may take issue with this analysis. He may challenge the sequence or the whole procedure. In such cases he should prepare his own procedure and test it in practice. The important point to remember is that such a technique can be reasoned about, that the conclusions can be weighed and tested, and that the executive can advance in management by virtue of such considerations.

Q. *Do you agree that the above procedure offers an effective method of dealing with complaints? If not, just how would you alter or amplify it?*

Q. *Suppose that a machine operator comes to you and complains that the operator on the night shift does not leave the machine in proper order. He further avers that he spoke to the night operator about it, but to no avail. The night shift is in charge of an executive holding the same position and authority as you. How would you handle this case?*

> What is the first thing you would do? Obtain the necessary facts? Would you take the matter up with your coexecutive or with your superior officer? If the former, what would you say to him? Would you offer reciprocative inspections? Would you tell the employee to work it out himself with the night operator?

Methods of approach to other executive difficulties which are commonly met with will be suggested in the following pages. It should be emphasized that the solutions offered are but suggestions. The wide differences which are found in personality preclude the formation of an inelastic procedure which will fit any and all cases. The value of the suggestions and the problems offered will be found in their stimulating effect upon proper habits of executive thought, which, when coupled with a fund of experience, will go far to improve the individual technique.

Open Opposition. Open opposition rarely is offered to the established executive. It may occur in the case of a new executive who is unpopular owing to the circumstances of his appointment, in which case the opposition is intended to reflect the objection of the employees to the acts of the management.

EXECUTIVE CONDUCT. The best cure is prevention. Learn to sense impending opposition and to avoid issues of this nature until you are in the proper strategic position. In such cases time almost always works to your advantage. If you face a situation which is in danger of becoming unruly, your vested authority will allow you gradually to alter conditions to strengthen your position. The opposition will tend to disappear as soon as its disadvantages become obvious to the employees.

Should an instance of open opposition develop, however, face it calmly and intelligently. The eyes of the entire organization will be upon you, and your behavior will inevitably affect employee opinion. In the first place, do not view such opposition as directed at you personally but rather as an act of mutiny toward organization authority which you represent. If the employee plainly tries to make his disobedience generally known in order to show his disregard for authority, you may find it necessary to dismiss him from the department at once. Such dismissal should be made without the slightest evidence of anger or excitement. Be mild but firm. If the disobedience occurs without attempt at publicity and is evidently in a spirit of sincere revolt, deal with the employee as outlined in the preceding section. If you are unable to convince him of his error in resisting authority, the employee must be dismissed; but do it impersonally and courteously, so that he may feel that your action is not the product of anger or rancor.

Q. *You have recently been appointed to an executive position in a new organization. You find that one of the employees who has been assigned to you is an elderly man who sharpens the saws and other similar tools in the department. He was an old personal employee of the late president of the concern and spent the majority of his time on the president's estate. When the plant was smaller, he would come down at odd times and sharpen tools, but he always considered himself as reporting directly to the president. With the president's death, he has been placed on your payroll. You have been told that he has made the following remark: "I don't intend to take any instructions from anyone around here. I know what my work is and nobody need give me any orders; and if they start to, I'll tell them where to get off." He is an excellent worker and very loyal to the company. How would you handle this situation?*

Is his attitude essentially disloyal? Will it affect the prestige of your position if you do not face the issue and require the employee to follow your orders? Will you make it a point to give him an order at once? Will you avoid dealing with him? Will you approach him on the basis of the similarity of your loyalties to the company?

Covert Opposition

EXECUTIVE CONDUCT. Do not respond in kind. Do not act until you are certain of the presence of opposition. Sometimes rumors are purposely brought to you to influence your attitude. When you have the facts, act in the open with your opponents. If you find the opposition to be real and powerful, do not force an issue until you have built up a position of strategic advantage. Never use underhand methods in retaliation for covert opposition; this would lower your status to the level of your opponent and would be a degradation of the position which you hold. When you are assured of the presence of opposition, its source, and its causes, face the issue fairly and in the open. Deal directly with the persons involved. Make it clear that the essence of organization is cooperation, that without it an organization is but a gathering of people, and that all must pull together if success is to result.

Q. *Does the statement that an executive should build up a position of strategic advantage before forcing an issue with his opponents imply that the executive must use underhand methods as a preliminary step to fighting in the open?*

> When covert opposition is suspected, what information do you require in order to act justly? The source of opposition? Its nature? Its direction (whether at you or your superior officers or the company as a whole)? Its causes? Is not discharge a legitimate remedy?

Q. *Assume that on entering an executive position you find that one of your employees feels that he should have been advanced to the vacancy to which you have been appointed. He has a number of sympathizers among the employees who are not giving you full cooperation. What method would you use to obtain effective support and at the same time maintain the department morale?*

Would you discuss the matter frankly with the sympathetic employees? What would you say? Would you discuss it with the employee himself? What would you say? Why would he be likely to be distrustful of your attitude toward him? Might he fear that you would find an excuse to discharge him? Would you prefer to show your friendship through your acts? To so establish your superiority? Is this not an instance in which the executive method would to an unusual extent be determined by the personalities involved?

Sullenness

EXECUTIVE CONDUCT. First, find the reason for sullenness. Second, do not react in kind. It is not reasonable to become angry at machinery when it refuses to run. Likewise, it is unreasonable to become irritated by an employee whose productiveness is decreased by his state of mind. Therefore, find the underlying cause. If it is personal animosity, the obstacle is not serious. Once the employee understands that you are aware that all people are not drawn instinctively toward one another, that he may quite humanly take a personal dislike to you, and that you will not allow this fact to influence your attitude toward him as an employee, he is likely to do his work and not let his antipathy affect it.

If sullenness is caused by conditions over which you have no control, it can often be eliminated if the employee knows that you are aware of his reasons and thoroughly understand his point of view. There are some people with whom sullenness appears to be a deep-seated trait. Their presence in an organization is not particularly harmful, as the other members discount their habitual tendency. It is sullenness in the employee who ordinarily is not of this disposition that requires executive attention and remedy.

Q. *How would you go about discovering whether an employee was chronically or temporarily sullen?*

> Would you ask other employees? Would you observe the attitude of other employees toward this person? How would you go about discovering whether the cause of temporary sullenness was to be found within or without your organization?

Q. *You have been appointed recently to an executive position. You are informed that a certain employee, who is several years older than you, is a chronic grouch, and that the other employees are awaiting your first encounter with him with considerable interest. How do you plan to approach him and gain his cooperation?*

> Would you infer that the employee was inclined to glory in the publicity which his attitude produced? Would you endeavor to approach him on some ground in which he is known to have a friendly interest? Would you determine to disregard his attitude—to refuse to acknowledge its presence? Would you call him into your office and so contrive to talk to him where other employees are not within hearing?

Stubbornness

EXECUTIVE CONDUCT. You should try to understand the basic cause of stubbornness. If the characteristic is innate in the employee's personality, you may find that he will respond readily to suggestion or other approach in which his stubbornness is not aroused. Often such persons can be made cooperative by appealing to their pride, when a direct request of an unusual nature would meet with little enthusiasm. If the stubbornness is deliberate, it is evidently the beginning of a spirit of mutiny. Proceed directly to acquaint the employee with the impossibility of organization work under such circumstances. Often this message can be effectively presented if the employee perceives that it is not your personal pride, but rather the necessity of discipline, which makes you demand obedience.

Q. *As sales manager of a concern employing a number of salesmen, you find it necessary to ask them to make a daily report of territories visited and calls made. You are certain that this innovation will meet with strong opposition, particularly among the older salesmen who have covered their territory for many years. These men, while in the minority, are of great value to the business, but the request cannot be fairly made of only the newer salesmen. How will you manage to avoid the stubborn opposition which will undoubtedly be evidenced if such a request is made in the form of a command?*

> Will you deal with the older salesmen individually or as a group? Will you follow a policy of exerting increasing pressure upon them to carry out your suggestions? Will you seek to prove to them that this plan will work to mutual advantage—that daily reports, for example, will show the central office ways in which it can be of greater assistance?

Discourtesy

EXECUTIVE CONDUCT. If the discourtesy of the employee is directed toward you, first take care to see whether it is not due to a previous discourtesy on your part. Discourtesy to a superior officer is an uncommon happening, and when it occurs it is often the result of the employee's retaliatory attitude—"he handled me rough, so I'll handle him the same way." A man with the natural qualifications of an executive rarely faces discourtesy from employees except from this cause. Should discourtesy occur otherwise, it is best to overlook the first instance. If repeated, a private conversation with the employee indicating that his offense is disregarded entirely from a personal basis but that the executive office cannot properly function in such an atmosphere should effect a remedy.

The discourtesy of employees to customers or to other employees requires different treatment. This defect often appears in employees of relatively low intelligence who are somewhat egotistical and delight in lording it over their associates. This can often be overcome through the setting of the proper example. Employees are quick to imitate you in such characteristics. Discourtesy of this sort may often result from overtaxing the nervous resources of an employee to the point of chronic irritability. The only cure in such a case lies in a lightening of the work or replacement by another employee of greater capacity.

Q. *Assume that you have charge of a group of sales girls in a department store. You receive complaints to the effect that one of the girls is discourteous to customers. Whenever she is under your surveillance her attitude is excellent, and you do not wish to spy upon her work, nor do you wish to bring the matter to the attention of the other girls in the group. How would you approach this problem, with the aim of correcting the fault without going to the length of discharging the employee?*

Should you place especially courteous employees adjacent to her, that she may tend to imitate them? Would you talk to her, explaining that, though a complaint may not be just, it at least indicates a misunderstanding of attitude by the customer—who may require a more convincing form of courtesy? Compare the employment of test shoppers in merchandising with inspectors in manufacturing.

Disloyalty

EXECUTIVE CONDUCT. Take care in defining disloyalty. Divergent opinions on the part of employees regarding policies or methods are not an evidence of disloyalty. While the open discussion of these opinions is a disloyal act, it is not always understood as such by the employees. Intentional disloyalty is clearly shown only by a definitely subversive act. If employee antagonism is the result of misunderstanding, it should not be cause for discharge. If disloyalty springs from an active enmity, safeguard your position against such attacks by acting decisively in the removal of the dangerous element.

Q. *You learn that one of your employees is continually criticizing existing policies and methods. The attitude of the employee to you is always cooperative, and his work is moderately well done. The employee seems, however, to take delight in talking with other employees out of hours and telling them at great length how he would run the business. What should you do, if anything, to eliminate this form of criticism?*

> How might the presence of such criticism be explained? By egotistic tendency showing itself in conversation with other employees? If so, does such criticism do material harm? Why? By lack of proper channels for complaint drainage? If so, who is at fault? Would you be inclined to think it probable or improbable that this employee had executive possibilities? Why?

Prejudice

EXECUTIVE CONDUCT. Do not interpret prejudice as a form of antagonism. It is an unfortunate tendency in mentalities of limited ability and background. In younger persons prejudice is often coupled with low intelligence. In older people its presence may foretell the cessation of constructive thinking. While prejudice is sometimes the offspring of opinionative stubbornness, it usually reflects a lack of intellectual power. Therefore, in dealing with prejudice you must patiently reiterate your ideas until they are absorbed, or good reason for their rejection is given. Often prejudice can be overcome only through actual demonstration of an idea. Do not take offense if forced to this extreme, but view such a difficulty as a challenge to your skill as an educator.

Q. *An executive proposes a new plan of operation to one of his employees. The employee, who is a conscientious worker and a man of many years' service, objects strenuously to the change, prophesying many difficulties if it is put into effect. The concrete objections which he raises, while numerous, are of little importance. He is evidently sincere in his attitude and is much disturbed over the prospect of the change. How should the executive proceed so that the new method may be given a fair trial and the morale of the employee maintained as well?*

> Should he aim to win agreement through continued discussion? Through fear of penalty? Through show of irritation? Through visual proof of effectiveness of the new plan? Through personal acceptance of all blame in case of failure? Through personal appeal to the loyalty of the employee in conducting the test operation?

Conceit. One of the lesser vices is conceit. It often overbalances its unpleasantness by providing a self-incentive to the individual to make good his estimate of himself. If it becomes intolerable, it is sometimes difficult to save the employee for the company. Conceit is distinguished from boastfulness in that conceit is a sincere though magnified opinion of one's own abilities whereas boastfulness is often deliberate exaggeration. In either case, the executive's procedure is the same.

EXECUTIVE CONDUCT. Never challenge an employee's opinion of himself until you have incontrovertible facts to support your attitude. Give him a fair chance to prove his claims, and see that he can have no excuse for failure. The boaster is usually very clever in finding plausible excuses for his inability to produce results. Sometimes unusual physical resources are found coupled with a low intelligence, and the employee so endowed delights in telling others how easy the job is for him and how early in the day he can complete his work. In such a case do not hesitate to agree that the employee has unusual capabilities, but see that he is given enough additional work so that his daily effort equals that of other employees less favored by nature. For additional work, additional wages should, of course, be given, but you should tell the employee that you expect more work from him than from the others.

A common instance of conceit very annoying to executives is found in the employee who believes that "the company cannot get along without me." Here again there is no value in opinionative controversy. The only cure is to be found in the test. An effective antidote for this attitude is an unexpected vacation with pay. If, upon return, the employee finds his job running better than before, he is usually cured. If this method is found too expensive, it may be approximated by finding an excuse to transfer the employee to other work for a temporary period.

Q. *One of your employees, a young man of limited experience and undeveloped personality, comes to you and says, "I thought you would be interested to know that I am taking a night-school course in business methods, and whenever you have any hard problems to work out, I'll be glad to help you." Outline a method whereby you will give him a sense of the importance of practical experience and maturity of thought and action and still not discourage his creditable efforts to improve himself.*

Do business problems have to do with the past, the present, or the future? If a present difficulty is to be overcome, does not the problem include means for its future avoidance? When problems deal with the future, what characteristic of judgment is called for? If imagination must be constructed out of bits of experience, how only can business judgment be acquired? Are there also intangible and unmeasurable factors in business problems which require the judgment of experience in their evaluation?

Discussion. What is your response to the following comments?

1. *A man of real executive talent never faces open opposition from individual employees, for they are intuitively aware of their inability to succeed.*

Is opposition to an executive always directed at him, or may it be directed, through him, at the company? Do you favor a quality of executive technique which founds its prestige upon superior power? Does a man who uses such a technique have real executive talent?

2. *The best way to overcome covert opposition is to beat your enemies at their own game and prove your right to leadership.*

Should an executive play the employee's game or the company's game? What are the rules of the game that win in the long run? Should an executive have to prove his right to leadership or should it be self-evident? Do employees judge the right to leadership from executive attitude or executive acts? Is not the attitude productive of the act? Is the attitude here recommended one of leadership?

3. *A man is sullen only when he dares to be. Sullenness doesn't appear when competent executives are about.*

What is the cause of sullenness? Is sullenness of no concern to the executive provided that it is masked by civility under pressure of fear? When emotional discomfort is evidenced, is there not more opportunity for its removal than when it is concealed? Does emotional discomfort tend to reduce output? If output is not decreased, does it not tend to increase the human cost of output?

4. *Never argue with a stubborn man. Action is the only language to which he will listen.*

Is there not a preventive method that is more effective? If an employee is known to be temperamentally stubborn, how would you attempt to reduce the tendency before giving opportunity for it to appear? What may be the basis for stubbornness? A sense of inferiority? A lack of understanding? A personal animosity?

5. *No man is discourteous by accident. Therefore nothing is to be gained by overlooking the first offense.*

When an executive overlooks an employee discourtesy, what may be the employee's inference? Should the executive give the impression of overlooking the act or should he make it evident that he views the act as unworthy of consideration? Need this attitude necessarily be an antagonistic one? May a discourtesy be "overlooked" in such a way that it will not tend to be repeated?

6. *A man whose loyalty to me is not sufficient to prevent him from outwardly criticizing my conduct is not a suitable member of my organization.*

Is it the employee's responsibility to be loyal, or the executive's responsibility to develop employee loyalty? Is outward criticism of method always interpreted as disloyalty by employees? Does a critical attitude toward executive method always imply a similar attitude toward the work or toward the company?

7. *An executive loses standing who wastes time with a prejudiced man. Employees will laugh at any boss who tries to convince a fool.*

Are fools always difficult to convince? Are there other avenues to conviction than that of argument? Does an executive lose prestige by showing patience with an employee weakness?

8. *Conceit may be effectively removed by continued criticism of minor errors in the presence of other employees.*

Is a show of superiority sometimes attempted to overcome a sense of inferiority? Would the proposed technique be desirable in such a case? Should any curative method be essentially destructive?

CHAPTER 11

Difficulties with Subordinates (continued)

Dishonesty. If we agree that the ability to distinguish right from wrong is proportional to the intelligence of the individual, it is clear that the dishonest employee may be placed in one of two classes: either he is *immoral,* that is to say, his act is willful and actuated by a subverted character, or he is *unmoral,* in that he does not realize the degree or consequences of his transgression. Those of the latter type may also be lacking in moral stamina and thus easily overpowered by temptation.

EXECUTIVE CONDUCT. With the willfully dishonest, action must be prompt, decisive, and impersonal with every regard to one's duty in the protection of the organization and society.

The case of the moral weakling or the employee of low intelligence must be dealt with differently. For example, if you question an employee of the latter type regarding an alleged misdemeanor, you may easily frighten him into lying. Such an act of dishonesty cannot rightfully be charged entirely against the employee. Likewise, if you, through lax system or carelessness, leave temptation before the moral weakling, you must shoulder a share of the blame if the employee yields to dishonesty. Even as the industry which presents physical hazards to its employees is held liable in case of accident, so the organization which presents moral hazards should be held partially accountable. The treatment of such cases must be constructive and remedial. The employee should be saved for society if possible, and, in many instances, the single experience of dishonesty provides the strongest type of incentive against repetition.

Q. *As superintendent of a factory you have several foremen reporting to you. Each foreman has been required to make up and submit his weekly payroll as part of his regular duties. The paymaster reports to you that he has evidence that one of your oldest and most trusted foremen has been taking money from the payroll by allowing employees to take vacations and continuing their wages, taking the funds himself, and forging the pay receipts. The foreman is a man well respected in the community, heretofore always loyal to the concern, and his work has been thoroughly satisfactory. How would you handle this case?*

> What sort of payroll system would allow this kind of thing to take place? Would the uses to which the money was put influence your decision? Suppose that the money could be returned at once; would you favor allowing the foreman to retain his position with an alteration in payroll methods? Would you favor asking for his resignation? Would you relieve him of executive responsibilities?

Q. *You have placed an employee in charge of the collection, assortment, and sale of waste metal and scrap produced in your department. Each week the employee brings you the cash from his sales to scrap dealers. The accountant* advises you that this procedure is loose, that the scrap taken from the department should be weighed and reported by an inspector, that running inventories should be maintained of the assorted scrap, and that the weight and type of the scrap sold should also be reported, so that it will be possible to account for the material. The employee objects, says he is no bookkeeper, considers this attitude an attack upon his honesty, and states that he will not be a party to such a system. His work up to date has been very satisfactory and you have no reason to believe that he is dishonest. What is the right thing to do, and how would you go about it?

> Is the suggested procedure an attack upon his honesty or a means of protecting it against false accusations? Does not the principle of accountability to stockholders require the maintaining of proper records concerning the use of their money? Have you the right to allow their money to be handled in this way?

Q. You have charge of a hundred laborers who do not seem to have a highly developed ethical sense. One of them reports to you that, on the day before, his watch was stolen from his clothes in the locker room. The watch belonged to his father and has a considerable sentimental value. He asks you to call all the laborers together and tell them that his watch was lost in the coat room, that on the following day you are going to ask each of them to go alone into the room and hunt for it, and that if it is not found you will call in the police. The employee says that the others will know what you mean, and he believes the watch will be returned. Obviously the thief cannot be detected by this method. Consider the ethics of this plan in the light of your responsibility to the employee, to the organization, *and to society, as well as the probability of success in regaining the watch by this method in comparison with others.*

> Should you do anything? Should not the employee suffer for his own carelessness? Is it necessary to catch the thief—in such a group of employees, is it not likely that there may be several such characters in the group at all times? Would you favor the use of the proposed plan with the threat of calling in detectives if the watch is not forthcoming? Would such a plan render the detectives' efforts ineffectual, if it should be necessary to employ them?

Immorality. A delicate problem confronts the executive when a subordinate is accused of immoral conduct with women employees, or when the morale of a group of women employees is affected by the employment of a girl whose moral standards are known to be low.

EXECUTIVE CONDUCT. Approach matters of this sort with the greatest care, for a mistake may irreparably injure a reputation. Remember that employees who seek revenge upon other employees or who wish to oust unpopular executives sometimes spread rumors of this sort in order to bring about the desired disgrace. In the case of the subordinate assistant who has been accused, you can only lay the situation frankly before him, if you feel that there are sufficient grounds. If he admits guilt, dismissal is the only alternative. This should be done quietly and any further discussion of the matter frowned upon.

In the second case, it is obvious that the original error lay in the employment of a girl of this type. Nevertheless, remember that the maintenance of morale is of dominant importance to the success of your department. Give the girl every reasonable opportunity to obtain a position elsewhere without a loss of wage, and consider such expense chargeable to errors in employment.

Q. *You have received an anonymous letter implicating one of your assistants and suggesting that you investigate his whereabouts on a certain evening. This assistant is a young man of considerable promise. His work has been excellent and he has appeared to be a person of moral stamina. He has always been frank and straightforward in his dealings with you. What steps, if any, should you take in this matter?*

> Would you turn the letter over to your assistant? Would you attempt to trace the sender? Would you investigate your assistant's moral record? Would you disregard the matter entirely? Suppose that you later received another similar letter; would you continue to disregard the matter?

Uncertainty, Worry, and Fear. The consideration of fear as an executive weapon is discussed in Chapter 7. Fear and worry are often occasioned by the presence of uncertainty; and it is a rule of executive conduct that uncertainties of all sorts should be reduced to a minimum. An employee who has requested a transfer, an increase in wages, or a cash advance against his accrued earnings should be given a definite answer as quickly as possible.

Rumors are often very harmful to morale because of the uncertainty and consequent worry which they may bring. The best way to strip a rumor of its strength is to acquaint the employees with the facts before the rumor has opportunity to spread. In a period of poor business, for example, it is far better for a concern to formulate a policy in regard to retrenchment in wages or in employment and to publish it than to allow things to drift along, leaving the employees in doubt.

There are also cases of intimidation among employees; these represent an especially difficult problem since their presence is hard to discover.

EXECUTIVE CONDUCT. It is usually impossible to reassure the employee who has been intimidated. Often the case is one in which the employee has been threatened with ill treatment if he allows his production to exceed a stated amount. Do not urge the employee to place himself in personal danger, but proceed against the alleged intimidators as outlined in section on Covert Opposition in the preceding chapter.

There are instances in which the employee has an unfounded fear of the hazards of the machinery or of the process. Fear of this sort is founded upon mystery. Do not assail the employee for his attitude, but see that he thoroughly understands the machinery or process. The safeguards which have been erected should be examined. Fear is an emotion and should be conquered through the use of the mind, and you should approach this problem as outlined at the beginning of this chapter.

Q. *An accident has occurred in your department. The employee has been removed from the scene of the accident but the extent of the injury has not been determined. You later learn that the accident was a very serious one. Is it advisable to relieve the uncertainty among the employees by giving them the doctor's report immediately or would it be advisable to wait until the following morning when the employees are in a less excited condition?*

> Would you post a notice, or would you inform only those employees who were adjacent to the workplace? Would the cause of the accident affect your decision? Are employees interested in the nature or seriousness of the accident or in the resulting condition of the employee? Could not the latter be better determined on the following day? Should the employees be immediately informed of the exact nature of the accident?

Grief

EXECUTIVE CONDUCT. Grief is an emotion that flourishes on solitude. Someone has said, "Grief is halved when told to another." Be receptive to those who are afflicted, and be sincere in your sympathy. The fact that the boss seems to care is of great comfort. Find work for the employee in close proximity to others. The most effective technique consists in turning the mind and will toward something constructive. Work is a great antidote for sorrow.

Q. *Word has come to you by telephone that the daughter of one of the women working in your organization has been injured and is at her home two miles away. The mother is of a very excitable nature. How would you handle this situation so as to give the mother the greatest cooperation and minimize any possible disturbance in the department?*

> When would you inform her? After means for her quick transportation home had been obtained? Where should

she be informed? At the workplace? In the executives' office? Outside the department? Who should inform her? A matron who would ride home with her?

Irresponsibility

EXECUTIVE CONDUCT. It should be remembered that a sense of responsibility is rarely an inborn virtue. It is something to be cultivated. Executive conduct should therefore vary with the amount of opportunity that the employee has had to develop the right feeling. Irresponsibility in a young man, for example, calls for educational measures, while irresponsibility in an older employee calls for the pressure of discipline. Often the error lies in large part with the executive for failing to define the responsibilities of the employee. This should be the first point for investigation. In training an employee to a sense of responsibility, it should be remembered that the problem is one of developing a true appreciation of the importance of the task. Once this appreciation is gained by the employee, his further progress depends upon character. If he is well-meaning, he will shoulder his load. If his viewpoint of life is superficial, he will tend to repeat his old errors.

Q. *Is it logical that a young unmarried man will tend to treat more lightly the responsibilities of his job than a man of similar age who has a family? If so, would the increased necessity of keeping his job be a reason? Would this be the only reason?*

Does family life tend to develop a sense of responsibility?

Q. You have a young man in your office doing clerical work. He has been instructed to lock the door upon leaving at night. You find that he has neglected to do this on several occasions. You are considering two plans: the first, to tell him that the next time you return to your office in the morning and find the door unlocked he will be automatically dismissed; the second, to advise him to put the office key in his hat after entering the office so that he will be automatically reminded to use it when leaving. Which of these plans is the better in principle? Can you think of an improvement over both?

Can habits be developed overnight, even under pressure of fear of discharge? Is the act of locking the door entirely to be considered one of habit? Does placing the key in the hat tend to strengthen a sense of responsibility, or merely provide a safeguard against failure? Suppose that you told the clerk that the night watchman had been instructed to test the door and keep a record; would this be a better method in point of principle? Why?

Unreliability

EXECUTIVE CONDUCT. Unreliability arises from many causes. When it is due to occasional dissipation on the part of the employee, warn him that, in justice to the work, this cannot continue. Ultimatums are not considered wise by the best executives, for improvement may be gradual, showing itself through greater intervals between instances of failure. Your task is to make a deep impression upon the mind of the employee. The fear of losing a job often offers much less of an incentive for right living to such an employee than does the risk of losing the friendship of a superior officer whom he respects and admires.

If poor health is the cause of unreliability, cooperate with the employee in facing the facts. If his condition cannot be remedied, a transfer to work of lesser importance should be considered, rather than termination of employment. If the condition can be remedied, exercise your personal influence upon the employee to adopt constructive measures, for he may lack the will power to carry out by himself the requirements of a cure.

Family difficulties often are the cause of worries which materially reduce employee effectiveness. Particularly is this true of work requiring concentration or unusual attentiveness. Acquaint the employee with his growing ineffectiveness before the situation becomes serious, giving him to understand that your attitude is not critical or meddlesome but that the demands of the organization upon executives and employees alike leave no room for a lowering of productiveness.

Q. *One of your employees has been appointed captain of the factory baseball team. The amount of time and thought he is giving to this responsibility is seriously affecting his value during working hours. In determining the proper allocation of his time, what factors should you consider?*

> Will this condition be permanent or temporary? Is the manager of the team doing his share of the work? Will it assist your organization to have a successful baseball team? Why? Should such success demand sacrifice in operating effectiveness of employees? Should the captain be asked to carry on all activities out of hours?

Dullness

EXECUTIVE CONDUCT. Never criticize an employee for being habitually dull or stupid. These characteristics are evidence of a low level of intelligence. Decide whether the employee's intelligence level is adequate for the work demanded by his particular job. If so, be patient with him and do not force new ideas upon him faster than he can absorb them. There is no value in attempting to frighten him into more rapid thinking or understanding, for the presence of fear simply adds more confusion to his mind. Once you are assured that you have the employee's complete attention, be satisfied with whatever rate of absorption he manifests. Such individuals find it hard to think, and do as little of it as possible. Encourage rather than threaten.

Q. *You are having difficulty in giving instructions to one of your employees. When you ask the employee if he understands you, he says, "Yes," but later he may do something entirely different. He appears to be well-meaning but is slow and probably stupid. How should you make sure that you are thoroughly understood?*

> Ask him to repeat instructions? Give instructions in writing as well as orally? Supervise initial operations? Instruct through performance as well as description? In testing an employee's understanding, is it effective to say, "Do you understand?" If not, what would you say?

Lack of Perseverance

EXECUTIVE CONDUCT. Loss of interest is a common failing among employees, particularly in work where the evidence of accomplishment or its reward is some distance in the future. It is often one of the prime tasks of the executive to supply the needed perseverance and to call upon different forms of incentive to keep the employees working satisfactorily. There are many instances where an executive's own perseverance and his never-failing ability to inspire it in others have carried a project through great difficulties to success. You can lighten the employees' burden considerably if you develop the habit of accomplishment in your men. If you insist upon their accomplishing the little things which they set out to do, you will find it of great help when more lengthy tasks are undertaken. One successful executive constantly emphasizes the importance of doing a "finished job." This is an example of the proper technique.

Q. *You have charge of a group of bond salesmen, and experience has taught you that the sales of a given week are in large measure the result of previous cultivation of the client extending over a period of four months or more. How will you set about keeping the new salesman encouraged to carry on his work effectively until the first four months are past, and to continue thereafter to spend a portion of his time developing future clients?*

> Should you interpret initial results in terms of number of calls made, percentage of total time spent in actual interviews, etc., rather than in terms of sales?

Lack of Initiative. The executive desires initiative of thought in his employees for the same reason that the administrator or chief executive desires initiative of thought in his subordinates. It is probable that the presence of initiative is largely an inborn trait evolving from a surplus of energy which the individual finds at hand after he has accomplished his normal tasks. Nevertheless, it is not uncommon for executives to stifle whatever initiative of thought is available through not clearly understanding its significance in organization.

EXECUTIVE CONDUCT. You should not desire initiative of action on the part of your employees. Action must be coordinate and must be initiated by the administrators and executives. Constructive thinking, on the other hand, should be welcomed from every employee. When these sources are properly tapped, a large additional thinking power is often made available to the organization and great benefit results. The executive who publishes the fact that he will sincerely welcome and value such expression of initiative from the employees is adopting the proper procedure. The use of suggestion systems and shop committee organizations is a means to this end.

Q. *Is the prestige of an executive lowered in the eyes of his superior officer if he is continually receiving valuable suggestions from his employees? Should he not be expected, as a good executive, to do all the constructive thinking necessary for the improvement of his department?*

If management is properly defined as the conscious direction of forces, is management confined solely to executives? To what extent do employees manage? Do greatest advances through industrial thought come as the result of individual or group thinking? Is the point of origin of an idea of as much significance as the care with which it is surveyed and the breadth of experience and judgment by which it is measured?

Q. *You have told your employees that they should show initiative in studying the problems of their job, and you find that you are constantly importuned by one employee, who brings you a stream of suggestions. They are largely visionary and impractical and are not well thought out. He gives so much time to the development of new ideas that his regular work is suffering. How can you set him right without giving the impression that you have been insincere in encouraging initiative?*

What is the distinction between good and bad ideas? How would you test the practicality of an idea? What do you mean by "thinking out" an idea? Suppose that his ideas were very good, but regular work suffered, what would you do? What other requisites besides imagination are necessary for the production of valuable suggestions?

Religious Difficulties. The executive will find that troubles which have their origin outside the workplace will often affect the spirit of the organization. In some cases the feeling of animosity between individuals or groups of employees is a serious impediment to cooperative effort. It is not uncommon to find employees of differing religious faiths showing such active antipathy toward each other that the coordination of the organization is injured.

EXECUTIVE CONDUCT. There is no hope of eliminating this trouble by a discussion of religious creeds. Make it evident that such differences in belief should not be used as a basis of shop dissension. Concentrate the employees' attention and interest upon their work and draw their minds away from religious differences. Indicate by your attitude of impartiality to employees of all beliefs that you are open-minded and feel that any religious belief is to be respected.

Q. *You receive a request from a group of women employees of the same religious belief. They ask that their workplaces be arranged adjacent to one another, as they believe they will enjoy their work better under these conditions. They are not in the majority in the department and have been industrious and cooperative in the past. How would you handle this situation?*

> In what ways might such an arrangement cause unpleasantness from which the group might suffer?

Differences due to Nationality. The differences in customs and modes of living found in peoples of different nationalities who have been in this country but a short time are so great that an executive cannot expect any great homogeneity. One investigation in an industrial establishment showed that the labor turnover in the dominating nationality was much lower than the turnover in other nationalities.

EXECUTIVE CONDUCT. Unless it is possible so to intermingle nationalities that no one group can assume importance in numbers in any department, it would seem wise to select the people who are best fitted by their background for a certain type of work and favor them for use in a given department, varying the dominating nationalities in the different departments of the organization. There is little doubt but that this policy will lessen friction among employees and decrease labor turnover.

Q. *Do you think that the method proposed violates the principles of Americanism in industry?*

To what extent does the first generation of immigrants seem to respond to Americanization influences? The second generation?

Q. *Can you think of any disadvantages in this plan?*

Is there danger of too much power through unusual group unity? Would racial antagonisms with other groups of employees tend to be increased through these segregations?

Social Differences. There are a number of fraternal orders of a social and beneficent nature which are popular among employees. The men in an industrial organization who meet each other regularly in the lodge room find freer opportunities for discussion of shop matters than is afforded other employees. Such groups are often able to exert considerable influence in forming employee opinion. Often their power is grossly exaggerated in the minds of the other employees, who attribute to them a vast amount of underground machinations.

EXECUTIVE CONDUCT. Remember that no reputable fraternal order of a social nature would knowingly allow the significance of its membership to be misused in influencing shop opinion. Let your employees know that you are aware of their fraternal relationship, that you respect and admire them for their desire to broaden their interests through these channels. Make it clear that you rely upon them not to degrade their organization through the misuse of the relationships which it has made possible with other employees. If you find that such misuse has occurred, have no hesitancy in approaching the head of the organization and enlisting his cooperation in applying remedial measures.

Q. *You find upon taking charge of a group of employees that a large number of them are members of a fraternal organization of which you are also a member. Should you make any use of this point of outside contact to strengthen your control over your employees?*

Do you think it would be desirable to attend organization meetings in the interest of executive prestige? Is there danger that employees may expect favored treatment because of these affiliations? How would you prevent the spread of such a surmise?

Family Differences. If relatives are employed in the same department, it sometimes happens that family difficulties develop which create undesirable feeling among these and other employees. Some executives guard against this possibility by refusing to employ relatives or members of workmen's families in the same group. One executive followed the opposite policy advantageously by telling the related members that the entire group would be judged by the conduct of any individual in it. If dissension broke out among them, or if any one of them proved noncooperative, the entire group would be dismissed. As he employed workers from a cultural group in which family bonds were very strong, this method proved effective.

EXECUTIVE CONDUCT. In cases where animosities between related employees occur, do not hesitate to discuss the matter with them. Refrain from any interest in the cause or justification of the feeling between the employees, but remind them that it must not be allowed to interfere with the work. If the condition does not improve, you face the necessity of dismissing both employees.

Q. *You are acting as management engineer in a small plant. The owner has gone away for a month's vacation and left you in charge. One of the younger workmen in the organization has recently been advanced to the position of foreman. In his department are many workmen older than he, one of whom has a boy employed there also. You arrive at the plant one morning to find this particular department in an excited state. The bookkeeper tells you the happening from hearsay. The foreman gave the boy an order. The boy refused to carry it out. The foreman told the boy to report to the office for his money. The boy refused, so the foreman took him by the arm and marched him out of the department to the office, where he was paid off. The boy then left the plant. The foreman returned to the department and was confronted by the boy's father, who denounced his actions as tyrannical, said he was unfit for his job, that many older men in the department were more deserving, and that he (the father) was going to see justice done. The foreman made no response, and the father returned to his work. Both the father and the foreman have been popular employees. The bookkeeper says that everyone is "worked up about it," that opinions are evenly divided in favor of the father and the foreman, that everyone is waiting to hear what you are going to do about it and that he (the bookkeeper) thinks you had better do something at once in order to avoid further trouble.*

Analyze this situation carefully and outline your procedure to the end that morale will be reestablished in the department.

> What influences are affecting the father in his attitude? Would you call the father, son, and foreman together and get the facts? The father and foreman? Would you talk to the foreman alone? What would you say to the father about the responsibilities of the foreman? How does the foreman earn his salary? Would you talk with the father alone, after a conference with him and the foreman? If so, what would you say to him?

Difficulties due to Wages. Where a wage system which rewards the employees proportionately to their productive worth is in operation, executive difficulties are much less than in those cases where the decision as to wage rate must rest upon executive judgment. A common difficulty occurs when the executive is approached for a raise which is manifestly deserved but which may be impossible because of a general policy of denying all increases in payroll during a period of business adversity. The executive is prone to pass the blame to his superior officers, saying that he advocated the raise but could not get it approved. This is poor organization procedure. The executive should present the viewpoint of the company to the employee and face the issue squarely with him.

EXECUTIVE CONDUCT. In all cases where pay increases require the approval of superior officers, be very careful not to arouse false hopes in the mind of the employee. In the case of the deserving employee requesting an increase, tell him that his request will be considered and that he will receive his answer within a stated time. Then approach your superior officer for approval and, at the stated time, give the employee his answer. If you do not follow this plan, but tell the employee that you favor the increase and will apply for it, experience has shown that the employee will assume that the increase will take place and will further assert that it should date as of the day upon which you favored the idea.

When undeserving employees apply for wage increases, do not summarily dismiss their requests unless you are armed with incontrovertible facts. Such an occasion offers you a chance to show the employee exactly why he is not progressing. This kind of executive action can be constructive and lead to improvement, while arbitrary denial, however justified it may be, merely arouses hostile feelings and lowers morale.

It should be remembered that the employee is often concerned more with the relation of his wage to that of others than with the exact sum which he is receiving. The fact that someone else, apparently less deserving than he, is receiving a larger wage arouses his sense of injustice.

Employees are quick to resent the employment of new workers at a starting wage in excess of that which is paid the older employee for the same work. This situation is obviously unfair but it may occur at a period when wage levels are fluctuating greatly and the executive has not been active in keeping the departmental rates in tune with outside requirements. If the executive does not increase his rates throughout his department, he should not advance his starting rates for new employees, even if this means that he must forego hiring additional employees.

Employees often feel that their wages should be increased as a result of length of service. While length of service is usually entitled to a reward, the recognition should not become a part of the wage but should be given separately and clearly in return for loyalty rather than for productive value. Nevertheless, it is true that an employee's wage should show a tendency to increase as his service lengthens, for logically he should be increasing his productive value to the organization. Employees who have remained on the same job for a considerable time and have not been found worthy of increase above the starting wage are not desirable members of the organization.

Difficulties caused by a poorly designed wage system may confront you. No attempt can be made here to discuss the subject of wage systems other than to indicate the qualifications of a satisfactory method, so that you may examine the system you are working with and compare it with standard requirements. The ten elements of a satisfactory wage plan are said to be as follows:[1]

1. A plan of wage incentive must be accepted by both employer and employee as the fairest under the circumstances.
2. It must be based on fair and agreed-upon standards of production.
3. It must be so simple that both workers and employers can figure it out for themselves without expert aid.
4. It must provide for an increase in reward at least proportional to increased effort and thought expended in realized production.
5. It should recognize that the mere attendance of a worker ready to work is worth a wage. The management must pay interest upon idle machinery: by analogy it must pay for those human beings whom it requires to be present but for whom it does not provide work.
6. It must safeguard both the employer and the workman against unfair rates or conditions.
7. The incentive is largely weakened when payment is deferred. Therefore the reward must quickly follow the effort.
8. To the extent that the reward is for individual effort it should be paid for individual effort. The real efficiency of an individual depends upon the extent of the cooperation he gives to and receives from others; but to the greatest degree possible his personal reward should be responsive solely to his individual effort.
9. The incentive should not be such as to stimulate an abnormal effort, for an abnormal effort must, by the law

[1] From a report prepared by Miller, Franklin, Basset & Company.

of nature, be succeeded by a subnormal effort, and thus the ends of production are not furthered. It is not necessary to have recourse to the so-called humanitarian arguments to demonstrate the futility of spasmodic, abnormal effort.

10. Any plan adopted should include the maximum number of elements that have been successfully demonstrated in practice.

Q. *You have recently been appointed executive in charge of a department in which the employees are engaged in day-work. Within the first few days you receive numerous requests for wage increases. The first employees who approach you are found to be chronic troublemakers, and it appears that they have urged the others to make like advances. How would you handle this situation?*

What is the motive behind these requests? Would you definitely refuse to consider them at this time? Would you deal somewhat sternly with the situation or would you find humor in the coincidence in requests? Would you offer any reason for delaying consideration of requests, and, if so, what? Assuming that you have been able to avoid an immediate issue, what would be your next step?

Discussion. What is your response to the following comments?

1. *It is a difficult matter to determine the unmoral or immoral quality of a dishonest act, and such decisions are best left to courts of justice.*

Is it difficult to determine the presence of management's failure to provide normal safeguards against the possibility of dishonest acts? If safeguards are present, would you favor a liberal or conservative policy in estimating their influence? Why? In the presence of dishonesty, why should you feel obligated to do anything? Does the answer to the preceding question clarify the problem of what should be done?

2. *If an employee lacks sufficient courage to withstand intimidation from other employees, he is not the type that I care to retain.*

Are you buying courage or operating effectiveness in your organization? Is courage an important element in operating effectiveness in industry? Is not the intimidation in reality an act directed against the management rather than the employee? Should the nonpartisan employee be made to suffer under these conditions? Is the presence of employee intimidation indicative of previous errors in management-employee relationships?

3. *The surest way to cure a man of irresponsibility is to let him suffer full penalty. Experience is the best teacher.*

Who will provide a just measure for the exact amount of the full penalty? Is experience always the fastest teacher? The cheapest? Are penalties always forces for progress? Should a sense of responsibility be built upon a foundation of penalties?

4. *The attempt to reform unreliable employees is commendable, but their shortcomings may cause the executive to lose his job during the process.*

If unreliable employees show promise of improvement and seem worth saving, cannot temporary safeguards be set up which will prevent errors from escaping unnoticed? What would indicate that unreliability is curable?

5. *Most dull people are too lazy to think, and the more patiently you treat them, the lazier they become.*

Is it true that indolence is usually found with dullness? Do not people, in general, dislike to do those things for which their capacities do not fit them? Is the use of patience justified except in the presence of improvement?

6. *I arrange to have employees of different nationalities and religions work together. The less they have in common, the less talking they will do.*

Is it necessary to make use of such a method in order to have the necessary attention given to the work? If the job is made interesting enough, can it not successfully compete for attention? What more legitimate reason may be given for the intermixing of employees of different races or religions?

7. *I have little trouble with wages. When a man objects to his piece-rate, I study the job and usually find some way to rearrange the work and reduce rather than raise the rate. The men know this now and bring me no more complaints.*

Has this executive eliminated trouble with wages, or merely insulated himself from it? Is it necessarily a permanent insulation? What is the proper procedure to follow when an employee objects to a piece-rate?

CHAPTER 12

Difficulties with Associates

The executive often must work in conjunction with men of equal rank who report to officials in other parts of the organization. For example, a foreman in a factory production department may have much to do with the accountant in charge of the factory cost department. Differences and difficulties may arise.

To settle such troubles through organization paths means a complaint sent up one line of authority and a decision returned down the same channel—a time-consuming and often unsatisfactory procedure. The executive who fits in the organization smooths out his troubles with associates by informal man-to-man talks. He gets together with the other fellow and discusses (not argues) the matter. Then, if a solution has been reached, all necessary changes in procedure are taken up with the respective chiefs and their approval requested.

Q. *You are an executive in charge of a group of office employees. The office has a system of routing important letters from one executive to another, but these letters have been badly delayed in reaching you because the secretary of the executive whose name precedes yours in the route lists does not dispatch them promptly. What steps would you take to correct this delay?*

> Would you suggest that your secretary talk informally with the other secretary? Would it be preferable for you to talk with the other secretary? With the executive? Would you write him a note on the subject? Would you approach the difficulty through informal channels first and deal with it formally after the first approach had failed, or vice versa?

The Newcomer. Not infrequently the executive who enters an organization from the outside experiences coolness on the part of his associate executives. This is, in some measure, to be expected. Aloofness is common among strangers. In some instances it may be sharpened by the fact that the executive group had hoped that someone from within the organization would be picked to fill the position. This handicap may be surmounted by the newcomer through the subsequent demonstration of his executive ability.

EXECUTIVE CONDUCT. Take this condition for granted. There is little doubt that you will find as fine a group of associate executives here as in any other plant of similar size, because the ability of higher executives to select such men does not vary a great deal in different organizations. Search for things to admire in every man you meet. You can put down his weak points a little later. Be natural and fair. Remember that acquaintanceship always takes a little time. If the coolness seems pronounced, develop your sense of humor. Time will play to your advantage if you continue to show friendliness.

Q. Upon entering an old and established industrial concern in an executive capacity, you find that the majority of your associates have been with the company for many years. Practically all of them are members of a company club which has as one of the requirements for membership a considerable number of years' service with the company. This club has become strong and active, and its members enjoy the facilities of an attractive clubhouse provided by the company. It is obvious that under these circumstances it will not be easy for you to come to know any of the executives in a social way. You find these men extraordinarily pleasant as a group, but you are concerned as to the possibility of social acquaintance with them in view of this situation. What should you do, if anything?

> Is this a situation over which you have any control? Is this a situation which you can fairly discuss with your chief? Are there methods of compensating for this limitation upon your contacts? Is this situation one for which your associate executives are in any way responsible?

Opposition from Other Executives. The executive may meet with opposition from his associates. This may be covert opposition carried on in ways which make it difficult for him to do his work, or it may take the form of efforts to discredit him in the eyes of his chief by magnifying the importance of errors which are committed in his department and spreading criticism concerning his methods and personality.

EXECUTIVE CONDUCT. Follow the suggestions given in Chapter 12 for dealing with the covert opposition of employees. Ignore the attitude unless it seriously affects the success of your work. Inform your chief when you are sure of such opposition, but do not attempt to color his viewpoint in the matter. Let him determine the justice of the opposition. Open discussion should be approached frankly with a sincere desire to find the reason and cooperate in the removal of the cause. Be careful to treat the matter from an unemotional and judicial standpoint without evidence of rancor or malice. Such an uncalled-for attitude on the part of associate executives is to be pitied rather than assailed.

Q. *Soon after accepting an executive position in charge of a new department, you realize that your associate in a similar position in an adjacent area is distinctly uncooperative. You then discover that several years previous, when floor space was allocated to the two departments in the new building, your department was expected to grow more rapidly and, as a result, a larger area was assigned to it when partition walls were erected. The executive in the other department felt this apportionment to be unfair to his prospects and since then has shown no desire to be of assistance to his neighbor. How would you deal with this situation?*

> Are you in a position to affect this point of view? Would it improve matters if he understood your willingness to have the partition moved, if it were necessary? Should you talk with your chief about the situation? Should you overlook the matter and ignore your associate's noncooperativeness?

Plant Politics. In organizations where competition between departments has been too highly stimulated, or where opportunities for advancement are unduly rare, an executive may find his associates giving an unwise amount of time to the establishing of personal influence.

EXECUTIVE CONDUCT. Steer clear. If your associates play plant politics, it is important that you guard your statements against misconstruction. As far as you can, avoid all discussion of personalities. If this is impossible, make it a rule never to say anything about any individual that you would not say to him personally.

Q. *You are an executive in the production division of a large manufacturing plant. The treasurer of the company, who is several stages above you in organization rank, is a distant relative by marriage, and you meet him occasionally in a social way. He has charge of the financial and accounting divisions of the company. A chief clerk in one of the accounting sections with which you have routine dealings asks you if you would be willing to intercede with the treasurer in his behalf with respect to a vacancy which has occurred in the department. The chief clerk tells you that there is keen competition to obtain this job and he is very anxious to get it. Your relationships with him have always been very satisfactory and you have reason to believe that he is capable of carrying on these increased responsibilities. What should you do?*

> Is he entitled to the type of assistance which he asks of you? Would you consider such an activity to be classed as "internal politics"? In what way, if any, can you rightfully be of assistance to him?

Cliques. Someone has defined a clique as "a group which has not invited you to membership." The significance or assumed influence of cliques in the average industrial organization is more a matter of smoke than of fire. Human beings have a way of enjoying comradeship in relatively small groups. These develop quite naturally where there are large numbers of men of the same organization rank. Frequently these social groupings provide real value in the form of opportunities for recreational and social activities.

EXECUTIVE CONDUCT. Don't become concerned about such groups. Take fullest advantage of any congenial opportunities. Frequently there may be a good deal of speculation and discussion of company policies and related events. This does no harm among any such group of executives; there are usually enough sensible heads present to assure that reason will prevail.

Q. *Upon entering an organization you find that a large number of your associates are active members of a fraternal organization. While there is no evidence that this outside association is misused in any way, this particular group of executives seems to hang together much more than others. You learn that a considerable number of the higher officials in the company are also members. You have never given much thought to lodge affiliation. In the past you have rather favored selecting your friends individually. You have been approached by a member to join this organization. On what basis should you form your decision?*

> Should you base your decision on the number of personal friends who are now members of this organization? On the possibility of being of greater service and worth to the company through wider contacts and relationships with

your associate executives? On the possible value which such association might be to your own advancement in the organization? On the value and worth of this particular fraternal organization and the assistance and cooperation which you might be in position to provide through membership in it?

Technical Difficulties. With the growing tendency in industry for material to be processed in thin, swiftly flowing streams, it is obvious that technical difficulties make themselves felt over wide areas and frequently are the cause of friction between executives in coordinating departments.

EXECUTIVE CONDUCT. Your procedure is clear. In such matters, concentrate your attention upon the situation rather than the personalities involved. Find where the difficulty originates and how it can be remedied. As soon as your associates discover that you are not searching for a culprit, and that you are willing to accept your full share of the fault, they will cooperate with you in detecting and overcoming the difficulty.

Q. *A new and highly integrated system of conveyor manufacture has been introduced into your department. As it is experimental, there has been some difficulty in its operation. You find that under this arrangement your output is much more dependent upon the effectiveness of various service departments supplying materials, power transport, and machine maintenance. Nevertheless, your chief has not discarded his habit of looking to you for results. Conditions must be improved in the near future if unhappy consequences are to be avoided. What should your procedure be?*

> Should you lay the whole situation before your chief? Should you endeavor to familiarize yourself with the new technical problems in order to regain your position of command over these facilities? Should you cultivate closer coordination with material control, machine maintenance, and transport? Should you be patient, realizing that this period of difficulty is characteristic of new installations?

Responsibility for Errors. Employees may make errors which will bring criticism from other departments.

EXECUTIVE CONDUCT. It is a principle of management that criticism of a formal nature should reach the employee only from the same source as his orders—namely, from his superior officer. If there is to be criticism of your employee, you should accept full personal responsibility before the complainant. Then you may pass the criticism on to the employee in such degree as is merited. The reason is clear. You should be personally responsible for the errors of your employees; for if the error is due to misunderstanding, you are at fault for inferior instructions, and if the error is due to unfitness you are at fault in your assignment.

Q. *You are in charge of a group of clerical employees. During the vacation period you find yourself facing a temporary shortage of labor, and it is arranged as a favor to you that a clerk from another department will work in your department every afternoon. The clerk will remain on the original department payroll, but one-half of this expense will be charged to you. You find that the clerk is inaccurate, which is probably due to lack of interest in the work, as it is manifestly a temporary job. Would it be advisable for you to insist upon a better grade of work from him? If so, should you talk to him or to the executive to whom he regularly reports? Is the arrangement a sound one from the organization point of view?*

> How could this difficulty have been avoided? By planning vacation intervals so that a temporary shortage would not occur? By careful selection of the clerk to be used on half-time work? By a definite understanding as to the degree of your control over the clerk? By establishment of more rigid supervision of his work? By arranging that records of the employee's accomplishment while in your department form a part of the record maintained in his department?

Changes in Rank. Organizations are not rigid structures. They are constantly changing in order to meet new objectives, conditions, personnel. Executives should anticipate that there will be frequent readjustments in the relative rank of their associates and themselves.

EXECUTIVE CONDUCT. These adjustments are the responsibility of the higher officials. It is probable that they have been made as the result of much thought and study. Though you may disagree with the changes as they affect your associates or yourself, you may be sure that the officials strongly desire that they will be accepted in good spirit, that they will be given fair trial. If you appear to have benefited by the change, remember that you have yet to prove your ability to make good. If you appear to have lost ground, do not interpret the change as a gesture unfavorable to you. This test of your primary interest in and loyalty to the company may bring your turn next.

Q. *As an executive in charge of a department you have for many years reported directly to the factory manager. You have come to know him intimately. During the past several years your associations with him have been one of the pleasantest aspects of your working life. As the company has increased in size, branch plants have been established. The duties of the factory manager have increased to a point where a change in organization has become necessary. Three plant superintendents have recently been appointed to supervise and direct the work in each factory. These men report to the factory manager. This adjustment means that you will no longer be in close touch with your former chief. Henceforward you will report directly to a man who has hitherto been of the same rank as yourself, to whose personality and point of view your activities must now conform. While this cannot be called a demotion for you, it has certainly been a loss. What should be your point of view?*

> Should you seek other means of keeping in contact with your former chief? Should you begrudge the new plant superintendent his position? Should you accept the situation as an inevitable but unhappy consequence of company growth? What would your former chief want you to do?

Overambitiousness. A rather common failing, particularly among younger executives, is an impatience for immediate advance. But it is one of the least of the executive vices. It is a sin of commission rather than of omission and frequently has a way of purging itself in most surprising fashion. Nevertheless, it demands attention.

EXECUTIVE CONDUCT. Be sure that what you take to be overambition on the part of others is not underambition on the part of yourself. The truth is that the industrial world, under the pressure of sad experience, is becoming distinctly more ambitious in temper. What was considered enterprising a few years ago is today called conservative. Overambition in its most unpleasant aspect takes the form of maneuvering on the part of an associate, with his own advancement as the direct objective. Your technique is clear. Find out what he is aiming at. If his objective, even though it be a personal one, will be of benefit to the company, don't stand in his way. If he plans to advance himself by climbing upon the shoulders of others, don't hesitate to let him know that you understand his game, but do it with a smile. Friendly frankness is your defense.

Q. *A younger man has been put in charge of a department which closely relates itself with yours in a sequence of processing. In the few weeks that he has been employed he has introduced a number of new methods and procedures. Some of these seem to be particularly good. Others, your experience leads you to feel, will not prove successful. He seems to be earnest and anxious to make good. On the other hand, he is overconfident with respect to the soundness of his methods. His verve and energy have delighted his chief, who is also your superior officer. You learn that the chief hopes you will look favorably upon the new suggestions because of the close juxtaposition of the two departments and the increased efficiency which may result if a common routine is adopted. But you doubt the soundness of some of the proposals and you fear criticism should you introduce the ones that seem acceptable and they be found superior to those which you have been advocating. Your associate believes that his ideas cannot be given a fair trial unless both departments cooperate in the experiment. How should you handle this situation?*

> Should you oppose him? Should you delay him? Should you remain aloof until his plans have been somewhat more seasoned? Should you attempt to bolster up your own enthusiasm about cooperating with him in the application of his ideas? Should you discuss the general question with your chief?

Pompousness. Executives frequently encounter associates who assume an air of superiority or pompousness justified in their own minds by their longer period of service in the company, greater experience in its methods, and general plant wisdom.

EXECUTIVE CONDUCT. Not infrequently this attitude is a direct result of an inner sense of inferiority and even of fear. Such men are literally "whistling to keep their courage up." It is desirable to set their worries at rest by being very frank about your shortcomings in the way of information and specific plant experience. If you show willingness to take their point of view into careful account and even to learn from them, you will quickly win their friendship and cooperation.

Q. *An executive in charge of a neighboring department has a habit of entering your office and interrupting any conference which you may be conducting. His missions are always on business matters but are not of more than normal urgency. He seems to enjoy giving the impression that he is of sufficient importance to make such action permissible. His office is only a short distance away, and on one occasion he remarked, "Easier to step in than to telephone." Just how would you handle this situation?*

> Would you retaliate by calling upon him in a similar fashion? Would you suggest to him that he telephone rather than make a personal visit? Would you indicate by your manner that you do not favor being interrupted?

Q. *Upon your entrance into an executive position in a large organization you have been deluged by advice from an associate. Having taken it upon himself to be your guide and mentor, he initiates lengthy discussions with you concerning your departmental activities. He considers himself an authority on company policy and feels that you should be safeguarded from any possible errors. While it is clear that he is sincere in his desire to be helpful, he is rapidly becoming a nuisance. What is the proper method of dealing with him?*

> Should you tell him tactfully that you no longer need his advice? Should you make it difficult for him to contact you? Should you advise him that you feel he must be taking too much of his own time from his work in giving you this assistance? Should you suggest to your chief that he be called off?

Plain Meanness. Chronically unpleasant individuals do exist, and once in a while one of them attains the position of executive. There are doubtless a variety of psychiatric explanations for this unfortunate point of view, but we are concerned only with the fact and the method of dealing with it.

EXECUTIVE CONDUCT. The important thing to remember is that such characteristics rapidly gain notoriety for the person who shows them. You may be fairly sure that you are not the only executive who has experienced difficulty with this associate. The easy procedure is to retaliate. But meanness feeds on meanness, and your relationships will become worse rather than better. The hard thing is to protect yourself intelligently against further difficulties and then to forget it. Unless you are to make your own life miserable, you must overlook unpleasant things in other people.

Q. *You have been placed in charge of a newly formed instruction section in a processing department of a manufacturing company. Your work is to train new employees in methods of operation until they are fitted to undertake the regular activities under the wage-incentive system of the department. You have no difficulty with your associates, with the exception of the executive in charge of the department which supplies you with raw material. He is well liked by the management, for he keeps his operating costs low, but because of his lack of cooperation he is cordially disliked by other executives with whom he does business. He consistently delays the issuance of material to you and makes it necessary for you to give considerable time to the following up of requisitions. In his personal contacts with you, however, he is entirely amiable. Because of the inability of the processing department, which you serve, to maintain its schedule, it was decided to eliminate some of the increases in production which your employees were required to reach and to permit these employees to carry a portion of the regular production at their present rate of output. You learn that when the general superintendent reviewed the production schedule and remarked concerning the absences of increases for these employees in your section, the executive supplying raw materials, instead of explaining, said, "It looks as if someone were slipping in the instruction section." How would you handle this situation?*

> Would you take the matter up directly with your chief? Would you take the matter up with your associate executive? Would you make any attempt to correct the erroneous impression which the general superintendent has received? If so, how would you go about it?

Difficulties Caused by Worry or Fatigue. There is no question that worry and fatigue have definite effects upon personality. A man under great strain may become completely irrational in action. Fatigue may not result so seriously, but it is apt to cause increased irritability and loss of control.

EXECUTIVE CONDUCT. Treat such situations thoughtfully. Don't interpret the behavior of your associate under such circumstances as being normal or permanent. You may not be able to excuse his errors, for it is part of the executive's job so to conduct his affairs that he does not become unduly fatigued or concerned. Nevertheless, these factors are not always within one's control. Your procedure should be the same as that which you would adopt with anyone suffering from an illness.

Q. The organization with which you are employed has been working for some time on a heavy schedule. Executives have been doing overtime work and dispositions are ragged. The executive in charge of the department which performs subsequent operations to yours has become increasingly dictatorial concerning delivery schedules. Finally, he charges into your office and delivers a lengthy oration on the poor service which he has been receiving from you. It so happens that a considerable number of employees are about and overhear his remarks. You restrain your temper and tell him that you will be glad to review the situation with him. You later learn that word has gone around your department that you have received a severe tongue lashing from your associate, that you were afraid to fight back. How should you handle this situation?

Was there any error in your conduct?

Religious, Racial, and Social Differences. Ideally, executives are selected because of their managerial ability alone, irrespective of religious affiliation, race, or social standing. As a result, it is not to be expected that there should be any homogeneity in these areas among the executive group. Difficulties traceable to these differences are, among this more intelligent group, much less prevalent than among workmen. Perhaps the greatest obstacle which they raise is the difficulty of developing fully the family spirit within the organization.

EXECUTIVE CONDUCT. Racial status is a matter of birthright over which we have no control. Religious predilection is deep-seated, and religious freedom is one of the tenets of our civilization. Social position is also affected by the fortunes of early background and family standing. It is clear, therefore, that these differences in the executive organization should, so far as possible, be ignored in their relation to company affairs. Take your associates at their face value. Measure their worth in terms of industrial accomplishment.

Q. *One of the executives in your organization has a racial background and religious affiliations somewhat different from those of the rest of the group. He is a competent manager and well liked by his associates in the plant. However, he has few acquaintances in the community, and out of hours he leads a rather lonely life.*

> Should you and your associates take it upon yourselves to contact him outside the plant to a greater extent? Or would you advise that he find, if possible, a position in another plant where there are a large number of executives of similar background and affiliations with whom he could form more intimate acquaintanceships? What constructive suggestions have you for dealing with this situation?

Age Differences. There is no question that differences in age are a frequent source of friction between executives. Youngsters consider oldsters too conservative and staid. Oldsters consider youngsters too impetuous and even erratic.

EXECUTIVE CONDUCT. No matter which of these age groups you are in, the technique is the same. Tolerance and consideration of the viewpoint of others are among the most useful graces in industrial relationships. The young must have a chance to gain experience through mistakes; the old should not be expected to reflect the tempo of youth. An exact similarity of viewpoint is not to be expected, but under conditions of friendly relationships each can learn from the other.

Q. *One of the executives with whom you have frequent contact is constantly referring to the many years of service which he has given to the company and the great wisdom which he has gained thereby. He disagrees frequently with your ideas, and a favorite remark is, "After you have been here a few more years you will find that won't work." He is extremely opinionated and feels that the seal of time is always the seal of correctness. At times you wonder if he is not trying to undermine your self-confidence. You are making no headway in gaining his cooperation or willingness to discuss a situation on an equal footing. How will you handle this situation?*

> Should you let him take the initiative in making proposals? Should you defer entirely to his point of view? Should you lay down plans for coordinating your work with his, and present them to him, making it appear that you are taking it for granted that he will cooperate? What other means might you consider for gaining his collaboration?

Social Responsibilities. Distinctly opposing points of view are found in different industrial organizations concerning company social relations. Some companies feel that the outside associations of the executive should be with entirely different groups of people from those with whom he is associated in the plant, that change and variety have a real recreational value and are to be fostered. Another school of thought argues that the family spirit engendered within the plant can and should be carried outside the gate. Executives and their families should mingle socially, as it is through these external contacts that acquaintanceship ripens into friendship and mutual understanding and cooperation are enhanced.

EXECUTIVE CONDUCT. If your company has a definite policy or point of view in this matter, it is important that you should familiarize yourself with it and determine whether it is one to which you can cheerfully and readily adhere. If there is no fixed policy, base your reliance upon the principle that real friends are rare and to be cherished. Whether they are found within or without the plant is a matter of secondary consideration. If you really enjoy the organization of which you are a member, it goes without saying that you will find real friends within it. On the other hand, outside activities of a religious, social, or fraternal nature may bring similar opportunities.

Discussion. What is your response to the following comments?

1. *Difficulties with other executives are bound to occur. You owe it to yourself to cultivate your standing with the higher officials so that when trouble comes you will be in a favored position.*

> Should legitimate difficulties be overcome by strategy, by compromise, or by the integration of conflicting ideas? Is the cultivation of a certain standing with administrators necessary to protect the executive against the stresses of organization politics?

2. *A new executive should not encourage social relationships with others until he has something to show in the way of accomplishment. After he has won his spurs he is in better position to increase his contacts.*

> Is it desirable that the new executive should take the initiative in making friendly overtures to other executives? Should he tend to stress or suppress the fact that he is new to the job?

3. *If you anticipate opposition from other executives, remember that the best defense is a strong offense. If you beat a man at his own game, he respects you and becomes your friend.*

> Is it better strategy to follow this proposal or to remove the basis of difference before hostilities commence? Is there a value in persistent discussion of subjects around which a difference of opinion exists? Does hatred usually thrive upon an increased acquaintance with a personality? Is there a value in persistent friendliness?

4. *A man is a fool who does not use every resource to increase his area of opportunity and usefulness. Friendship is a resource in business and its benefits are a fair return to any one who can earn them.*

> Is there a distinction between the capitalization of friendship and the playing of politics? What, if anything, may an executive rightfully do to increase his opportunities other than to show competence in his work?

5. *Make it a point to become a member of as many clubs and societies as possible. The more you meet your associates on the outside, the better you will get along with them on the inside.*

Is this an improper procedure? Are its objectives open to criticism? If you were president of a society would you object to membership on these grounds?

6. *In dealing with technical service departments, remember the saying that it is the squeaking axle that gets greased. A little temperament, when it comes to technical service, will get you attention.*

Are there other and better ways of gaining attention? If so, what are they? Is there a distinction between temperament and an insistence upon high standards?

7. *The real source of employee errors lies with the employment manager. The right sort of employee doesn't make errors.*

Are there other good reasons? Inadequate training? Inadequate method? Equipment? Material? Incentive? Working conditions?

8. *The world takes you at your own measure. If you admit that rank means nothing to you, you will not be considered when changes in rank are contemplated. If you show the company that you value your standing, the company may use this means of rewarding you when you have shown results.*

What is the purpose of rank? Why do executives have titles? Is it position that you really want, or is it the opportunity to do your very best in terms of your own capabilities?

9. *It is much better to be over- than underambitious. The sooner a man discovers his upper limit of accomplishment,*

the sooner he will be satisfied. Overambitiousness accelerates this process.

Can a man be overambitious? What should be the nature of executive ambition? Is personal advancement an unworthy aim? Does difficulty result from excessive ambition, or from ambition poorly directed?

10. *The best way to deal with a pompous executive is to submerge him with questions. As soon as he has to say that he doesn't know the answer it is likely that he will become normal.*

Is this a good antidote? Do you know of a better one? Does pompousness demand a countertechnique?

11. *A mean man is usually a coward. The best protection against his tricks is to arouse his fear of consequences.*

How far should you go in attempting to compensate or neutralize unfortunate characteristics in other executives?

12. *There are many good reasons for becoming irritable and there is one good reason for not doing so—namely, that it may get you into trouble. Executives can usually control their irritation when it is to their advantage to do so.*

Are there other ways than this of protecting yourself? Under what conditions is it undesirable to submit to irrational conduct? Is a good reason for irritability necessarily a good excuse?

13. *There are people of certain nationalities that I dislike intensely. It seems hypocritical to me to assume an attitude of friendship which I do not sincerely feel.*

Does common courtesy necessarily imply a friendly attitude? What sort of treatment would you favor from a person who had a strong, but impersonal, dislike for you?

14. *The best way to handle the oldster is to agree with him and cheer him along. And then do whatever necessity dictates.*

Just why should this procedure be acceptable to the older executive? Are there conditions under which it would be justified? Is deception ever justified? How can a younger man win the compliance of an older executive of opposing viewpoint?

15. *I am a company man for eight hours a day and no more. Outside the plant my time is my own and my companions are of my own choosing. No company has the right to ask me to mix my social interests with business.*

Should a man be criticized for taking this point of view? Should the executive view the possibility of outside contacts with his associates as a necessity or as an opportunity?

CHAPTER 13

Difficulties with Superiors

We have seen that the executive is chiefly concerned with the organization of employee will, and we have also seen that the administrator must obtain a like cooperation from his executives. It is clear that group action thus developed among executives may require of them personal adjustments and possibly even sacrifices. This exacts a degree of unselfishness and an ability to keep the prime objective of the entire organization clearly in sight. Organization does not call for habitual unthinking obedience. The best organization is composed of individuals of *common purpose*. Assuming a common purpose, there may be many ways to its accomplishment. One must be chosen and adhered to by all. Hence the need of an administrator who will decide and executives who will work as one with him along the paths of his choice. Orders must be carried out. One able student of management has said:

> If your boss asks you to do something with which you do not agree in the matter of method or policy, do it three times as energetically as ordinarily. If you are right, the error will be evident three times as quickly as otherwise. If you are wrong, you have learned your error at no cost to yourself.

Disagreement with Orders

EXECUTIVE CONDUCT. You may ask the privilege of voicing objections to orders issued by your chief with the understanding that you wish them answered in order that you may learn. But make it clear that your attitude will in no measure affect your willingness and alacrity in following instructions. Remember that your chief may not be in a position to state all his reasons for demanding certain action. He expects your confidence in him and his judgment to be sufficient reason for obedience. This is a measure of loyalty.

Q. *You receive an order from your chief which violates certain ethical principles which you uphold. Should you express your objections only to your chief or acquaint your employees with your attitude so that if your chief does not change his order and you feel obliged to resign your position, there will be continuing opposition to the order on the part of the employees?*

> Should you attempt to impose your ethical standards upon other employees in the organization? Should you resign or should you continue to raise objections to your chief until policies are changed or you are discharged? Should you say nothing, follow orders, and wait until you are in an executive position with sufficient power of discretion to adjust practices in accordance with your own standards?

Q. *Your immediate superior has suddenly been called out of town, to be gone for a minimum period of one month. You have been elevated to his position in his absence. Before leaving, he did not have time to discuss with you in detail your new responsibilities; however, you are rea-*

sonably familiar with the job. In the past you have abided by the decisions and policies laid down by your superior, even though you have not always been in complete agreement with them. Now that you are in charge, you feel you can change some of his policies to conform to your well-considered beliefs. What is your responsibility here?

> Would it make any difference if your superior had told you specifically to carry out his policies in his absence? Could you act differently if you had been appointed by your superior's chief instead of being designated by your superior to fill his position in his absence? Would the nature of your work affect your actions? Would it make any difference if your own supervisor was to be gone for just a short period of time? What if you had in the past discussed your differences of opinion with your supervisor?

Appeal to Higher Officials. At times the executive finds himself opposed to the policies laid down by his chief. Although the executive may carry out orders with which he is not in accord, he may feel that by so doing he is working against the welfare of the department and the business. In discussion with his chief he may encounter what he considers to be an unreasonable and obstinate attitude. He may then weigh the desirability of appealing to a higher official whose attitude toward his ideas may be more cooperative.

EXECUTIVE CONDUCT. Experience proves that in the long run little is gained by going over the head of your chief. Executive relations are human relations, and good will and mutual confidence are indispensable factors. It has been said that "the hardest way is usually the surest."

This axiom applies here. Your chief will be more amenable to your point of view after you have convinced him of your dependability in carrying out orders.

Q. *A recent visit to a factory manufacturing an allied product indicates to you that a radical change in the arrangement of machinery and flow of work in your department would lead to marked reductions in unit costs. Your chief, with whom you are on the best of terms, is generally regarded as a conservative person. You anticipate that any proposal of yours concerning such a change would require long incubation before any alterations would occur. Your brother is a lawyer and a close personal friend of the president of the company. He suggests that he be permitted to mention your interest in these newer methods and drop a hint that it might be well for the president to send your chief to the factory you visited to consider the desirability of adopting its procedures. Your brother feels that your chief would respond to this approach much more readily and effectively than to any suggestions of the sort coming from you.*

> Would you consider this going over your chief's head? Assuming that this plan proved successful and your chief later learned of your indirect contact with the president, would he have grounds for objection? To what extent should you allow organization etiquette to interfere with, or delay the introduction of, technical improvements?

Criticism versus Morale. The executive may hear adverse criticism of his chief. He may believe the criticism to be sound. His own opinion may be invited.

EXECUTIVE CONDUCT. If you are loyal and believe in

your organization, you will refuse to voice your feelings. While criticism may be justified, its expression is not. Intrinsically, it may be based on truth, but its utterance will corrode morale. Elbert Hubbard said to the organization man, "Get in line or get out." If you feel that the support of your chief will demand a lowering of character standards, get out. Otherwise, your attitude should be one of full confidence and cooperation.

Q. *You have received an order from your chief with which you disagree in point of method. You discuss the matter with him, but he does not believe that your differing ideas are sufficient grounds for change. You issue the order to your workmen and although you have not expressed your attitude to them, they find objections similar to yours. One of the employees comes to your office and asks permission to discuss the order with you. What attitude should you take in this case? Should you refuse to discuss the matter with him? Should you present the attitude of the chief, identifying it as his? Should you strongly support the chief's position (in which you do not concur)? Should you present the chief's attitude as the "company" attitude, with which every employee should cooperate?*

> Suppose that the employee asks your permission to talk with your chief about the order, should you encourage or discourage him in doing so? Should you notify your chief of his coming?

Delays in Important Administrative Decisions. Changes in administrative policies are sometimes forced upon a concern by economic conditions. The need of the change may be felt first by the executive, who appeals to his chief for a decision. For example, a rapid increase in business may require overtime work or the formation of a night shift. A delay in obtaining a decision upon such matters may cause considerable annoyance.

EXECUTIVE CONDUCT. Whatever your uncertainty or mental discomfort, be careful to conceal your feelings from the employees. When you have laid the problem before your chief you have reached the boundaries of your authority and responsibility. Now devote yourself to maintaining your organization in the best condition possible under the circumstances until you receive further directions. Guard against repeated appeals to your chief for action. These are likely to retard, rather than hasten, decision.

Q. *A neighboring organization which is employing the same type of men as you are has recently increased wages 15 per cent. Your organization has not duplicated the increase, and this has caused considerable feeling between the administrators of the two plants. Some of your best employees resign and obtain employment in the competing plant. Your production schedule suffers. You present the situation to your chief, the factory manager. He tells you to do the best you can until the officers of the company formulate a policy but gives you no encouragement concerning the certainty of a similar wage increase for your men. How will you interpret his instructions until you obtain definite information on the company attitude?*

May there not be advantages in connection with your organization, such as continuity of employment, which you can suggest for employee consideration? Would you favor the use of a personal appeal? Would you favor threatening employees with blacklisting if they accept employment with the neighboring concern? If the present situation is temporary, will the employees want to change? If it is permanent, can your organization avoid an ultimate readjustment in wages?

Delays in Administrative Action. There are certain tasks which can be accomplished only by the chief, and which must be performed before the executive can function properly. For example, changes in the duties of associating executives are sometimes necessary. The chief is clearly the only person who can authorize such a change. He may agree that this should be made but delay unaccountably in making it.

EXECUTIVE CONDUCT. Remember that the element of time is a very important one in administrative action. To agree that a thing ought to be done is not to agree that it should be done at once. One must wait until the time is ripe. It rarely occurs that the time of discovery of a constructive change coincides with the moment when the change should be put into effect. Therefore, be patient. You can gain nothing by urging the matter, for often the chief cannot explain in detail the reasons for his delay.

Lack of Access. Executives often feel hampered by their inability to keep in close touch with their chief. They complain that the chief seems too busy, that he is not sufficiently available, that they find themselves delayed in their work.

EXECUTIVE CONDUCT. First determine whether you are getting as full a share of your chief's time as are other executives. If you find that you are not, probably the fault lies with you. Administrators will cut down their time allotment to you if you waste it by lengthy presentations of unimportant matters which you should decide for yourself. The chief will also dislike talking with you if you habitually preface your problem with the question "What shall I do?" The executive who is effective in conserving his chief's time will always receive a welcome. The executive who never sees his difficulties until they demand solution finds himself running to his chief several times a day. Look ahead and analyze your difficulty before it becomes urgent; be in a position to suggest a solution, group the problem with others, and see your chief at a convenient time when the material which you have collected can be methodically discussed.

The writing of memoranda, while subject to misuse if overdone, can be made very valuable in conserving the chief's time. You can express yourself more clearly and concisely in this way. Often the chief may note his answer immediately upon the memorandum and return it, thus eliminating the need for a conference.

Q. *You have recently been appointed to an executive position and have sent several memoranda to your chief. He sends for you, and when you enter the office he picks up the letters and says: "I have received these letters from you but I've been too busy to look at them. What are they all about?" You take the papers, give him a brief summary of each, finding him attentive and willing to make decisions.*

Should you continue to send memoranda? Would your chief have read them had they been shorter? Would he have any reason for preferring to have you come in person to present your business?

> Is it probable that the chief knows you intimately? Does the spoken word convey more than the written? What more? Would your chief be likely to explain why he would like to see you personally? Might he later desire to have you return to the use of written memoranda? If you plan to see him personally for a time, would you discontinue the preparation of written memoranda?

Difficulties in Obtaining Wage Increases for Employees. Under certain forms of wage systems it becomes the recurrent duty of the executive to obtain his chief's approval to wage increases for employees. The difficulty here is that the executive must ask for an increased company expenditure, which has sharp significance to his chief, in return for an increase in employee worth which may be hard to evaluate.

EXECUTIVE CONDUCT. Do not approach your chief on this subject until you are armed with all available facts. Administrators hesitate to approve such requests because they fear that the employee has asked for a raise as a matter of dicker and the executive has merely passed it along, expecting the chief to do the thinking. If the chief sees that the request has had careful thought and investigation, he will be more likely to grant it. The ideal condition is one in which such illuminating employee records are maintained concerning productivity, attendance, promptness, attitude toward work, and cooperation that the record itself determines the justice of the request without further comment by the executive. Some executives acquaint their chief with employee requests for wage increases which have been rejected. This emphasizes the fact that the executive is using discrimination and is not asking approval of all requests which come to him.

One method of reducing the number of approvals necessary consists in the preparation of a standardized employee roster indicating the normal number of employees required and the maximum and minimum wage available for each job on the list. This roster is approved by the chief, and thereafter the executive is allowed to replace any terminations, in order to maintain the number of employees agreed upon, and to adjust the wages of any employee between the minimum and the maximum amount without further approval by the chief. Where the administrator finds it possible to give the executive this area of discretion, the plan works admirably.

Pressure from Superiors. Emphasis is constantly changing in business. Executive pressure must vary likewise. It is therefore not only logical but proper that there be fluctuations in the demands made upon executives by their superior officers.

EXECUTIVE CONDUCT. If your chief becomes unusually strict in holding you responsible for results, you are to be congratulated, for you may be sure that he considers your work important and he has some reason to believe that you will accomplish it satisfactorily. Otherwise he would either bring no pressure to bear or he would replace you. There is exactly one thing to do. Meet his expectations and more. The surest test of loyalty is quick responsiveness.

Q. *The work of your department is so similar to that of several others that close comparisons can be made. Though you frequently win first place in competition, your chief seems to expect even better results. During your last interview with him on this matter, when your ranking in relation to other departments was pointed out, he remarked, "Yes, I understand all that, but I don't believe that you are giving me the fullest measure of ability of which you are capable. You could be much further in the lead if you would put your mind to it."*

What is your attitude toward his point of view? On what basis, if any, has he a right to ask more of you than the maintenance of the leading position? Are you entitled to sufficient competition to stimulate you to do your very best? What reasons might your chief have for taking his position?

Q. *Because of unforeseeable irregularities in raw materials, your department has had to perform extensive reprocessing operations. Your superior, the division superintendent, is aware of your troubles and has said, "Do the best you can under the circumstances." However, production from your department has caused such serious delays in departments performing subsequent operations that the plant manager has come directly to you and said, "Increase production." What would you do?*

What if you could increase production by dispensing with some safety precautions? What if you could increase production by lowering the quality of the product? Would it make any difference if your immediate superior had been present or had given the order to increase production? Would your answer be the same if the request were entirely unreasonable? What if you had assured them (before you knew about the defective raw materials) that you would get out the specified production?

Determination of Area of Discretion. Every executive has a certain area of authority in which he may act upon unusual matters without obtaining approval. This is his area of discretion. In many cases its boundaries are vague and the executive is at a loss to know just how far he may rightfully go. He hesitates to ask his chief for more precise information, and the situation usually results in the executive's asking for approval in more cases than necessary.

EXECUTIVE CONDUCT. If you are new to your work, your area of discretion is undetermined. The chief does not yet know how much he can leave to you. In time, as your judgment and ability become more apparent, your chief forms more definite opinions. You can assist in determining this area in the following way: After you have suggested a decision regarding a matter of non-routine nature, have obtained the chief's approval, and have handled the matter successfully, you may conclude your final report with the question "Do you want me to take up matters of this sort with you hereafter, or shall I go ahead on the basis of my own judgment?"

Q. *A little problem has arisen in your organization which involves an interpretation of company policy. There are three possible interpretations, and you have prepared an answer for each and taken the matter to your chief. He has selected the proper interpretation and approved your solution. You then have dealt with the situation satisfactorily. This being the case, would you expect him to allow you to deal with similar problems without consulting him in the future?*

> Is company policy necessarily unchangeable? Is it the job of an executive to interpret company policy or to act upon interpretations of company policy? Should you attempt to choose an interpretation or should you concentrate solely on a comprehensive analysis of the situation?

Determination of Scope of Authority and Responsibility. An executive should be thoroughly informed concerning the scope of his authority and responsibilities. When he faces a situation in which his position is not clear, he fears to overreach his authority and may err in the opposite direction. This is frequently the case when the vagueness lies in an area between his authority and that of an associate executive.

EXECUTIVE CONDUCT. You have every right to ask for light on such a matter from your chief. Be careful, however, that your chief does not misunderstand your motive and assume that you are trying to extend your area of supervision. When the decision is forthcoming, look to your chief to advise all those who are affected. For you to do this might lead to misunderstanding and ill will.

Q. *You have recently joined an organization as storekeeper. You find that the traffic manager is held responsible for all incoming materials. The plant has a rather elaborate system of railroad sidings, and a considerable amount of the material comes in flat cars. There has been stealing of material at night. One of your employees tells you that the traffic manager has authority to place the incoming cars on different parts of the sidings but that you are held responsible for the safety of their contents and your department stands any expense of guarding them. You find that two night watchmen are required to guard the yard at night because the cars are widely scattered. If they were brought together, only one watchman would be necessary. You have been given no information regarding your authority in this matter. How would you present the situation to your chief in order to gain careful consideration and yet not appear to be trying to cause trouble between yourself and the traffic manager?*

> Would you talk with the traffic manager first? If so, what would you say to him? Would you discuss the problem from the standpoint of departmental expense or company expense? Should you both approach your chief with a joint plan for readjustment of responsibility and resulting decrease in company expense? Assuming that your newness in the organization and the personality of the traffic manager make such a development impractical, what plan would you propose?

Emergency Decisions. From time to time the executive is called upon to deal with emergencies calling for immediate decisions. Conditions may not allow opportunity to obtain the authorization of his superiors.

EXECUTIVE CONDUCT. Remember that a great enemy of good management is surprise, that emergency situations are unfortunate at best and to be avoided so far as it is humanly possible. When an emergency has to be faced, do the best you can, realizing that no one should be expected to make a perfect score under such conditions.

If the decision required is beyond the area of your discretion, your first thought should be the possibility of communicating with your superiors. If time does not permit and it is clear that a delay will seriously aggravate the situation, it is your place to act. Consider two or, preferably, three possible decisions. Choose the one which, over the long pull, will best serve the interests of the company. State your decision clearly, definitely, vigorously. Irrespective of the final outcome, there is no need for apologies. You have done the best you could.

Q. *You have charge of the branch processing unit of a large establishment situated in a Southern city. This plant is located just outside the city limits. Most of the employees live in the city. To reach it, they must pass across a bridge which seems rather rickety and which is now being replaced by a more modern structure. The factory superintendent is on vacation and cannot be reached. The president of the company lives in a distant city where administrative offices are maintained. Heavy rains have caused the river to rise rapidly. During the early afternoon the weather bureau reports an additional cloudburst in the upper watershed, which will undoubtedly cause a further rise and render the use of the bridge increasingly dangerous. The output of your branch bears a key relation to the production of the main plant. Present conditions demand that your unit be operated to full capacity. If you hold the employees until the usual closing time, there is some possibility that the bridge may be temporarily blocked to traffic. It would be possible but not desirable to attempt to take care of the employees overnight. When your chief left for his vacation, his final words to you were: "Spring rains will probably push the river up again. Don't let anybody scare you into shutting the plant down because of a few inches more water." What will be your decision?*

> Will you attempt to telephone to the president? To get further information concerning the probable rise of the river? To get further data concerning the condition of the bridge? Will you consider giving each employee a choice of going home immediately or waiting until six o'clock with the possibility of staying in the plant overnight?

Attitude of Superiors. Attitude is extremely important in executive relationships. It is the wave length upon which communication and contact operate. The executive who does not give thought to the attitude which his chief displays toward him is not completely fulfilling his responsibilities.

EXECUTIVE CONDUCT. If you notice a change of attitude, find out what lies behind it. Probably it has been brought about by some previous act or relationship. If it is for the worse, lose no time in discovering the cause. If it is for the better, be sure that you have the correct reason therefor. In either case make certain that you deserve it.

Q. *You supervise the processing of a product which is becoming less important as time goes on. During the past few years the company has turned its attention to newer and more promising developments. Your relationships with your superior have always been pleasant and satisfactory. Of late he has been particularly amiable. A certain official brusqueness has disappeared and he seems even more sympathetic to and considerate of your point of view than hitherto. When you mention this situation to your brother, he remarks, "Looks as though he was getting ready to lay you off." What should you do about this, if anything?*

> Should you talk with your chief? If so, what would you say to him? Would you discuss the matter with any of your associate executives? Would you try to get indirect information concerning the company's policy with respect to your department? Should you do nothing?

Incompatibility. While warmth of personal regard between executive and chief is of value, it is not essential if respect and mutual confidence are present. We all have our innate preferences. Indeed, our choice in these matters is one of the outstanding traits of personality.

EXECUTIVE CONDUCT. Remember that coldness, aloofness, or lack of congeniality in your chief is no basis for antagonism. Do not forget that humanity is not perfect and that the presence of honesty, squareness, and good judgment may well overbalance the lack of personal charm.

Q. *On certain subjects relating to the routine operation of your department you find your chief entirely approachable. On other subjects, such as changes in wage schedules, introduction of new equipment, important changes in processing, and the like, you find him reserved and uncom-*

municative. There are a number of such matters which you would enjoy discussing with him, for you feel that a mutual consideration of certain problems would lead to improvements. It is extremely difficult, however, to make any headway in these areas without arousing signs of impending irritation.

> Should you omit these topics? Should you present your ideas in the form of written reports bearing specific recommendations? Should you be mild but firm in your insistence upon a hearing? Should you talk frankly with your chief, telling him that you find it difficult to discuss these matters with him and asking him just what he wants to do?

Senescence. Human age is not measurable in years. Some men retain their intellectual and physical vigor much longer than others. You will doubtless be one of the first to notice any decline in the powers of your superior.

EXECUTIVE CONDUCT. Remember that you too will some day pass your zenith. When that time comes (and it will not be a happy one), you will hope for a degree of understanding and consideration on the part of those about you. During his lifetime your chief has doubtless given much to his subordinates in the way of tolerance and patience. He is deserving of a return.

Q. *For some time you have been assisting the superintendent of a mill. This man has been with the company for many years and is in no small measure responsible for its success. An excellent technician, he has maintained high quality standards and reduced costs as a result of improvements in manual and mechanical processes. The company has appreciated his efforts and paid him a considerable annual bonus, which he has saved, so that now at the age of sixty he has attained a competence that makes retirement possible. The company has favored this step, as he has been in poor health and has been forced to be absent from work for lengthy intervals. You have carried on well as an assistant and are now virtually in charge of production. You find it difficult to institute new plans or policies, as your chief objects to any developments which do not originate with him. Even minor changes made during his extended absences are in strong disfavor. You have appealed to the president for more authority and a clarification of your position. The president, while entirely friendly to you, refuses to force the retirement of the superintendent, in view of his many years of valuable service. Furthermore, the president says that he does not wish to overrule the dictates of the superintendent, even though your counterplans are obviously superior.*

The trend of your situation is unfavorable. Employees appear bewildered about what actions will make their employment most secure. The superintendent's ill health renders his attitude increasingly temperamental. The president shows a certain irritation when recurring difficulties at the mill are brought to his attention. You have been with the company for seven years and have fitted yourself for the executive responsibilities involved. On the other hand your experience would be of considerably less value to another concern. How should you proceed?

What are the important factors in this problem? How will they be affected by the passing of time? Is the decision here one which you or someone else should make? What do you surmise to be the employee's point of view in this stiuation? What is the right thing to do? Would your answer be affected if you were a heavy stockholder in the business? If not, why?

Assumed Mistreatment. Nothing cuts the morale of the executive more keenly than the feeling that he has received a "raw deal." Nor is there anything more likely to disturb his emotional balance and cause him to act in ways which he may later regret. Sheer mistreatment in the form of injustice, dishonesty, or deception is unquestionably a rarity. The reason is plain. Superior officers know only too well that these tactics fail in the long run. More than this, they would most probably not have been promoted to their present jobs had they previously made use of such devices. In the large majority of instances, then, the appearance of mistreatment is brought about through misconception or misunderstanding.

EXECUTIVE CONDUCT. When trouble of this sort appears to descend upon you, you must watch yourself closely. At such times your feelings will be poor guides. The natural tendency is to run to friends for sympathy and support. Since all the facts are not available, this conduct almost always serves to make matters worse. Moreover, you will have a strong desire to strike back immediately, and in so doing you will only feed the flame of your growing resentment.

Your procedure is clear. First, don't talk. Second, delay action until you are in position to think with some degree of cheerfulness. Then go to your chief. Point out the aspects of the situation which seem to you unexplainable and ask for light. Maintain a pleasant attitude. If he is unable to clarify the situation completely, ask his permission to talk with his superior officer. If this subsequent interview is granted, be sure that you cast no aspersions upon your chief.

If, by this procedure, you discover that the difficulty has all been a matter of misunderstanding, you will be doubly grateful that you handled the matter in this way.

Q. *You have been employed for some years as a general foreman in a small plant manufacturing leather specialties. The company is managed by the president, who owns the controlling interest and, with four other members of the board of directors, is active in the business. Poor business conditions have caused several wage reductions, and your income has been reduced commensurately. You discover, however, that other executives, who are on the board of directors, have not had such extensive wage reductions. At this time you are approached by the factory manager of another concern, who offers you a position at your original salary if you will agree to bring with you a foreman who has developed with you a new line of leather specialties which is meeting with an accelerating sales demand. You have decided to refuse this offer when you learn that there are further wage decreases in prospect and that if you reject the offer the competing company will probably approach your foreman and obtain his services. You feel that were you in a position to talk the matter over with the president, arrangements would be made to meet the competitive offer. On the other hand, you have agreed to make no statement to the president except in the event that you and the foreman accept the offer. You also feel that to be favored by salary increases at this time would not be in line with the company's situation, inasmuch as it is losing money even though surplus is large. However, you have family responsibilities to consider, and the acceptance of the offer will reestablish your living standards. What should you do in such a situation as this?*

What are the important factors to be considered in this problem?

External Relationships. Superior officers, out of hours, are usually natural, unaffected people; not infrequently their personalities seem entirely different from those which they display while on duty. Such men characteristically enjoy the presence of other people and sometimes are happiest when in the company of their business acquaintances or associates.

EXECUTIVE CONDUCT. Don't be afraid of your chief. He is no different from other human beings except that he is a little more conscious of life and all that it means. Although it is not your place to initiate external contacts, by all means make use of them if they should be made available to you. Through them you may become familiar with new aspects of your chief's interests, recreations, and personality. Be natural and sincere when you are with him. Do not stress your subordinate relationship, but do not forget it. Let him choose the topics of conversation. Do not enter into a business discussion unless he initiates it.

Q. *Not infrequently when driving to work you overtake your chief, who lives a shorter distance from the plant and who makes it a practice to walk to his office.*

Should you offer him a lift? Should you make it a point to speak to him when passing? Should you choose another route?

Q. *Your newly appointed chief, having come from a distant city, affiliates himself with the local chapter of a fraternal organization in which you are an officer. In certain initiation ceremonies you are called upon to place your chief in rather undignified situations for the amusement of the other members. How should you conduct yourself?*

Should you proceed without reference to your relationship? Should you make it a point to speak to your new chief, indicating your realization of the awkwardness of the situation? Should you ask to be relieved of your duties in the initiation?

Q. *You have membership in the same golf club as your chief. On several occasions you have been called to fill in a foursome of which he was a member. He is not a good golfer, and in each instance your score has been much better than his. He takes his golf rather seriously and you question the desirability of continuing these unhappy comparisons. How should this situation be dealt with?*

Should you play a poorer game in subsequent foursomes? Should you avoid playing with your chief? Should you give the matter no further thought? What factors should affect your decision?

Discussion. What is your response to the following comments?

1. *If I disagree with my chief, I don't see why I should hasten to do as he says. I think an administrator respects*

his executives more if they show the courage of their convictions.

Is this a proper method of showing the courage of one's convictions? How should it be done? It is said that an executive responsibility is the maintenance of the momentum of production. Does this statement explain the significance of action in executive work? Does an executive lose prestige through the carrying out of orders with which he does not concur in point of method?

2. *To deny me freedom of speech in criticizing my chief is to challenge my rights of personal liberty. The proper sort of superior officer will not give his subordinates any cause for criticism.*

Is it the presence of the right, or the desire, to criticize which is under discussion? Is it possible for a superior officer to obtain complete agreement with his subordinates in matters of method in the attaining of an objective? Why?

3. *When our chief gives us an order, he expects it to be complied with at once. When we ask a decision of him, he should reciprocate by giving us a prompt response.*

What determines the timing of an order? What determines the timing of a decision? If an order is not carried out promptly, what may happen? If a decision is not made promptly, what may happen?

4. *If I go to my chief and ask his advice, he always wants to know what I would advise. If I do not talk with him but follow my own judgment, he reprimands me for overstepping my authority. He is a hard man to please.*

Is the chief in a better strategical position in case of the failure of the plan if it is suggested by the executive or by himself? How may a chief develop an executive for increased responsibilities? Is anything to be gained by a comparison of viewpoints and opinions?

5. *I never suggest anything to my chief without finding him opposed to the idea. He isn't unfriendly about it, but he seems to be distinctly negative. Usually he agrees ultimately to my proposals but not until I have used every available argument. He would be an excellent administrator if he were not so difficult to deal with.*

Why do administrators purposely assume a negative attitude toward the proposals of their subordinates? What effect does a chief's reputation for fair-mindedness, coupled with a negative attitude, have upon the executive? Upon the quality of his proposals? Is the vigor with which an executive supports a proposal one measure of executive ability?

6. *I don't believe in discussing wage increases for my workmen with my superior officer. If he hasn't sufficient confidence in my judgment in these matters, then I am not fit to be his executive.*

May other factors besides that of merit enter into the problem of wage increases? Should wage increases be founded upon executive judgment? If not, upon what?

7. *I do not work well under pressure. Tell me what is required and I will get the desired results. But I don't want anyone following me around when I am doing it.*

Is there any harm in the unusual interest which your chief may have in your work? Is there any value in it?

8. *I always try to avoid full responsibility for emergency decisions. Then, in case of error I do not have to shoulder the entire blame.*

> Are joint decisions necessarily improper? On what basis would you decide for or against them?

9. *My chief does not play favorites but he frequently reverses his attitude toward a subordinate with no apparent reason. I have given up trying to forecast my standing with him. I do my work as well as possible and take my chances.*

> Upon what should a chief base his attitude toward subordinates? Should a subordinate attempt to forecast or to explain his standing with his superior? Of what value to an executive is the knowledge of, and the reason for, his chief's attitude?

10. *Life is too short to work for a man whom you don't naturally like and respect. A large part of your waking hours is spent on the job. If it isn't a pleasant experience, search until you find one that is.*

> Review your experience with superior officers. Did your attitude toward them change as time passed? If your enjoyment in working for them increased, what were the reasons? Is it true that first impressions are always correct impressions?

11. *Young men who try to compensate for the growing inefficiency of their chief frequently are deposed along with their boss. It is poor policy to allow sentiment to cloud facts or to support or condone poor work in any form.*

As a subordinate, is this your problem to solve? What is your responsibility to the company under such conditions? To acquaint higher officials with the situation? To use your influence to effect a change? To do your job as well as possible under the circumstances?

12. *There is a place for everything, and righteous anger is the proper response to mistreatment. Show your chief that you have a capacity for vigorous resentment and his respect for you will increase.*

Do you disagree with this statement? Is righteous anger a proper or a natural reaction, or both? When, if at all, is the proper time to show your chief that you have a capacity for vigorous resentment?

13. *The surest way to become unpopular with your associates is to be seen in your chief's company out of hours. Whether it is true or not, they will immediately assume that you are playing for position and conclude that you are using unfair methods in trying to win advancement.*

Is there any way in which you can prevent the spread of this point of view? If it is not true, should you give it any further consideration? Should you allow it to affect your contacts with your chief?

CHAPTER 14

Executive Improvement

Improvement today brings security tomorrow. As buyers of factory-made products we expect constantly to obtain better and cheaper goods, and in the competitive market we choose those products that give us the most for our money.

As producers and sellers we cannot avoid the responsibility of introducing improvements into the goods we manufacture and distribute; otherwise we must expect that a more progressive competitor will get the business.

And as executives we should develop methods steadily to advance the performance of the work which we supervise. Unless improvement is a current part of our activities, our own future is probably in danger. The rapidly changing and developing environment in which we live provides growing application of the motto "Improve or perish."

EXECUTIVE CONDUCT. Let the necessity for constant improvement constitute a normal part of your existence. Take it for granted as part of your daily thinking and acting. Enjoy its spice. Learn to look forward to the challenge it brings to your intelligence and your versatility. When you have made improvement, take full satisfaction from it. Review your progress. Measure your gain. Take pleasure in your advance. Thus you will build enthusiasm to improve further.

Q. *You experience difficulty in finding personal enjoyment in improvement. It is more comfortable to run on your own momentum. Furthermore, your superior seems satisfied with things as they are. How should you approach this personal problem?*

> Should you argue, scold, frighten yourself into taking interest? What should you do?

Improvement: Habits and Novelty. We may find difficulty in making improvements stick. We may develop a new and better method of operating. We may meet little or no opposition. But after a short time we may see workers returning to old ways.

Most of us can remember getting out of bed on cold mornings to take setting-up exercises via the stimulation of a radio program. We continued for a while and indeed felt better for it, but after a bit we found ourselves staying in bed just as we always had done.

As we look back, we find that it was the novelty of the activity that engaged our interest. When the novelty wore off, our old habits were still present and influential. It is hard to change basic habits in ourselves and in others, yet change them we must if progress is to be made permanent.

EXECUTIVE CONDUCT. Try to find ways to burn your old habit bridges behind you. In improving the preparation of payroll records, for example, the introduction of payroll accounting machines mechanically assures that new routines will become permanent. Another device is to maintain running records of gains made, and continued, by your subordinates so that commendation for steady improvement can be objectively given.

Remember that a change of habit, to become lasting, requires the attainment of a new kind of "automaticity." It will take you twice as long as it does now to write your name and leave out every other letter, until the new way has built new habit paths.

Q. *You have an employee who entered upon an improvement program with great enthusiasm. Definite progress was made and continued. Now he comes to you and says that he would like to return to the old method of doing his work, which he says is less effective but does not draw as heavily upon his effort and attention. How will you handle this situation?*

Improvement and the Expert. There is a place for the expert in improvement. The management counselor, the industrial engineer, the methods specialist, all have their functions to perform. Among appropriate activities are the installation of radically new techniques, the coordinate study of operations covering a wide band of departments, the carrying through of long-term highly technical or statistical studies. Such responsibilities offer unique opportunity for the expert to be of valuable service to industrial production.

But here the executive has no less important opportunities, which serve to complement and to support those of the specialist. Not only are there a number of ways, to be described later, in which he can discover new and better methods of doing things. He can also build a spirit of improvement into the personnel of his department to the end that everyone feels, with him, that the ever-better is the ever-surer in terms of job continuation. Improvement with morale is the goal to which every modern executive aspires.

EXECUTIVE CONDUCT. Learn to work comfortably with the experts, for there will be more rather than fewer of them about as time passes. They are human beings, like the rest of us, with families to support, mortgage interest to pay, and a salary to earn. They are often heavily dependent upon you for their own accomplishment, for you frequently can make or break the effectiveness of their installation by the degree of your cooperation, or even by your outward attitude toward it. Knowing external conditions and trends in their field, they can keep you informed of the steps you should take to keep abreast of your competitors in other establishments.

Q. *You have been placed in charge of a new departmental process which represents the last word in modern planning. A wide variety of expert knowledge has been brought to bear to make this departmental installation completely up to date. What chance is there here for improvement?*

Improvement with Morale. We hear the expression "the pain of a new idea," but experience tells us that the new idea is painful only when it is inadequately presented. Millions of people gladly accepted a new idea that required the forming of new habits in an activity directly affecting their personal safety when they bought new car models with the gearshift transferred to the steering column.

We resist a new idea about our work for two reasons:

1. We fear that the new idea may rob us of our job.
2. We fear that it may rob us of our prestige.

When it can be clearly and surely shown that neither of these results will follow, that instead our security and our standing are to be increased, we find little trouble in maintaining morale as improvement takes place.

EXECUTIVE CONDUCT. To build morale, build confidence—confidence that improvements will not hurt the improver or the improved, confidence that full credit will be given to him who discovers the better way.

As a young industrial engineer, I was instructed by my senior officer to describe to the employee's boss, *in the presence of the employee,* any improvement resulting from the employee's suggestion, so that he could be absolutely sure that we, as consultants, were not taking the credit for his ideas.

Q. *Your department is part of an organization supplying an established but limited consumer demand which will not be increased by the offering of lower prices. Therefore, cost-saving improvements may tend to result in a smaller working force. How can you maintain improvement with morale under these circumstances?*

Intensive and Extensive Improvement. We may divide improvements into those which are *intensive* and those which are *extensive* in nature. Intensive improvements are *expressed out of* a given situation or activity as we would express juice out of a lemon. Extensive improvements are those which are *impressed upon* a situation or activity from without (a new product, a new market, a new material).

Usually intensive improvements follow upon extensive developments. An organization hits upon a new product, opening a new market and an attractive source of revenue. Once this extensive improvement is fully under way, intensive improvements in the form of lower prices, better quality, and quicker service should follow in order to enable the product to hold its own in the growing competition which it will arouse. There seems to be no end to the possibilities of extending these two types of improvement, as each is constantly being stimulated and nourished by the other.

EXECUTIVE CONDUCT. Do not become discouraged when extensive improvements come along and wipe out products or processes in which much intensive improvement has been made. If in automobile design we had been content merely to improve intensively, we should today have only a highly refined version of the original prototype. Extensive improvements involving over-all design changes were needed in order to introduce the more fundamental changes which modern design incorporates.

Q. *You are in charge of a department manufacturing small gear parts for lathes, millers, and gear-cutting machines. Much work has been done in the form of intensive improvement. It now appears that these parts may be more cheaply produced by the process of powder metallurgy, whereby parts are pressed and processed from "micronized" metal.*

How will you deal with this situation?

Finding Ways to Improve. Once the executive has convinced himself and his subordinates that constant improvement is the surest road to long-term job security, his next step is to discover the opportunities for betterment within his own department. Most such opportunities will be in the nature of intensive improvements, and it is to these that we shall turn our attention in the remainder of this chapter.

A number of devices for applying calipers to working methods are commonly found in the tool kits of industrial engineers. They are equally adaptable for use by the progressive executive. Once he has become accustomed to their use, he can capitalize upon an important advantage, namely, that his close knowledge of the work at hand enables him and his employees to make improvements at lowest cost. In many instances executives and employees have shown themselves to be as ingenious in reducing the cost of an improvement as in instituting the improvement itself.

EXECUTIVE CONDUCT. The trick of steady departmental improvement is the building of a backlog of opportunities from which you can select those best fitted for the time and the budget. The establishment and maintenance of a considerable reserve of constructive ideas and projects is just as normal and important to good operation as a reserve of cash.

Once a reserve of opportunities for improvement has been established, the next step is the determination of the minimum cost of installation and operation of each. This is the point where your detailed operating experience as an executive will enable you to get minimum costs.

Q. *In estimating the cost of work-saving facilities for a certain operation, you find that costlier facilities will bring lower unit costs of operations on long runs of work, while less costly facilities will bring minimum though lesser unit economies for smaller lots of output. How will you formulate your decision here?*

The Questioning Attitude. The easiest question to ask—often the hardest to answer—is expressed in the little word "Why?" Bright children wear their parents out with this incessant interrogation, and bright parents exert every effort to provide a reasonable answer every time the question is asked.

As we grow older, we become more accustomed to living comfortably with our ignorance. We take things for granted when we should be taking them apart. An able executive once remarked that the surest way to discover the basic value in any facility or activity is to ask, "If the facility is not used, or the activity not performed, exactly what will occur?"

When railroad executives raised these two questions about the huge train stations with sheds to shelter incoming engines and cars, they could not provide suitable answers; narrow overhead shelters were ample to protect passengers, and the trains were as weatherproof when standing still as when in motion. So the great sheds were taken down. No one had asked "Why?" when they were built.

There is a third question which has paid big dividends to the industrial engineer, and which is entirely appropriate for the executive to ask about every operation in his department, namely, "Can we simplify, shorten, or combine?"

Opportunities here are often traceable to increases in the amount of production or to growth in the regularity of demand which has developed since the operations were first laid out.

EXECUTIVE CONDUCT. Constantly question. A good answer last year may be a poor answer today. Challenge the simplest activities, for frequently they conceal the greatest opportunities for improvement. The "capacity to wonder" is one of the executive's greatest resources in these days of increasing readjustment to the new.

Q. *You question a current procedure in your department and ask why it could not be performed in what would appear to be a much simpler and quicker fashion. You are told that the work was carefully studied two years ago, when alternative methods were tested by actual performance and that the present method, all things considered, was found to be the best. What should be your response? Your next step, if any?*

Visual Examination. We have a way of thoughtlessly accustoming ourselves to our surroundings. Frequently we live with marked defects about us—poor lighting and ventilation, congestion, confusion, and delay. We accept conditions unconsciously which we should have to recognize as bad were they to be brought forcibly to our attention.

Artists face the same problem when they paint pictures. When they do not have the services of a critic, they must use another method to bring defects into relief. It is what they call "new eyes." That is to say, they undertake more than one painting at a time, thus returning to each project with a fresh viewpoint. For a few moments they can see defects which quickly disappear as they become once more accustomed to viewing their previous work.

EXECUTIVE CONDUCT. Approach your department with "new eyes." If you arrange your work so that your first activity of a Monday morning—when you are refreshed by the change of scene provided by the week end—is a quick turn about your department, you will be surprised at the suggestions for improvement that result. Instances of unnecessary fatigue, hazard, noise, grime, inconvenience come to light as a result of this weekly round with a fresh outlook.

A second technique employing this same principle is to enter into a compact with several associates in executive charge of departments similar to yours that you will, as a group, visit and report upon conditions and activities in each department. In this way you will be given several opportunities to criticize your associates constructively, as well as to gain the advantage of their critical findings as they look over your bailiwick.

This procedure has netted extraordinary gains where the mutually confidential nature of the comments contributed has enabled each member of the group to speak frankly and unequivocally.

Q. *You undertake the plan of walking through your department after a week end of absence but are advised by one of your associates that you will soon be marked as a snoop, if not a faultfinder, when it becomes generally known that you use this method to uncover opportunities for improvement. What should be your response?*

The Study of Change. We can often uncover opportunities for improvement by studying the changes in departmental activities which have taken place and those which will occur over a period of time. Many such movements come about so unobtrusively and gradually that their full import is not realized.

Particularly is this true of the production demands upon the department. Only too frequently we wake up to find that our equipment, arrangement, personnel, quality standards are attuned to a demand for our product quite different in magnitude, variety, or quality from that which we are currently experiencing. Unless we are watchful, our customers' requests become disproportionate to our original facilities and methods and lay us open to serious competition from more vigilant organizations.

EXECUTIVE CONDUCT. Slow-motion pictures are valuable in revealing movements that the eye cannot otherwise see. So are fast-motion pictures, and for a similar reason. The human memory can rarely recall variations in demand, in machine precision, in quality requirements, in materials extending over, say, a five-year period.

When these are put down on a single piece of paper, surprising trends of difference may appear, and they may point immediately to improvements in more closely relating our facilities to our current needs.

Compare, for example, for the same two-month period in several consecutive years (1) the nature of actual physical products manufactured, (2) the customer specifications, (3) the rate of production, and (4) the extent of diversification, and you will often discover marked changes hitherto unobserved, which justify improvements in present methods or facilities.

Study past successes. In one instance the detailed examination of costs, output, and inventories of a department during a previous year when it had given an unusually good account of itself revealed the hidden principle which, when applied, restored it to its original effectiveness.

Q. *As a new department head you find some difficulty in attempting to obtain data on operating conditions in your department for previous years. You learn that word has gone around that you are searching for facts to prove how badly the department was operated prior to your coming, and further that you are searching for evidence to implicate certain individuals. What should you do about this, if anything?*

The Use of Pictures. Layout diagrams are pictures and charts are pictures, no less than tracings, blueprints, and photographs. At times these visual devices disclose opportunities for improvement much more plainly than rows of figures or pages of type.

For example, a series of vertical bars placed side by side across a sheet, indicating the height from the floor of a given part in process at each stage of its fabrication and transport through a department, will indicate more vividly than figures or words the opportunities for eliminating unnecessary liftings and lowerings in process.

Again, the plotting of wage rates against length of service for all employees in a given department throws into strong relief those instances where unusual ratios of income to experience call for review and justification.

EXECUTIVE CONDUCT. Find ways to make pictures of comparative conditions. They may not point directly to improvement, but they are likely to raise "questions to answer," which is the first step toward advance. More particularly, discover the way in which your superior officer prefers to have his data presented. Depending upon personal training, experience, and habit, such men vary widely in the ways in which they can most readily absorb and remember facts. Some prefer tables; some favor charts; some are accustomed to written presentations. For each of us there is a best form in which we may view the new. Find and utilize your boss's predilections here, and more of your ideas will be absorbed and weighed than otherwise.

Q. *You prepare a bar chart as outlined above, covering fabrication, transportation, and storage heights in your department. A considerable number of unnecessary vertical movements are revealed. Before showing it to your superior, you let the plant industrial engineer have a look. He tells you that if you show it to your chief it will be interpreted as a criticism of the industrial engineering department and that he, the industrial engineer, will personally resent any such action on your part. What should you say and do?*

Bringing Facts into Focus. Facts sometimes come before us in a form which robs them of their significance. For example, to analyze the output of defective work for a given day may yield little. Yet to assemble defective pieces for a month will provide a devil's harvest permitting of critical analysis and remedial decisions.

At times translation of facts into financial terms gives new perspective and incentive to improve. A concern engaged in the manufacture of brass parts found that information to employees of the monetary value of parts at each stage of the process gave new stimulus to the study of waste elimination.

EXECUTIVE CONDUCT. Treat the problems of improvement with the dignity they deserve. Present facts in terms that are commensurate with their importance. It may be true, for example, to say that a certain improvement might produce a saving of 3 per cent in annual operating costs. But to say that it might produce a saving of $50,000 (which is 3 per cent of annual costs) is to present the opportunity in a more effective way.

Q. *You are in charge of the payroll department in a very rapidly growing business. Despite a complex wage-incentive system, you originally succeeded, with one thousand employees on the payroll, in keeping payroll complaints due to departmental errors down to less than 1 per cent of the payroll. As the company expanded, the ratio of errors decreased until, at twelve thousand employees, payroll errors are barely .5 per cent.*

The payroll department is close to the president's office, and he informs you that he counted fifty people standing in line for payroll corrections after payday; that this is too many and should be reduced. How will you handle this situation?

Verification. Opportunity for improvement is sometimes disclosed through figure-control checks which leave no avenues for concealment of marginal defects.

For example, placing a given weight of raw material into process, noting precisely the weight of (1) completed units and (2) legitimate and (3) preventable waste at each operating station permits the executive to complete his analysis of the entire process, finishing with exactly the same total weight (now divided between the three subclasses mentioned above) as was introduced at the first operation. Failure at any station of these components to total the original weight introduced is cause for investigation.

Many of my former students have used this analytical device with effectiveness. In at least three instances serious leaks of materials were disclosed.

EXECUTIVE CONDUCT. Use control checks to reveal the many minor losses that may mount to significant figures in a month or year. These small drains upon resource often mark the difference between profit and loss.

Furthermore, such checks protect against collusion and dishonesty in areas where the temptations resulting from loose controls are greater than human nature can well withstand.

Q. *You are newly employed in a plant in a mill town whose business is the reconditioning of textile-machinery parts. Parts are collected, repaired, and renewed, and returned to mills on a routine annual contract basis. A control check shows that, as a result of a very loose record system, about 20 per cent of the work has been returned without proper charge to the mills. Carelessness rather than dishonesty seems to be the cause. How will you proceed in correcting this situation with the mill customers?*

The Suggestive Comparison. We should not expect best results from a baseball player unless we tell him not only what he is supposed to do and what every other player is supposed to do but where his team stands in the league. As executives we may also find stimulus for improvement in measuring conditions in our department against what might be called "good standard practice."

The comparison of our lighting, heating, and ventilation standards with those found in other first-class establishments is frequently enlightening. A healthy and sometimes upsetting comparison is that made between our factory practice and state laws governing working conditions.

Any area in which we can compare our practice with the advancing state of the art is worthy of our study.

Finally, ambitious executives use every possible avenue to stimulate themselves to improve. One such is the comparison of their efforts with those of others dealing with similar difficulties and opportunities.

EXECUTIVE CONDUCT. Find fun in gauging your standing in the team. If you are red-blooded, to be in the lead will spur you to stay there, to be in the running will spur you to get there, to be in the rear will spur you to leave there.

The reason golf holds the interest of so many of us is the presence of comparative stimuli: the par of the course, your own past record on it, the score of your partner, who performs at his best when playing with you.

Q. *Your comparison of working conditions in your department with good conditions elsewhere reveals the status to be distinctly old-fashioned if not well-nigh obsolete. You find that the company has for some years considered the building of an entirely new plant and has cautioned against any temporary improvements until this step is taken. At present, the date for starting the new building is still indefinite. What can you do, if anything?*

Arraying Opportunities for Improvement. The program here outlined should reveal many opportunities for departmental improvement. Indeed, many more should result than can practically be undertaken at any one time.

Some order of priority or preference should next be established. One such arrangement gives first place to those opportunities where improvement may result at minimum expenditure. Such a sequence permits the executive to initiate improvement at little or no cost to the company. Resulting accomplishments build personal credit with superiors, which in turn provides reason for increasing appropriations of funds as accomplishment continues and prestige increases.

EXECUTIVE CONDUCT. Begin by gaining approval of projects that call for little or no special cash outlay. Stay with these projects until measurable improvement is indicated and their continuance can safely be left to others. Then propose further undertakings where costs can be repaid from economies in the shortest possible period of time. As your proven reputation for results increases, you will ordinarily be able to increase the size of the appropriation requested and the length of time necessary to recoup the expenditures from savings made.

Q. *When arranging your projects as indicated above you note that your associates and employees, no less than your superiors, have an interest in the sequence which you propose. Some improvements are badly needed and wanted although costs are high and returns slow. Again, certain projects have had a long background of proposal and discussion and there will be some impatience aroused if these are not given early preference in your schedule. How will you deal with this situation?*

Time for Executive Improvement. Executives sometimes argue that the pressure of routine tasks is so exacting that they have no time or strength for improvement. It was Henry Ford who pointed out that every man of whatever rank in industry has exactly as much time as every other. When a man holds that he has no time for a given activity, he is usually saying that there is something else he would really rather do with his time.

EXECUTIVE CONDUCT. It is not necessary to discipline yourself here. The trick is to begin with *the kind of improvement that fascinates you.* Every one of us likes to improve. But we enjoy the privilege of choosing our own method where it is possible to do so.

Discussion. What is your response to the following comments?

1. *Improvement may be a normal part of anyone's existence, but to retain old habits is more normal than to change them. Changes of habits require discipline and self-control, which are acquired rather than natural traits.*

   How would your attitude toward this comment be affected if you lived in a static civilization where change did not occur? When we can adjust ourselves to life in a moving world, can we not act naturally thereafter?

2. *People return to previous methods of doing things because they are lazy and it is easier to do them the old way. Improvement takes more than incentives to make it last. It must be insisted upon.*

   Is helping a person to persevere in the use of improved methods the role of the taskmaster, the teacher, or the friend? Can it in part be the responsibility of management to see that employees are not allowed to backslide?

3. *Specialists in methods may be all right but they are apt to upset steady production and make the workers uneasy. Things run better in my department when they are not around.*

Should this necessarily be so? If not, what should be added to, or subtracted from, the situation in order that specialists may be made sincerely welcome? After all, are we not all specialists of a sort and to some degree?

4. *If I have to wait for morale to develop, I won't have a chance to make many improvements. Most people dislike change because it may make them think. Morale naturally lessens when changes of any sort are made.*

Do we need to wait for morale to develop or can we help its development? If so, just when should the inspiration be applied? Before or after the improvement? Do people object to thinking? Is there a difference between helping people to think and telling them to listen to what is said?

5. *There should be some way of forecasting extensive improvements (new processes, new materials, and the like) so that we do not waste our time intensively improving ways of doing things only to find that the process itself is becoming obsolete.*

Is research susceptible of forecast? If so, is it really research? What is necessary in order to be granted maximum time to change over from one basic method to another?

6. *I have a large backlog of opportunities for improvements now in my department. My problem is that top manage-*

ment will not approve action upon them or provide the money to go ahead with them.

Do you feel that it is management's primary responsibility to accept your ideas, or that it is your proper responsibility to persuade management that your ideas are good and should be tried?

7. *If we begin to take everything apart in the department, we soon won't have anything left together. Too many "why's" disturb employees.*

In actual practice what limits the number of "why's" that can be asked? Do all questions necessarily have to be asked when they are thought of?

8. *I can see plenty to do in my department without "new eyes." What I need are more employees who will keep their old eyes on their work and concentrate on output and quality.*

Will we find the kind of employees that we want, or will we have to develop them ourselves? What should we do when employees do not want to keep their attention on their work?

9. *There is no value in comparing the present with the past. What is done is done. Today's problems are different from yesterday's.*

When yesterday's equipment, arrangement, methods are applied to tomorrow's needs, is there not value in looking at yesterday's demands? In a changing world we cannot learn so much from the past as we can when there is no change. But can we not learn something? If so, just what?

10. *Pictures on paper may be all right, but it is straight-from-the-shoulder word pictures that count the most. If you tell your story straight, most people will listen and learn.*

> Word pictures certainly have their place, but is it always an appropriate place? Would we find it as easy to describe a motor tour without a map as with one? Are there not values that are found in charts, graphs, tables, and drawings that are not found in verbal reports? If so, just what are they?

11. *I doubt if facts have to be dressed up to make them effective. A fact is always in focus for the man who is trained to use it.*

> Can we risk the release of facts that are safe only in the hands of those trained to use them? Is putting facts in proper focus necessarily dressing them up? Cannot facts be misused to cause wrong inferences? If so, just how? And how can wrong inferences be safeguarded against?

12. *Verification sounds good, but I want men in my department whose work and whose loyalty I don't have to verify.*

> When men are working with other people's property, are they not entitled to the safeguarding of their own reputation by the use of verifications which prove the honesty of their acts?

13. *Comparisons are helpful but a competent executive should constantly be aware of what standard practice is in his field, without dragging it in to make an "improvement" out of it.*

How can we be sure that we, as executives, do know the exact state of the art at any given moment? How standard is standard practice in a constantly advancing industrial technology? Are improvements which bring us up to par with competition enough to enable us to overcome competition? How far are effective comparisons helpful? What do they lack? Does a knowledge of where we stand with respect to standard practice permit us to determine how much improvement is necessary to establish our leadership in the field?

CHAPTER 15

Executive Creativeness

In a world of increasing newness and rapidity of innovation the call upon human creativeness affects every aspect of industry and each stratum of the hierarchy of management. Not only is management called upon to manage the function of creativeness. Management must itself become increasingly creative.

Couple with this trend in our industrial requirements the presence of growing magnitude, growing mass detail, and growing complexity in the nature of our executive responsibilities, and it becomes obvious that fresh resources must be sought and drawn upon if we are to meet the challenges inherent in our work of today and tomorrow.

This entire development is still in its early stages. The purpose of this chapter is to consider historical aspects of these procedures and to describe certain devices for the stimulation of creativeness which experience has proved effective.

Background. In 1926 a distinguished English author and administrator, Graham Wallas, published his first edition of *The Art of Thought.*[1] Here he laid down the hypothesis that there appears to be a cycle of events pre-

[1] Jonathan Cape, Ltd., London, 1926.

ceding and following the discovery of a new idea or concept, which can be identified and employed in solving realistic intellectual problems where quantitative devices are still too limited to afford a solution by themselves and where creative thought is essential.

In his fourth chapter, entitled "Stages of Control," Wallas suggested four stages in the thought process, namely:

1. *Preparation*—in which the problem is investigated
2. *Incubation*—during which the problem is not consciously considered
3. *Illumination*—where the creative idea appears
4. *Verification*—when the validity of the solution is tested

In 1944, and quite without knowledge of Wallas's reasoning, James Webb Young published an essay, based on an address he had delivered to graduate students in the School of Business at the University of Chicago, entitled *A Technique for Producing Ideas*,[2] in which he summarized his procedure as:

1. The gathering of raw materials
2. The working over of these materials in the mind
3. The incubating stage
4. The actual birth of the idea

The similarity is at once obvious. Since this time other publications have appeared supporting and enlarging upon these general procedures.

[2] Advertising Publications, Inc., 8th ed., Chicago, 1953.

With the growing consciousness that creative thinking is not a privilege granted to only a favored few, there came the stimulus of new and effective procedures involved in research and development departments, which, though applied to technical problems, had equal pertinence in fields of management.

A number of homely devices have been employed by executives to capitalize more effectively upon the extraordinary capabilities of the human intellect when it is provided with untrammeled and stimulating opportunities for original thought.

The Nature of Executive Creativeness. Creative activities appropriate to the executive are characteristically not related to such matters as new products, new processes, or new operative methods. Such concerns are normally the bailiwick of technical specialists.

Executive creativeness is primarily addressed to the solution of problems involving dynamic relationships between people, incorporating such obstacles as the presence of important but intangible factors, competitive unknowns, and the ever-present difficulty of foretelling human response to yet untried stimuli. To find a solution to these complex and ramifying issues requires as high a degree of creative ability as do the creative responsibilities relating to products, processes, and facilities.

Executive creativeness is more heavily drawn upon as the speed of change, reflected in the enterprise and in the industry, increases. In these days of accelerative change, to keep a business running smoothly and effectively is as much a challenge to inventiveness and controlled imagination as to keep a product or a process competitively up to date.

Devices for Creative Thought

SLEEPING ON A PROBLEM. An old and well-tested device for dealing with a difficult executive problem has been that of charging the mind with facts of all sorts relating to the situation at hand and then sleeping on them. The next morning it is not unlikely that a simple solution will find its way into consciousness. In some instances this period of incubation has been extended to a week end or longer.

Q. *A distinguished American industrialist was approached by an acquaintance who asked whether he was willing to listen to a troublesome executive problem of long standing. The industrialist agreed. Subsequently he asked a number of searching questions, and then said: "Let me mull this over for a while and I'll drop you a note." Some three months later the inquirer received a letter from his mentor with an unorthodox but fundamentally sound suggestion which was successfully put into practice.*

The story is told that in the early days of the Ford Motor Car Company Henry Ford went to the Eastern seaboard to raise additional funds. He approached a prospective investor with a request for $10,000. After listening to the proposal, the capitalist informed Mr. Ford that he would advise him the next day of his decision, as he had made it a rule to sleep on all investment questions. Mr. Ford responded by saying that he was leaving for the Midwest on the night train and would require an answer before his departure. As a result, the investment was not *made. In later years the capitalist became widely known as "the man who did* not *invest in the Ford Motor Car Company."*

> Do these anecdotes throw light on areas of use for this technique?

OBJECTIVE AND OBSTACLE. A closely allied procedure often yields interesting practical results. Bisect the first page of a pad of writing paper with a horizontal line. Above the line state a given executive objective. After this statement put down the obstacles or difficulties in the way of attaining this objective. Repeat this procedure on additional pages until all executive problems are listed. Just before going to sleep, review these objectives and the corresponding obstacles.

The following morning upon waking, reread the list and jot down on the lower half of each sheet any ideas for overcoming the obstacles. By this process the mind is nightly fed with current objectives and obstacles and is as often milked for the results of the mulling process.

This procedure is not recommended for those who sleep poorly, for the mind so charged seems to remain subconsciously active and adequate rest may not be forthcoming for the normally light sleeper.

READING AND LISTENING. One executive has devised a slightly different technique. He procured a comfortable semi-reclining chair with an attached magazine rack at one side and a writing board with pencil and paper at the other.

One evening a week he would first review a pocket

notebook which contained a list of both current and long-term problems. He would then turn to his magazine rack, which contained periodicals and other literature allied to his field, and read a miscellany of articles, sometimes on subjects far removed from the issues immediately concerning him.

As he read, ideas would come to his mind, frequently having no relationship to the printed page but connected subconsciously to the problems with which his mind was charged. When this occurred, he would quickly jot down the notion, having found from experience that the best ideas were often the most evanescent and difficult to recall. He carried on this practice for many years.

SOLITAIRE. When the mind is tensioned with a problem, the playing of solitaire has been found helpful by more than one industrialist. The game seems to activate the mind in semi-routine ways which permit "the filaments of brain tissue, in a hidden and mysterious process, to make innumerable couplings and at last send through into consciousness an opinion." [3]

PHYSICAL EXERCISE. A friend of mine who is athletically inclined has found the interspersing of physical exercise, such as squash, badminton, or strenuous canoe paddling, with periods of intensive thought to be helpful when he has particularly difficult problems to solve.

ENVIRONMENT. Again, we find Helmholtz, a great German physicist, describing the way in which his most important new thoughts had come to him. He said that

[3] Edward D. Jones, *The Administration of Industrial Enterprises*, rev. ed., Longmans, Green & Co., Inc., New York, 1935.

after previous investigation of the problem "in all directions . . . happy ideas came unexpectedly without effort, like an inspiration. . . . They came particularly readily during the slow ascent of wooded hills on a sunny day."

There is a widespread belief among those of the Quaker faith that the presence of a scenic vista is particularly helpful when there is an involved problem to solve. In some unknown fashion the optical perspective seems to stimulate the intellectual.

All these devices as presented are merely indicative of possibilities for the development of executive skills in the industrial art of creative thought.

An Example of Creative Executive Thought. The president of a medium-sized company manufacturing jewelers' supplies found himself with a sense of uncertainty and a concern for the future of his business. Economic conditions had been increasingly favorable over a period of years and were still showing signs of further advance.

The president set out to obtain as many facts as possible concerning the current and future situation. In this endeavor he approached his own sales department, his statistical division, his banker, the secretary of his trade association, and an economic consultant. Gathering together the resulting data, he proceeded to acquaint himself completely with their contents.

Then, said he, "I let the matter drop and for the next few days gave my thoughts to other matters. One night at

3:00 A.M. I found myself sitting upright in bed with the answer clear before me."

Thereupon the president proceeded to liquidate inventories, trim unnecessary activities, and in all ways prepare for a decline. When the break in business conditions eventually occurred, the company assets were in liquid form and inventories at a minimum.

As the decline continued, he studied and prepared for a decision as to the turn of events. Once again he chose an effective moment in which to stock his plant with necessary supplies and materials, to purchase new equipment, and to make other preparations for the rise which ultimately occurred.

Upon being questioned, he stated that the procedure was nothing new in his experience; it had been the result of a great deal of thought following upon his appointment to the presidency, for in the years before he took over this office the vacillating day-to-day policies of his predecessors had nearly wrecked the company.

Conclusion. The application of creative techniques in industry is multiform. Problem seminars, buzz sessions, brain storming, to say nothing of highly developed procedures in the technical areas—all reflect the widespread interest in and necessity for consideration of this important facet of industrial management.

This chapter has dealt in a fragmentary way with only one aspect of this problem—namely, the ways in which the executive can increase his own creative and constructive abilities as he finds himself forced to deal with new and rapidly evolving change, with its multiplication of human and economic problems, difficulties, and opportunities.

Discussion. What is your response to the following comments?

1. *The assembling of facts before undertaking the solution of an executive problem merely reflects common sense. There is nothing particularly unusual here. Given the facts, any problem can be solved.*

   Are all the facts usually available in executive problems? What type of fact is particularly difficult to obtain?

2. *Incubation of problems is an attractive alternative to prompt attack upon a current difficulty. It appears to be a polite excuse for procrastination.*

   Why are executives urged to think and plan well ahead? What difficulties face an executive who is attempting to solve a problem—other than its inherent complexity?

3. *Happy ideas are always welcome. My experience has been that they are more often the product of perspiration than of inspiration.*

   How does the mind function when it is hard at work? Precisely what is hard mental work? Is it entirely a conscious activity?

4. *I see no more reason for creative thought now than at any previous time. We always have need for imagination, provided it doesn't go too far.*

   Do you believe we are living at a more rapid tempo than ever before? What has been the history of industrial change? Has it taken place faster or more slowly as time has passed?

CHAPTER 16

Executive Self-development

Executive training courses originating both within and without the plant have been rapidly increasing in number. Yet a great unexplored area is that of executive self-development. The importance of this field goes without saying. We appreciate its significance when we realize the obvious necessity of executive self-development if our managerial leadership is to keep pace with the rapidly developing techniques of manufacturing which result from research and development. In our quickening, expanding, ramifying industrial world it is only logical that new and greater executive knowledge and skill are called for if we are not to become slaves to our growing responsibilities. Yet the opportunity for specialized formal training may not be vouchsafed to each of us. We then must rely upon our own efforts—our own self-development.

Self-development and Personal Objective. The objectives to be sought through self-development may properly vary widely. For example, we may find in entering upon executive responsibilities that our first task is working for others—fitting ourselves into accepted patterns. At this early stage, self-development may take the form of developing an understanding of the pattern of activity and how it works, of learning the routines and following the rules as laid down. Self-discipline is required to obey the requirements of the pattern, to fit into the complex and to become a part of it.

Once this has been established and our performance is satisfactory in the eyes of our superior, we may turn to ways and means for advancing our efforts toward the upper limit of our talents or capacities, and thereby find the optimum working accomplishment for us. Here discipline is required to restrict our ambitions to attainable limits and yet to urge us to press forward, beyond acceptable minimums of effort. To keep growing, we must try to grow.

Only then, it can be argued, are we ready for executive authority over others. The goal of self-development here is our ability to motivate others by setting them a stimulating and challenging example. Self-development is the road to self-control, and self-control is the beginning of executive control.

Q. *Are there other aspects of self-development that apply particularly to the executive on the new job? Is it desirable that the new executive should have "won his spurs" in the eyes of his subordinates, and this before he has been elevated to his new position? Are there any opportunities for executive self-development that are open to the beginner before he assumes executive duties but that will not be available to him after he receives his executive assignment?*

A second general objective for self-development may take the form of long-term goals. Many people attempt self-development without a clear idea of the end purpose to be accomplished. Most of us have no time or energy to spend upon aspects of self-development that will not be directly helpful to us in reaching our long-range objectives, either personal or professional.

But long-range goals and current activities may not harmonize with one another. Not infrequently the attainment of a long-term objective requires immediate self-denials, if not sacrifices. It is here that the presence of a general plan for one's future development is especially valuable.

Q. *A young man employed in a staff position in a medium-sized factory was assigned activities giving him the run of the plant. He decided to make use of this opportunity to develop as many first-name acquaintances among supervisors and employees as possible, with the thought that at a later time, should he be given executive status, these contacts would be valuable to him.*

In this instance, would the long-term objective create any current difficulty or need for self-denial?

A third objective for self-development may be that of all-round, or balanced, skills. One approach to this aim is the assessment of one's needs and lacks. Here we establish the areas in which we are found wanting and concentrate upon these fields rather than spread our efforts superficially over a great many fields in which only marginal values may lie.

A fourth approach is through the analysis of our accomplishments to determine upon those areas of personal activity where our self-development may produce the most definite achievements.

As executives we are confronted with a variety of problems. To them we apply our ingenuity, training, education, experience. Decisions are made, action is authorized, and a degree of accomplishment results. It is when we compare these results with the goals originally aimed for that we can measure our discrepancies and undertake constructive measures. This procedure forces us to be practical in the search for avenues leading toward personal improvement and to face squarely those instances where our concepts may be at odds with basic realities or trends in the environment in which our efforts take place.

Q. *Benjamin Franklin listed for himself all the "necessary or desirable" virtues and then concentrated upon each in sequence, for a period of time, thereby bringing a certain equality or balance of emphasis into his program of self-betterment.*

> Would you favor this procedure for the industrial executive?

A fifth and final objective is that of enabling the executive better to deal with accelerative change and its constantly shifting demands upon his capabilities. Here a new balance in the coterie of managerial skills is necessary. Newcomers in the spectrum of executive qualifications, such as versatility, increased awareness, ability and adaptability in adjustment to increasing change, assume new importance. A self-development program that emphasizes these executive requirements and qualifications is a program attuned to the future as well as the present.

Techniques of Self-development. With our objectives carefully chosen and sharply defined, we are in a position to consider the way we shall go about our task of self-development. Here the beginning of all wisdom is that self-development is a growth activity. It is something over and above our daily duties, our habitual activities, our regular work habits. It is an addition to our general scheme of things. It is a *plus* responsibility.

Once we face and accept this fact, the next step follows readily. If self-development is intrinsically something "over and above," it follows that the thought, the time, the energy to be given to self-development must come from our reserve, or surplus, resources. If we are to succeed in our endeavor to grow in effectiveness, we should assemble personal time, energy, and attentiveness to apply to our task. This means that *we should plan to withdraw such resources from other, less important, activities and concentrate them upon the special objective that we have set ourselves.* This is the rock upon which many well-meaning attempts at self-development have foundered. Entering upon our task of self-improvement with enthusiasm, we cheerfully take on additional demands upon our limited resources and sooner or later find that we are wearing ourselves out before our goal has been reached. One of the prerequisites of self-development is that we should grow in strength as we proceed; obviously this cannot be attained if we are drawing too heavily upon our reserves of energy. When we hear someone say that he has no time to read, for example, we know that he is really saying that there are other things he deems it more important to do.

EXECUTIVE CONDUCT. Make for yourself a reasonable estimate of the time and effort necessary to give your new program a proper chance of success. Then examine your day, your week, your month, and decide upon those present activities (loafing may be one) that you will dispense with in finding a place for your project.

Q. *A distinguished financier equipped his town house with a magnificent library. Each morning he arose early, breakfasted, and then spent exactly thirty minutes reading from his vast collection—usually on topics in no sense related to his current financial problems. Thereupon he would go to his office.*

Why did he choose this period of the day for this activity?

There is a further concern or hazard in connection with our final accomplishment that we should not overlook. It is what might be called the novelty factor. How often do we embark upon a new undertaking, filled with enthusiasm, interest, and a stimulating sense of newness, only to find, as the days pass, that it has lost its savor and has somehow been relegated to a less important place in our scheme of things.

Now there is no harm in the presence of novelty. Indeed, one of the characteristics of life in the United States today has been said to be the prevalence of newness. But we should make sure that we do not confuse its inherent temporariness with the steady, invincible, slogging, down-the-middle-of-the-road personal endeavor that is essential to our complete self-achievement.

EXECUTIVE CONDUCT. A good way to capitalize upon the element of novelty is so to plan your approach and initial activities that you can point to some satisfying mark of progress about the time that your initial enthusiasm begins to wane. If, when the newness wears off, you are able to see some definite advance, you will find in it a satisfaction that will more than compensate for the lack of novelty.

A second problem with which we must contend concerns a familiar human characteristic. We call it habit. Here is perhaps one of our most useful propensities, but one that has definitely mulish tendencies. Habits are extraordinarily hard to alter. More than this, they frequently give the impression of having been changed when in reality they have only been lying "doggo," awaiting a propitious moment to return to full influence upon our behavior. We set up a revised daily or weekly schedule in order to adjust our available time to a program of self-development, we put it into motion, it appears to work well; we swerve our attention, and suddenly we find ourselves back in the old routine.

Q. *A story goes that a farmer was approached by a young representative of the state agricultural department, who urged him to take advantage of the advisory services which were available. The farmer demurred at this suggestion, saying: "I know now how to farm twice as good as I'm doing."*

What was he trying to say?

The redesigning of our habits is one of the commonest difficulties to be found in the technique of personal improvement. There are at least four ways in which the permanent overcoming of previous habits has been approached.

The first might be described as the use of enforcement measures. Here the user finds a way by which new habits are self-enforced. For example, a person desiring to learn to speak a given language arranges to live in a family where only this language is spoken and understood.

Perhaps the most extraordinary application of such enforcement is in the regulations effecting daylight saving. Millions of people willingly arise an hour earlier by a trick of time-changing which alters old habits and enforces new ones—a desired accomplishment that few of the individuals affected would bring about by personal determination or resolution.

A second device may be described as the use of rewards or penalties. In this instance we so organize our project that it will either bring us some greatly-to-be-hoped-for satisfaction or incorporate a much-to-be-avoided penalty. An example of the latter would be enrolling in a course of home study and paying the entire tuition in advance. By this device the student-to-be ensures his continuing interest and application through his natural desire to get his money's worth.

Rewards for self-accomplishment are almost always present in some degree. Yet it often is possible to sharpen or clarify such returns in a way that will make them doubly attractive. For example, if the undertaking is one which may ultimately contribute to our advance in the organization, it is certainly to our interest to do well at it, but we are even more eager for results if there is a certain desired opening now available for which our new skill is a prerequisite.

A third device is the use of stints; these may take the form of short-term increments of progress which, when added together, comprise total accomplishment. The human creature has a curious tendency to rise to an immediate challenge—to measure himself against today's standard, to reach for the satisfactions to be found in the successful attainment of a stint which may be but a small part of the entire effort.

For example, so simple a device as the scheduling of daily stints of effort on the numeral faces of a monthly calendar, permitting of their being blocked out when the task unit has been performed, often provides an extraordinary visual stimulus toward the continuance and ultimate completion of self-imposed tasks.

A fourth device, if one may call it such, is the incorporation into the task of self-development of the spirit of good nature—of lightness of heart, of fun. It has long been recognized that growth is highly dependent upon environment and that when the environment is pleasant, learning is advanced and memory strengthened. There are those who feel so strongly in support of this principle that they will refrain from any community activities where their services are contributory if they cannot be assured that there will be, for them, pleasure and satisfaction in the doing. We change our habits more readily when we are convinced that the new way is more satisfying, more enjoyable, than the old.

In self-development there are certain precautions to be observed. Our first concern should be to find ways of compensating for the absence of the formalized teacher contacts to which we became accustomed in our school days. More than this, there was the stimulus of the group of which we were a part. In beginning a program of self-development, we should be sure that we make up in some way for these lacks.

Again, self-development is a dynamic activity. For example, we should properly proceed somewhat modestly at the outset. Then, as we progress, we may increase the effort. Thus when laying out a program we should take care, first, not to become overambitious and aim for too difficult an accomplishment and, second, not to become overconfident and undertake too long a program.

There is another principle at work here. We have heard the old saying that soldiers must taste blood. In less gory terms the same is true in the area of self-improvement. Visible, measurable accomplishment is a remarkable motivator. If we are continually to carry forward our own self-development, we must take care to arrange for ample encouragement along the way. To attain the satisfaction of self-development we should begin in a small way; we should set subgoals and goals that are not too difficult and not too far distant.

Q. *A teacher of hobby handicrafts first assigned tasks which yielded a simple finished product after half an hour's work. At the end of the course his students had built up staying power and perseverance, resulting in the completion of thirty-six-hour projects.*

Is this idea applicable to executive self-development?

A further precaution: Self-development activities are curiously delicate things, especially at the beginning. Always they carry a strong tinge of experimentation. They require for best usage a considerable degree of flexibility and an atmosphere of privacy, not to say secretiveness.

So we wisely will not talk too much about our objectives, plans, and accomplishments outside the friendly environment of our homes or of the boss's office. Little by little, as we gain facility in progress, we may be better able to discuss our problems, our opportunities, and our achievements with others.

Finally, we can go too far. We know people who have so fully dedicated themselves to the improvement of their future that they have sacrificed the homely joys and pleasantries of the present and the immediate responses to immediate happenings, with the result that they seem not of this world. When we talk with them, we get the feeling that their attention is not really upon us or our topic but upon something over our shoulder that is coming nearer. We leave them with a mixture of uncertainty and awe and are glad when we may return to less exalted folk. The person who lives largely apart from his neighbors in point of future time may be good medicine but he is not good company.

Opportunities for Self-development. Opportunities for executive self-improvement are precisely as numerous as the activities which the executive performs or wishes to perform. Indeed, in order to take advantage of these opportunities, the executive need only apply a single technique of self-development, one which is not only promising but convenient and well within his reach.

This technique is the discovery and use of evaluative devices to measure the effectiveness of our efforts in whatever we do. With this principle firmly rooted, we do not consider an executive task completed until we have applied some form of evaluation to our achievement and decided how to do it better the next time. In some cases we are in a position to measure our accomplishment almost as soon as it occurs and can be continuously informed as to the effectiveness of our efforts. This immediate evaluation, which has been nicknamed "feedback," is rapidly being applied wherever such immediacy of information allows us to better our efforts constantly as we go along.

It is fair to say that no other self-betterment device so surely makes us aware of the multiplicity and variety of opportunities for self-improvement as does the application of evaluative measures.

Q. *Does the use of feedback (immediate evaluation) satisfy all objectives in executive self-development? When is it particularly valuable? Under what circumstances does the evaluation of one's current efforts fail to offer complete satisfaction as a device for self-development?*

Any classification of executive opportunities for self-development invites criticism, because such opportunities do not truly relate to each other in simple linear terms (as do clothespins on a clothesline). Nevertheless, we must arrange them in some such sequential order so that we may write and talk about them. So let us first consider managerial opportunities.

Managerial Self-development. Curiously enough, this is the area where we are least troubled by our method of approach. This is because most of the principles of good management that we apply in our daily work as executives are identical with those that we may apply to ourselves. In other words, good management is good self-management.

Let us be specific. Each of the concepts, the procedures, the basic fundamentals that we apply at our executive workplace—such as the concepts of defining objectives, planning for their attainment, organizing for operation, control of procedures, motivation of personnel, and evaluation of results—are equally applicable to our own constructive endeavors. The development and use of standards of time, energy, and space, of economies through analytical devices, classification, and foresight and forecast are equally pertinent to personal or self-management.

Even personnel relations are not exempted from use. As we deal with ourselves, we find many instances where the direction of the mind and will may differ from the wishes of our physical selves.

I remember reading of a great warrior who, when he found himself responding to the hazards about him, said, "So you tremble, Body! You will tremble more when I take you to the top of yonder hill!"

Self-leadership is no empty phrase. The truth is that each one of us is managing himself constantly. Indeed, all the elements in the round of management which we have spoken of as objective, plan, organization, control, motivation, and evaluation take place whenever we light a cigarette!

Our problem of self-development in managerial areas, then, is to find ways to direct our present knowledge of good management so that we, no less than the job itself, may benefit.

Q. *As a young industrial engineer, the author was given access to a course of study in what was then called personal efficiency. Time-saving methods in daily routines of dressing, shaving, and the like were outlined; comparative studies of shortest routes between home and work were recommended; the planning of personal work schedules and the application of standardization procedures to wearing apparel and desk facilities were described. Today, emphasis upon managerial self-improvement includes many additional suggestions and opportunities.*

If so, what would they be?

Social Self-development. This category includes a wide gamut of possibilities. Chief among them I would place acquaintanceship. A great resource to the executive is an extensive range of acquaintance which affords him the privilege of comparing ideas, of trying out notions, and often of obtaining experienced and dependable counsel and advice. Many executives consider this opportunity sufficiently important to justify setting up filing systems and other paraphernalia to ensure against the loss of such contacts, once established.

EXECUTIVE CONDUCT. Time is necessary to improve your acquaintanceship, and memory is often fleeting. Therefore this opportunity does require some vehicle or implement whereby individuals are not overlooked or forgotten with the passage of time. An address book conveniently stored in your traveling bag and the practice of daily review and entry before sleep, when traveling about, especially to conferences or group gatherings, have been found to serve as a practical approach. In any event, don't trust your memory unless it is unusually dependable.

Another area for social self-development is that of extraplant activities, such as community work, associational activities, and church endeavors. Self-development here yields many returns. We have opportunity to meet and to work with high-minded folk. A wise person once said that our best friends are the people whom we work with. Again, we learn the important skill of getting things done when our collaborators no less than we are working without remuneration. And of even greater importance, we may discover latent talents of our own, the exercise of which will bring us much future satisfaction.

Finally, we become an indirect resource to our employer in that anything that we may accomplish in the way of betterment will redound to the company as well as to ourselves.

EXECUTIVE CONDUCT. The way to begin here is to begin. Accept, initially, some helpful responsibility that is not too entailing of time and energy and that can be undertaken at periods convenient to you, your employer, and your family.

Such opportunities are normally not difficult to find. To make yourself available for activities in which (1) you expect no remuneration and (2) you expect no credit usually provides a chance to get under way. The learning process here is largely one of cause and effect. You will have opportunity to witness individual and group success and failure. By making such observations you will gradually discover the principles governing effective contributive efforts. For example, one such principle is that human beings are naturally gregarious—naturally cooperative—and cooperation will normally proceed if there is nothing to prevent it.

There are many opportunities for executive self-development in areas of social skills. Here I do not refer to "parlor manners" but to those auxiliary skills of communication so essential in today's world. The preparation of reports and memoranda, the use of visuals, rapid reading, public speaking, conference leadership, and the like—each has a literature of its own where paths of self-improvement are clearly indicated. These developed abilities are now seen as essential implements in social relationships.

EXECUTIVE CONDUCT. Practice makes perfect. Pick out one of these skills that has a particular appeal for you. Find some literature dealing with its development. Prepare a schedule of progress to measure against as you proceed. Then go ahead and enjoy the process.

Intellectual Self-development. When we think of intellectual development, we think of books—and rightly. No one has yet discovered a more advantageous ratio in the transfer of knowledge than that of the time spent by an author in writing a book compared with the time spent by the reader in reading it. In a matter of a few hours, information can be comprehended that may have taken years to accumulate, organize, print, and distribute. And we should not omit from our statement the reading of fiction, for, though it is not truth, it must reflect the truths of human relationships if it is to satisfy its readers. Opportunities here are so numerous as to defy listing. Biography, history, philosophy, science—to mention only a few—are areas where literature for self-development is readily at hand. Indeed, the possibilities are so vast as to become formidable in themselves. The answer to the riddle lies in the application of a human quality which is to be found in some degree in each of us—the quality of curiosity.

EXECUTIVE CONDUCT. Find an area that you would like to know more about. Find a librarian. Tell her that you want to read the most interesting book in this field. Take it home. Find the most comfortable chair in the house. Get a good light. Then thumb through the book. If you come upon any chapter of special interest, scan it. Get acquainted. Then read a little—not too much. Leave yourself hungry for more. Then put the book in a convenient place. Don't let reading it become a duty. Read it for enjoyment.

Books are not the only road to self-improvement. Conversations are another. We may gain a great deal of value in these days of specialization by learning from people whose work involves disciplines other than ours. A successful industrialist spends a pleasurable amount of time with his neighbors who are largely professional men. He finds that their point of view, their facility in different fields of effort, and their widely varied experiences bring him new concepts and stimulate his thinking.

Last in this category we may place the opportunity for self-development in general awareness of the current state of the industrial art, of the general business situation, of the state of human relationships which exist within and without the plant. Here is a real challenge to both ingenuity and determination. One of the growing problems in the accelerating industrial world is that of maintaining a current familiarity with what is going on as it relates to your industry and thereby indirectly to yourself. There are few if any courses of study, books, or periodicals that may be relied upon in any major way to fill your needs. Your self-development here will be the ultimate mastery of the knack of finding the necessary source data and then contriving so that it will flow to you with completeness, immediacy, and accuracy, and with a minimum of demand upon your time.

EXECUTIVE CONDUCT. Your first business here is to find out precisely what you want to be continually informed about, then to discover the source of such information, if any, and finally to establish ways to sluice the data to you. There is rarely any completion point to this project, as new forms of information will frequently be required and the sources of your facts will also be changing. Such an activity undertaken as a way of developing your own industrial awareness may ultimately serve to increase your direct value in your enterprise. In any event, being well informed in this area will make your job and your relationships more interesting and profitable.

Emotional Self-development. Some people never grow up. As Joseph M. Dodge so trenchantly puts it: [1]

> Many people are grown up physically but not mentally. There may be instability, a running to extremes of thought and emotion or action. This can manifest itself in violent likes and dislikes; extremes of friendliness or antagonism toward business associates and subordinates; anxiety for action without proper counsel or consideration; and ill-founded or immovably fixed opinions.

For each of us there is much opportunity for self-development here. But the way is not too easy. For one thing, it is difficult for us to see ourselves truly. As Bobby Burns sang:

[1] *The Business of Managing,* Detroit Bank, Detroit.

O wad some Pow'r the giftie gie us
To see oursels as others see us!

For another, our emotional make-up is a complex business and the road to improvement is often difficult to perceive. Yet self-development in these areas is entirely possible. For example, an executive disability may take the form of a fiery temper. A distinguished judge, of Spanish background, in an address to a graduating class, described his struggle over a period of years to master this problem—which he finally completely succeeded in doing.

A challenging field for self-development closely akin to this is that of emotional consistency. There are those of us whose mood is unpredictable, whose outward state of mind fluctuates widely, depending upon a variety of influences, both within and without our work environment. Here again the desired quality of consistency may call for an objective appraisal of our situation and a planned program to introduce into our response to difficulties a greater degree of emotional balance.

Self-development may also turn from the correction of obvious personal weaknesses to the cultivation of constructive executive virtues. For example, the development of a positive approach to executive challenges or difficulties is becoming an important resource when dealing with people. Personality is made up of diverse constituents. We are all part angel and part devil, and the art of leadership is to a great degree the ability to appeal to the positive, constructive, forward-looking, optimistic, cheerful side of the personalities with which we deal. Yet to do this consistently and continuously often calls for self-development on our part.

One approach to these matters is to reverse the field of the problem and ask ourselves: "What are the positive emotional qualities which I should hope to find in my boss?" With this question answered, it is not difficult to ask again: "To what extent am I reflecting these qualities in my personal dealings with others?" Answers to these questions provide us with starting points for further emotional self-development.

A great administrator once remarked that "the art of influencing people is no art at all," meaning that leadership, to be effective, must contain a quality of naturalness as well as sincerity. This would seem to pose a problem, until we realize that each of us has, within his make-up, many differing facets to reflect his light. We have our greatest moments when our best selves come to the surface of our personalities. The trick of life is to keep them there—in their naturalness.

Avocational Self-development. An area of growing importance in our present-day world is that of our avocations, our recreations, our hobbies. With the trends toward greater leisure, it is becoming clear that lying in a hammock will not be enough, while to drive a car is merely to transpose a vehicle of transportation, which is already an adjunct to our daily work, into new applications. Something more is needed.

At this stage of inquiry we frequently find ourselves facing an unexpected obstacle. We have no difficulty with the idea of learning how to play—of self-development in the fun of doing some useless thing well. Indeed, as we ponder how to spend our leisure, we readily give importance to avocational pursuits and promptly make time for them. The obstacle which concerns us is just how to become proficient in this new skill without making public fools of ourselves in the process.

The trouble is that most of the outdoor sports or games of skill, such as golf, tennis, badminton, skeet, swimming, and the like, involve the inevitable presence of spectators, who appear to take satanic delight in commenting to their friends upon the exact nature of our initial deficiencies. No one likes to do poorly before an audience. Yet we must begin somewhere, and obviously we shall start out in an atmosphere of awkwardness, uncertainty, and error.

The truth is that we are witnessing within ourselves a full-blown demonstration of false pride. Everyone knows the problems confronting the beginner in any field. Everyone sympathizes with the novice. Those who watch us are hoping that we will do well; for they were novices themselves and they know how we feel. Self-development here, to be effective, will contain a goodly lump of humility, and this is as it should be. To put our pride in our pocket and do our best when our best is still none too good is a rewarding experience for all of us.

Q. *How may we allocate our time to create a balance between the fixed amount of time available for recreational* *activities and the considerable amount of time required to develop excellence in a recreational skill?*

Q. *How may we measure the effect of avocational self-development upon our working effectiveness?*

The returns from avocational self-development are large. Satisfaction in accomplishment may be realized to a degree which the executive task provides only on a longer-term basis. There is a certain pleasure in complete preoccupation with a hobby that cannot be experienced in any other way. And there is an opportunity for self-expression that can be present only when the task performed is without economic or social purpose. As in the instance of social self-development, the avocation once again offers us opportunity to test our accomplishments against our capacities and thus to grow in the knowledge of our natural talents and propensities.

Spiritual Self-development. We should not lay aside the opportunities for self-development without considering the ways in which we may approach the field of spiritual self-development.

With the Judaeo-Christian doctrine holding as it does that spiritual faith rests upon acceptance of belief in the fatherhood of God and the brotherhood of man, it might well be argued that any so-called self-development will inevitably include both relationships with the Deity and with one's fellow men.

Be this as it may, we can be sure that there are infinite possibilities for personal growth here for each one of us.

To suggest ways and means would be both unseemly and unwise. We may say only that there can be no greater human satisfaction than the certainty, as time passes, that we are steadily and surely growing and serving in the sight of God.

Conclusion. It may quite properly be questioned whether a chapter on such a topic as executive self-development has pertinence in a treatise on executive control. In 1924, when the first edition of this book came from the press, the author too would have been inclined to be skeptical. But times have changed and needs have grown over these more than thirty years.

Today we are living in a hastening world. Our thoughts, our decisions, our attitudes, and our relationships with others cannot help being greatly affected by the accelerations which are taking place all about us. That this geometric growth is good is attested by all who partake of it. The extraordinary powers of human creativeness, when released in orderly forms of research and development, are proving a mammoth cornucopia pouring out new contributions to our rising standards of living.

As executives we should fit our talents to the changing opportunities before us. To lead, we must be "men of the hour." To lag only renders us easy prey to obsolescence. These are days replete with growth and progress. Let us become worthy of the compliment that Abraham Lincoln once paid a man, when he said: "His powers are constantly expanding."

Discussion. What is your response to the following comments?

1. *My personal objective in self-development is to make more money. There are plenty of ambitions I can satisfy once I get the cash.*

Money-making ambitions have been known to put people in jail. What place should money hold in self-development? Is money the only return to be sought through self-development? Is money an objective or a reward for proper objectives?

2. *Good management may be good self-management, but I have known men who could manage themselves but could not manage others.*

Have you known any executives who were excellent managers of others and yet lacked control over themselves?

3. *I am not in favor of activities where we are called upon to do something for nothing. Too often enemies instead of friends result. People don't enjoy being objects of charity.*

Are there not areas where contributions of time and ability enable improvements to be made that otherwise would never occur? Is helpfulness necessarily to be viewed as charity?

4. *I doubt if reading for enjoyment ever results in self-development. To read for enjoyment is to entertain oneself, and entertainment is usually more amusing than instructive. Books that have helped me have been books that I have had to work hard over, and there was no fun in that.*

Is it possible to find both enjoyment and value in a well-written book? Must books be hard going in order to promote self-development?

5. *Current familiarity with what is going on in your industry is good in theory. But if your time spent in watching competition and the state of the art is devoted to improving your own business, you will be better off.*

What has been the history of companies that have maintained a policy of isolation in their industry? What does a company lose by such a policy?

6. *My problem is not so much dealing with the angel and the devil in us as it is battering sense into the heads of idiots and fools. Self-development for me is how to deal more forcibly with plain unadulterated stupidity in the people who report to me.*

How would you diagnose this point of view? Of what is it symptomatic? How may this problem be more constructively approached?

7. *This idea of taking up hobbies or outdoor skills leaves me cold. When I'm not on the job, I am resting and getting in shape to go back and hit the work hard. I have no desire to learn how to do some useless thing well. There are too many useful achievements still waiting to be accomplished to cause me to fool with activities that don't increase the pay check.*

Can we be sure that avocational pursuits are completely without influence upon our success? What seems to be the trend of the times? Is the trend good or bad? If the former, do we want to be leaders or followers? What is best for us in the long run?

CHAPTER 17

Executive Proficiency

To be proficient is to be well advanced in skill. To be proficient is to enjoy the thrill of finished technique. There is a kind of master craftsmanship in executive control, and it demands as much of you in the way of rigorous self-training, devotion to high standards, and constant self-discipline as does distinction in any art.

There are those executives whose crude technique barely covers the necessities, earning for them a sort of day-to-day continuance of their responsibilities. There are those executives who, believing in skill for skill's sake, operate on much higher levels of effectiveness. These men win admiration and respect, but their greatest satisfaction comes from the doing of a finished job.

There are well-defined ways in which this higher quality of accomplishment shows itself. There is a certain *quiet swiftness* which is characteristic of the department whose executive is master of his technique. The delight in silent dispatch makes the high-grade executive quite willing to pay the price of meticulous planning, careful relating of means to ends, and painstaking coordination of resources.

There is a certain characteristic *smoothness of operation* which marks the technique of the able executive. His department seems free from crises; activities are carried on evenly and steadily; one gets the impression of a well-oiled, smoothly running machine. Indeed, in some instances this virtue is misjudged, and onlookers remark: "What an easy job he has! No troubles ever come his way." Sometimes the executive does not disabuse them of their ignorance, does not tell them of the long hard thinking whereby future difficulties are detected and avoided or prevented. And he may not tell them of the strict self-discipline of supervision and review maintained in order that he may be completely aware of departmental happenings, that he may always be in command of detail.

The proficient executive has acquired a certain *ready responsiveness* to severe demands upon his department. Indeed, he takes pride in dealing easily with difficult assignments. Nothing that his chief proposes seems to disconcert him. This is not a pose; it is a quality of spirit which is effective only when it permeates his whole organization, when there is the feeling of solidarity known as *esprit de corps*.

Finally, there is a characteristic *habit of advance* in all the departmental undertakings. Improvement has been accepted as one of the normal accompaniments of operation. Employees expect and receive encouragement to this end, but they do not anticipate praise, because progress is commonplace with them. Only executives who have demanded continuous growth of themselves can understand the denials and disciplines which it entails. Yet its rewards are sweet, for it lies at the basis of security. No philosophy of proficiency is complete without the element of steady development.

There are other telltale signs of mastery in the relationship between the executive and his subordinates. When you find employees turning to their chief for advice concerning their personal difficulties, you may be sure that he is something more than a mere order giver. When you notice the contagious cheerfulness which he spreads, you know that there is something about his presence that is more than a symbol of authority. When you hear past employees speak well of him, when you hear men who have been disciplined say, "The best thing that ever happened to me was when he laid the cards on the table and told me some plain facts," you can be certain that he is something more than an impersonal dispenser of justice.

Proficiency reveals itself sharply in the relationships between executives. Men of this caliber who take real pride in their work tend to draw more closely together. Mutual understanding and confidence increase. Ideas ordinarily requiring lengthy presentation they may express to each other in a few words. Much time is saved in conference and collaboration. A family spirit develops. When mistakes are made, they are viewed only as such; motives remain unquestioned. When widespread differences of opinion develop, regard is not affected. Mutual praise among such men is rare. "He is a good man" usually represents the height of the compliment, but it will mean much.

The executive who has earned a reputation for proficiency enters into a new relationship with his superior, a relationship incorporating new elements of mutual admiration and respect. Formality tends to disappear, except on official occasions. Austerity is replaced by friendliness; compliments often take other forms than words. When the chief sends for his subordinate and says, "I have been considering a change in personnel policy; I'd like your opinion," this is a high form of praise.

EXECUTIVE CONDUCT. Don't miss the experiences which accompany proficiency. They provide some of the greatest satisfactions in life. To earn a living as an executive may be a vital and essential accomplishment, but the difference between doing merely this and attaining really high levels of accomplishment may be the difference between dull existence and a fascinating life.

There is a thrill in doing things well. There is a tremendous enjoyment in clean-cut achievement. The philosophy of quality for quality's sake brings rich returns.

Discussion. Assuming that the following complimentary remarks were made about an executive of your acquaintance, just how would you explain his proficiency?

1. *His department runs like a watch. No hurry or flurry, but everyone on the job and things getting done. I don't know how he manages it.*

2. *His department accomplishes more with less apparent effort than any other division. He certainly knows the trick of getting results.*

3. The thing that pleases us most is his absolute dependability. You can give him a difficult job and never have to think of it again. He doesn't require follow-up.

4. It's a curious thing, but I get more requests from employees for transfer to his department than to all the others put together. His wage scale is no higher, and the work is less pleasant if anything. But everybody wants to work for him.

5. They tell me that last spring some of the men learned that he was to put his boat in the water on a certain Saturday afternoon. Although no one was asked, between ten and fifteen of them "just happened to come down" to the beach to help.

6. His department has been a sort of incubator for executives. During the last ten years I should guess that a third of our new bosses have come from his division.

7. Everybody smiles when he comes into meeting. You like him, even when he's disagreeing with you. And he is a mighty good man when it comes to difficult labor situations. The men all swear by him, and he has a way of making the right thing seem obvious.

8. About once a year we call on him to explain how he gets his low unit costs, but he just says, "Well, I don't know. The boys could answer that question better than I could." The truth is, they work like Trojans for him—and enjoy it.

CHAPTER 18

Executive Reading

Much of the current data on executive techniques is in the form of periodical articles; these are particularly valuable because of their reflection of immediate problems and the equally immediate attempts at their solution.

Here the use of periodical indexes is most desirable. Practically all public libraries and many plant libraries subscribe to one or more of the following services:

The Industrial Arts Index

A subject index to periodical articles on industrial, business, and technical topics. Over 200 journals are indexed. Bulletins are issued monthly and are combined in one annual volume.

Public Affairs Information Service

A subject index to periodical articles, pamphlets, documents, and some books on public affairs, economics, and industrial subjects. Bulletins are issued weekly and are combined in quarterly and annual volumes.

Readers' Guide to Periodical Literature

An index to periodical articles under both subject and author. The journals indexed are more general in scope than those in *The Industrial Arts Index,* but several economic journals are also indexed.

Other special indexes to publications are: *The New York Times Index, Monthly Catalog of United States Government Publications, Cumulative Book Index, Accountants' Index,* and *The Engineering Index* (sections on "Management Engineering" and "Production Control").

In addition, the Cleveland and the Newark Public Libraries have prepared bibliographies on a number of management activities and will be happy to make them available to you.

Finally, such management associations as the American Management Association, the National Industrial Conference Board, and the National Office Managers' Association have extensive bibliographical material and are staffed to be of assistance to those desiring reference material.

It has occurred to me that perhaps my readers might enjoy a few references to supplement the topics which I have discussed. These suggestions, which follow the chapter sequence of the book, are selected from references which I have found particularly helpful in my own thinking:

THE EXECUTIVE

Henry, William E.: *Executive Personality and Job Success,* American Management Association, Personnel Series, no. 120, New York, 1948.

This paper throws new and significant light upon abilities essential to success. The section dealing with executive characteristics, based on a personality survey of some three hundred executives, is particularly enlightening.

Given, William B., Jr.: "Specifications for Management Material," *Bottom-up Management,* Harper & Brothers, New York, 1949.

The author, President of the American Brake Shoe Company, suggests twenty-six qualifications which were distributed to executives in his organization as a guide to the selection of executive timber—a list well worthy of study.

EXECUTIVE ATTITUDE AND MORALE

Likert, Rensis, and Daniel Katz: "Supervisory Attitudes and Practices and Their Effects on Worker, Productivity, and Morale," in Joseph M. Dooher and Vivienne Marquis, eds., *The Supervisor's Management Guide,* American Management Association, New York, 1949.

In this article, the authors discuss objectively the effect of supervisory attitudes upon employee morale, as indicated by the application of newly developed research tools of clinical and social psychology in an automotive plant, a public utility, and a railroad.

EXECUTIVE CONTROL

Pigors, Paul: "Technical Communication: Order-giving," *Effective Communication in Industry,* National Association of Manufacturers, New York, 1949.

This chapter describes order giving as a two-way process, made up of seven equally important phases—a revealing and interesting analysis.

EXECUTIVE DELEGATION

Joynt, Jack B.: "Effective Delegation of Authority," *Annals of the Thirtieth Annual Session of the Southern Indus-*

trial Relations Conference, Blue Ridge, Ga., July 20–23, 1955.

Unquestionably the presentation most filled with sound thought and practical wisdom in matters of industrial delegation that has come to my attention.

Corson, John: "Five Steps to Better Delegation," *The Nation's Business,* May, 1956.

A practical and basic discussion of delegation, this is well worth reading.

Baker, Helen, and Robert R. France: *Centralization and Decentralization in Industrial Relations,* Research Report Series, no. 87, Industrial Relations Section, Princeton University, Princeton, N.J., 1954.

Case problems and other data of a very useful sort are included in this publication.

EXECUTIVE STIMULATION

McCormick, Charles P.: *The Power of People,* Harper & Brothers, New York, 1949.

A practical and experienced viewpoint on "the things in human nature that make people enjoy their work and lead them to be more productive in their own interests" is found in this book; five basic factors that employees want from their jobs are outlined in some detail.

Overstreet, H. A.: *The Mature Mind,* W. W. Norton & Company, Inc., New York, 1949.

A fresh approach to problems of human motivation and behavior; in the chapter entitled "Psychological Foundations" the concept of psychological age as a prime determinant of behavior is presented.

EXECUTIVE DUTIES

Pigors, Paul, and Charles A. Myers: *Personnel Administration: A Point of View and a Method*, 3d ed., McGraw-Hill Book Company, Inc., New York, 1956.

Techniques of employee rating, promotion, transfer, layoff, discipline, and discharge are thoughtfully considered; illustrative case problems are also presented.

EXECUTIVE COLLABORATION

Gardiner, Glenn: "The Operating Executive and the Personnel Department," American Management Association, Personnel Series, no. 121, New York, 1948.

A provocative discussion of collaboration between the operating executive and the personnel department, directed especially at the personnel manager, is found in this study, which defines these relationships in no uncertain terms. This presentation has been widely commented upon.

EXECUTIVE PUBLIC RELATIONS

Gras, N. S. B.: *Shifts in Public Relations*, Business Historical Society, Boston, 1947.

A fundamental approach to problems of public relations is found in this pamphlet. Broad in scope yet basic in treatment, its historical approach is helpful as a background for these activities in any industrial field.

DIFFICULTIES WITH SUPERIORS

Niles, Mary C. H.: *Middle Management*, rev. ed., Harper & Brothers, New York, 1949.

Problems of the junior executive in relation to his superior are interestingly presented in a chapter devoted to this topic.

Getting action on recommendations is one of the several topics of particular interest and value.

Gardiner, Glenn, and Robert L. Gardiner: "How to Achieve Foreman Participation in Policy Making," *Vitalizing the Foreman's Role in Management,* McGraw-Hill Book Company, Inc., New York, 1949.

This chapter makes several suggestions for improvement of relations with top management.

EXECUTIVE CREATIVENESS

Osborn, Alex: *Applied Imagination: Principles and Procedures of Creative Thinking,* Charles Scribner's Sons, New York, 1953.

An excellent book in the field; it covers in detail the steps essential to creative thinking.

EXECUTIVE SELF-DEVELOPMENT

The Autobiography of Benjamin Franklin

Franklin's account of his project of arriving at moral perfection lists thirteen virtues which he aimed to strengthen in himself, each to be given "a week's strict attention." His project is a classic example of executive development.

Index